Working with
Unicenter
TNG®

que®

201 West 103rd Street, Indianapolis, Indiana 46290

Y0-BBW-147

Working with
Unicenter
TNG®

Rick Sturm

Que®

Working with Unicenter TNG

Copyright © 1998 by Que

International Standard Book Number: 0-7897-1765-4

Library of Congress Catalog Card Number: 98-86422

Printed in the United States of America

First Printing: August 1998

00 99 98   4 3 2 1

This book was produced digitally by Macmillan Computer Publishing and manufactured using computer-to-plate technology (a filmless process) by GAC/Shepard Poorman, Indianapolis, Indiana.

Trademarks

Warning and Disclaimer

EXECUTIVE EDITOR
Bryan Gambrel

ACQUISITIONS EDITOR
Bryan Gambrel

DEVELOPMENT EDITOR
Bryan Gambrel

MANAGING EDITOR
Patrick Kanouse

PROJECT EDITOR
Rebecca Mounts

COPY EDITOR
Tonya Maddox

INDEXER
Christine Nelsen

TECHNICAL EDITOR
Computer Associates, Inc.

SOFTWARE DEVELOPMENT SPECIALIST
Computer Associates, Inc.

PRODUCTION
Carol Bowers
Mona Brown
Ayanna Lacey
Gene Redding

COVER DESIGNER
Nathan Clement

BOOK DESIGNERS
Ruth Harvey
Nathan Clement

Contents at a Glance

Introduction 1

Appendixes

Table of Contents

About the Authors

Rick Sturm is a principal with and a cofounder of Enterprise Management Professional Services, Inc., and has over 15 years experience in network and systems management. In his role with EMPS, he consults with companies to help them determine how they address the problems of managing their networks, systems, and applications. He also works with vendors, helping them deliver products that will meet the needs of today's network and systems managers.

Rick is involved in a variety of industry activities. He was one of the founders of OpenView Forum and the OpenView users group, and served two terms as president of that group and four years as a member of the Board of Directors of that organization. Rick was the co-chair of the Internet Engineering Task Force (IETF) working group, which developed an SNMP MIB for the management of application software (applmib).

Rick currently writes a column on network management for *Internet Week* (formerly *Communications Week*) and occasionally contributes to other industry publications, including *Network World*, *Network Computing*, and *Computerworld*.

Audrey Rasmussen is a senior consultant with Enterprise Management Professional Services, Inc. She has over 15 years experience with mid-range and distributed systems. She was a systems engineer with the IBM Corporation for eight years, where her experience included small to medium-sized systems in standalone and distributed network environments, applications, communications, user training, marketing, project management, and teaching classes to users.

Her clients included Fortune 500 companies, as well as small businesses in industries such as manufacturing, distribution, consumer products, medical, petroleum, service industries, construction, retail, and more. In this capacity, she became intimately aware of the complexity of the management issues in a distributed computing environment. In addition, this experience helped her more fully appreciate the user requirements and frustrations associated with systems management.

Robert H. Taylor is a senior consultant with Enterprise Management Professional Services, Inc. He has over 20 years of experience in IT operations and market research, including having conducted market research for clients in a variety of industries and supervising over 400 research projects.

For eight years, he was responsible for the data center operations at the University of Colorado's College of Business. There he was responsible for overseeing the daily operations of the facility as well as the evaluation, selection, and implementation of new hardware and software. In this capacity he faced the full spectrum of network and systems management issues.

Dedication

To Marilyn and David, who put up with my long hours and supported me through the creation of this book.

—Rick Sturm

To Roy, Kristen, and Lisa for their love and support.

—Audrey Rasmussen

To Suzanne, who has long endured my daydreaming, muttering to myself, and strange hours at the keyboard.

—Bob Taylor

Acknowledgements

Many people assisted us in the creation of this book. However, above all we need to thank the team at Computer Associates: Reuven Battat, Larry Eiss, Zvia Faro, David Hood, Steve Mann, Charles Martin, Bill Merrow, Brandon Musler, Bill Nicotera, Anna Pelino, and Mark Sylor. They supported us through the process of writing this book in many ways. Most importantly they provided us with virtually unlimited access to information about Unicenter TNG, in many cases providing information not normally available to anyone other than employees of Computer Associates. (The truth is that without their experience, insight, and considerable work in reviewing the manuscript, this book might never have been completed.)

Tell Us What You Think!

As the reader of this book, *you* are our most important critic and commentator. We value your opinion and want to know what we're doing right, what we could do better, what areas you'd like to see us publish in, and any other words of wisdom you're willing to pass our way.

As the Executive Editor for the Client/Server Database team at Macmillan Computer Publishing, I welcome your comments. You can fax, email, or write me directly to let me know what you did or didn't like about this book—as well as what we can do to make our books stronger.

Please note that I cannot help you with technical problems related to the topic of this book, and that due to the high volume of mail I receive, I might not be able to reply to every message.

When you write, please be sure to include this book's title and author as well as your name and phone or fax number. I will carefully review your comments and share them with the author and editors who worked on the book.

Fax: 317-817-7070

E-mail: cs_db@mcp.com

Mail: Executive Editor
          Client/Server Database
          Macmillan Computer Publishing
          201 West 103rd Street
          Indianapolis, IN 46290 USA

Introduction

In this chapter

The operational challenges facing IT executives today are quite daunting. It is no longer sufficient to keep a handful of mainframe systems up and running. The entire IT infrastructure has grown in both the number and complexity of systems. Enterprise management is now the issue—monitoring and controlling all of the computing and communications resources for the entire enterprise, even if that enterprise spans the globe. Enterprise management must encompass everything, from the management of various network components (hubs, routers, and so on), network discovery, database performance, space management, and application response time to the traditional operations functions such as tape, help desk, security, and workload. In addition, enterprise management is not limited to the real-time monitoring of the environment along with necessary corrective action when problems occur.

A very simplified model can be constructed to give some idea of the complexity of enterprise management. It can be thought of as addressing all of the components in the enterprise information systems environment. A partial list of those areas follows:

Networks
Intranets
Extranets
Internet
LANs and WANs
Other private networks
Systems
Mainframes
UNIX servers
Windows NT servers
Desktop systems
NCs
Applications
ERP
Groupware
Other commercial applications
Custom applications
Databases
Relational databases
Data warehouses
Data mines
Data marts

Non-IT Devices
    HVAC systems
    Coolers and freezers
    Lighting systems

These areas represent just the tip of the iceberg. Further subcategories can be defined within each of the sub-areas. For example, there are hubs, routers, and network servers under LANs and WANs. In addition, there are functions that must be performed for each category. Several years ago, the International Standards Organization (ISO) identified five broad categories of management functions: fault, performance, accounting, configuration, and security. While this functional model is useful, at times it is not readily apparent what is encompassed by each of the categories. For this discussion, it is sufficient to recognize that within each of the areas to be managed there are many management functions to be performed.

While the scale of the problem increases with the size of an enterprise, this is a challenge faced by every organization.

Because of the magnitude of the enterprise management challenge, it is no longer possible to successfully address the issues without some type of automated assistance, which comes in the form of management tools. There are literally thousands of management tools available on the market. Most of these tools are specialized programs focused on some particular aspect (*niche*) of the enterprise management problem. That niche might be a particular type of hardware, or it might be limited to working with a particular protocol. Many of these products are standalone solutions that cannot be readily interfaced with other products. IT executives are faced with the problem of determining which types of products are needed in order to manage their company's resources effectively. This is a decision that is not to be taken lightly. Choosing the wrong management tools can waste money, hinder the effective management of the IT resources, and degrade the level of service provided to end users.

Of all of the enterprise management tools in the world, Unicenter TNG is probably the most widely distributed. It is a comprehensive, open product set that delivers a rich set of functions for end-to-end enterprise management, encompassing the diversity of environments and functions discussed. With Unicenter TNG, Computer Associates has sought to deliver an innovative, highly scalable product set with an open architecture and the capability to leverage industry standards. It is with this powerful product set that Computer Associates has been willing and able to take on all comers in the enterprise management market.

The Need for a Book on Unicenter TNG

When it was first suggested that we write a book about Unicenter TNG, we were somewhat skeptical about the idea. The need for such a book was not, as a former professor liked to say, "intuitively obvious to the casual observer." After all, Computer Associates produces extensive documentation for Unicenter TNG and its related products (in both electronic and printed forms). Literally tons of documentation are produced and distributed for these products annually.

However, as we thought about it and looked at the question more carefully, our feelings about this project began to change. We came to realize that there are many people who need to understand the functions offered by Unicenter TNG. The level of understanding that is needed falls between the very detailed instructions of the product manuals (*Unicenter TNG Administrator Guide*) and the brief summaries contained in the marketing literature. It is this gap that this book addresses.

It is a simple fact that Unicenter TNG is a massive product with very broad capabilities. Few people not working with it on a daily basis fully appreciate all of its capabilities. Because of the product's scope, it is even possible to use it regularly but be unaware of all that it can do. Even this book cannot address all of Unicenter TNG's functions. Instead, this book provides a survey of the major functions in the product set, with illustrations of what is required to implement each of those functions.

This book's aim is to provide the reader with a basic understanding of the major functions available from Unicenter TNG and a rudimentary sense of the effort involved in implementing, customizing, and using it. This is not a replacement for the extensive product documentation that is available, nor is it intended to be a substitute for formal training.

This book is neither an evaluation of Unicenter TNG nor a comparison of Unicenter TNG and other products. Given the rate at which products change, such comparative information is better suited to periodicals and industry seminars than a book.

Overview

The following paragraphs offer a summary of the contents of the individual chapters of this book.

The Architecture of Unicenter TNG

Chapter 1, "The Architecture of Unicenter TNG," introduces Unicenter TNG, its user interface, and the main functional areas. It discusses the extensibility of the product's design. This chapter sets the stage for a clear understanding of enterprise management solutions.

The Unicenter TNG Framework

Chapter 2, "The Unicenter TNG Framework," provides an overview of Unicenter TNG's framework and a closer look at the Unicenter TNG user interface, including how it is applied to the task of managing systems. A walk-through look at major components adds to the foundation laid in Chapter 1 and sets the stage for the rest of the book.

Basic Network Management

Chapter 3, "Basic Network Management," addresses network management with Unicenter TNG, beginning with implementation. It looks at how Unicenter TNG discovers the various components in a network and continues through the network management functions to performance analysis and reporting.

Server Management

Chapter 4, "Server Management," looks at the diverse functionality available from Unicenter TNG for the management of servers (distributed and centralized, UNIX, Windows NT, and others). It begins with the implementation of the fault management capability and goes on to discuss topics such as performance management, automated job scheduling, and the like.

Desktop Management

The number of desktop systems in any organization makes the management of those hardware and software components a daunting task. Chapter 5, "Desktop Management," looks at some of the Unicenter TNG functions that can be used to assist with the management of the desktop environment. It also considers how some of the Unicenter TNG components can be used to automate certain desktop management tasks.

Help Desk and Problem Management

The Help Desk is at the very center of the enterprise management function. Chapter 6, "Help Desk and Problem Management," looks at the available Help Desk functions. The most critical of those functions is the tracking of problems. However, this chapter also covers how Help Desk tasks can be automated to improve accuracy and efficiency.

Storage Management

Corporate databases are critical to the survival of most organizations today. Chapter 7, "Storage Management," considers how Unicenter TNG can be used to safeguard that data with a comprehensive strategy of backups while avoiding unnecessary capital investment by migrating seldom-used data to lower-cost storage media.

Security

Chapter 8, "Security," examines how Unicenter TNG can be used to protect an organization's information assets, beginning with access control through the use of user IDs and passwords to more sophisticated methods. It also looks at how the efficiency of security measures can be improved through the use of a single sign-on.

Web Management

Organizations continue to offer more and more information via the World Wide Web. This vehicle for disseminating information and for electronic commerce is becoming increasingly important. This increased importance forces companies to take seriously issues related to Web management. Chapter 9, "Web Management," looks at the Web management functions available within Unicenter TNG and its options.

Application Management

Only when IT organizations are able to manage their applications and databases can they effectively manage their IT environments end-to-end. Until recently, the management of both databases and application software has been haphazard and piecemeal. Chapter 10, "Application Management," looks at how with Unicenter TNG the management of these components can be integrated into the complete enterprise management strategy for an organization.

Intended Audience

There are two broad groups of people for whom this book is intended. First are those who may need to work directly with Unicenter TNG or who have a need to evaluate it (network and system management personnel, system administrators, planners, architects, and so on). They want to know what Unicenter TNG can do for them. Does it make sense to invest the time and effort to implement the product? While no book can answer that question, this book does attempt to provide the information readers need in order to answer the question themselves.

The other broad group for whom this book is written is the IT managers and directors who are responsible for the operation of an organization's networks and systems. This group is made up of people who will never have to implement Unicenter TNG. However, they need to understand what benefits the product set may offer their organizations and how much effort might be required in order to implement it. It is this book's intent to meet their need for that information.

The Architecture of Unicenter TNG

In this chapter

Governing Growth and Change

The more complicated, demanding, and unpredictable the environment for an enterprise becomes, the greater the need for its IT resources to be ordered, responsive, and useful. Managing such an enterprise requires more than an ad hoc approach or a fashionable consulting methodology. A bona fide solution encompasses the entire enterprise. It starts with a solid, adaptable foundation. Good architecture is based upon a combination of insightful design and pragmatic engineering that yields a consistently reliable approach for delivering solutions. Unicenter TNG is designed for business enterprise management. It is a template for governing growth and change.

Compare a business's IT resources to a city's, which is built over generations. The first settlers lay out the town center with a few dozen pedestrians in mind, but over time immigrants increase the population; new neighborhoods, buildings, and factories spring up; automobiles and public transportation are introduced. As the city grows larger and more complex, some form of traffic control becomes essential. Road signs can be relied upon, though navigating a city with stop signs on every corner wastes time and gasoline. In addition, even if traffic flows freely within neighborhoods, what is movement like between neighborhoods at rush hour, and over a bridge to the only airport in town? To address such problems, at a minimum city planners must add a centrally controlled system of automated traffic lights. Likewise, city plumbing, sanitation, sewage, health, public safety, and so on must all face these issues of scale, economy, performance, and reliability. Unicenter TNG does for IT resources what a municipal government does for a city—Unicenter TNG's architecture serves as a vehicle, a means of rationalizing the core management functions of dynamic business information processing.

Unicenter TNG's architecture consists of the following:

- *Real World Interface*—The fully integrated user interface is easily leveraged by computer users with any level of computing knowledge. All aspects of the Real World Interface are driven by the Common Object Repository.
- *Common Object Repository* (*CORE*)—The central storage mechanism for all components of Unicenter TNG, accessible by management functions and third-party applications.
- *Managers*—The core management facilities that provide resource management throughout an enterprise.
- *Agents*—The means to monitor and control all aspects of the business enterprise.

See Figure 1.1 for an illustration of Unicenter TNG's architecture.

The Real World Interface

Unicenter TNG's Real World Interface component provides the enterprise with a graphical user interface—specifically designed for management. The Real World Interface allows management applications to identify the business resources they manage, as well as the relationships among those resources.

FIGURE 1.1
The Unicenter TNG
architecture.

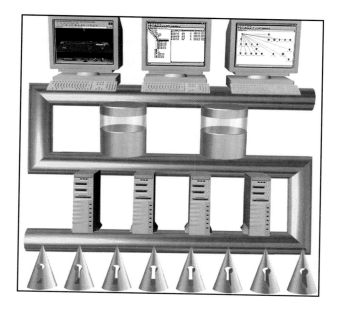

The Real World Interface provides browsers that present two-dimensional and three-dimensional views of the enterprise. Out of the box, these browsers offer an intuitive interface for working with the management environment. Customizing browser views provides an appropriate selection of information for many different types of users. A user can glimpse a consolidated view of resources spread across the enterprise, or different users can each visualize the same information from a personalized perspective.

The Real World Interface draws on the Common Object Repository (Unicenter's central storage facility, defined later in this chapter) to generate management maps dynamically. Unicenter TNG automatically creates these geographic and topological maps, which the user can immediately deploy without modification or customization.

Users can arrange objects on backgrounds manually or, if more convenient, automatically position them on maps using longitude and latitude, global positioning system (GPS) coordinates, city names, or telephone numbers. A representation of the entire IT world within an enterprise may be set up quickly using any or all of these methods.

The Real World Interface helps simplify the management of distributed resources by using three-dimensional animation and elements of virtual reality to visually represent the resources that users and administrators deal with, making them more realistic and manageable.

From a single point of control, administrators can more easily resolve problems via "traveling" throughout the enterprise, identifying and viewing the status of the system, network, database, application resources, and even the physical environment. This three-dimensional representation of real-time status information provides system administrators with an intuitive interface. Three-dimensional visualization is especially useful for managing non-computing devices; this capability is often indispensable for maintaining or servicing these resources. Figure 1.2 provides an example of a Real World Interface 3D map.

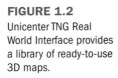

FIGURE 1.2
Unicenter TNG Real World Interface provides a library of ready-to-use 3D maps.

Unicenter TNG also offers a two-dimensional, graphical representation of your enterprise's logical structure. A set of menu commands provides for navigating the 2D map and manipulating data. The 2D map simplifies managing your IT resources by providing a set of powerful tools that can be used to customize visual representations of your business enterprise.

The maps' drag-and-drop capabilities make it easy to design views that simplify the myriad of IT assets Unicenter TNG manages. Assets managed by Unicenter TNG range from the global network to individual computers, hardware within those computers, and even abstract objects such as database processes and user IDs. The 2D map can illustrate anything considered vital to the organization's operation.

FIGURE 1.3
An example of the two-dimensional interface and related tools.

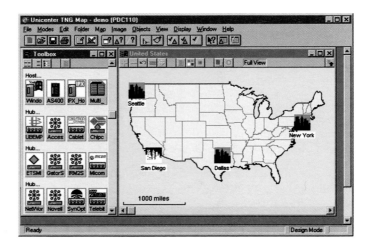

The 2D map also comes with built-in geographic maps that allow the visualization of managed resources by location. Other features, such as resource placement by telephone number, also eliminate the need to associate map locations to managed objects. It is also possible to add images, such as floor layouts, to your views in order to see at a glance exactly where a device resides or a problem occurs, an important feature of modern systems management.

The Common Object Repository

The Common Object Repository (CORE) is the location where all Unicenter TNG management functions store information about managed resources, their properties, and relationships. Third-party applications and all Unicenter TNG components access CORE. The information displayed in the Real World Interface, for example, comes from Unicenter TNG's CORE.

The CORE is a true object repository that provides all of the intrinsic benefits associated with object-based repositories. Accordingly, the CORE is database independent and has been designed for multi-user and multi-system operation.

Building the Common Object Repository and loading it with data that describes your enterprise—also called *populating the repository*— is performed automatically by Unicenter TNG through a process called Discovery. Chapter 3, "Basic Network Management," covers Discovery in greater depth.

Browsers   Besides the Real World Interface maps, Unicenter TNG offers views of information stored in the Common Object Repository and other data stores, which organize complicated information and allow a simplified yet comprehensive look at the IT infrastructure.

Unicenter TNG conveniently organizes tools for viewing and manipulating IT infrastructure information into three general categories:

- Browsers and an ObjectView that displays information in the Common Object Repository
- Browsers and viewers that work with data provided by Unicenter TNG agents
- Graphical User Interfaces (GUIs) related to Base Management Functions

Unicenter TNG provides five easy-to-use browsers—Class, Object, Topology, Link, and ObjectView.

The Class Browser presents the Unicenter TNG classes and their properties. It provides a comprehensive look at all the classes in the repository; see Figure 1.4.

FIGURE 1.4

The Class Browser displays Unicenter TNG's class hierarchy as well as the class-level and object-level properties.

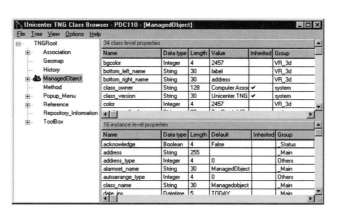

The Object Browser lists objects derived from each Unicenter TNG class. It allows the user to view class-specific and object-specific information; see Figure 1.5.

FIGURE 1.5
The Object Browser displays the object instances of a given class.

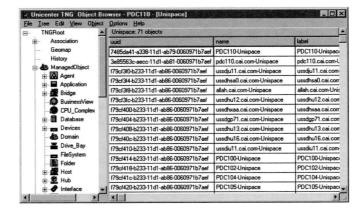

The Topology Browser displays the inclusion relationship between objects as they appear on the map. It provides you with a view of the relationships between managed objects.

The 2D map and Topology Browser demonstrate the multi-view approach used in Unicenter TNG. Different views of the same information are shown in Figures 1.6 and 1.7. In the first illustration, successive double-clicks drill down from the level of the city of Chicago to the devices on a token ring segment. In the second illustration, the Topology Browser displays the same information in file folder fashion.

FIGURE 1.6
In an example of the 2D map, the numbered gray arrows indicate double mouse clicks drilling down to successive (deeper) levels of information about a network.

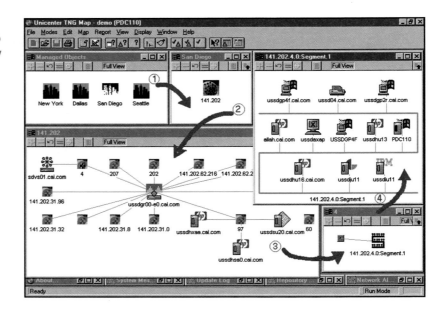

Figure 1.7 displays the same information in tabular format through the Topology Browser.

FIGURE 1.7

The same information that's displayed in Figure 1.6, viewed through the Microsoft Explorer-style Topology Browser.

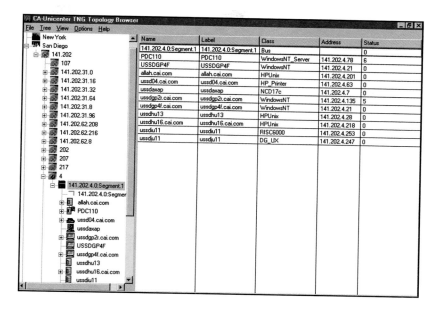

Many of the managed objects in the Common Object Repository represent network devices. ObjectView provides details on the performance of devices, the number of devices connected, which interfaces are down, and the number of packets coming in compared with the number going out.

Device performance can be graphed for further analysis via the Graph Wizard. The Graph Wizard, located in the DashBoard (accessed through ObjectView), provides the tools necessary for creating various types of dynamic graphs.

Agents and Managers

A distributed computing enterprise includes many varieties of hardware and software, often from different vendors, widely dispersed across a network. Indeed, even a single business application often consists of multiple software components distributed across multiple disparate platforms. Management software needs to monitor, manage, and control all of these hardware, software, and application pieces, regardless of location.

An infrastructure comprised of robust agents and managers is the key to handling the scalability and complexity demands characteristic of such distributed management systems and environments. The agents reside on or near the managed resources, gather data about the resources, and filter the data to identify and report the most important information to managers. The agents may perform some control actions themselves, and they execute instructions on behalf of managers.

In contrast to agents, which are located in or near managed resources, managers may be located anywhere in the network. They analyze the information sent to them by agents, correlate the various pieces of information in the environment to discover trends and patterns, and determine how to best control the managed resources in the context of management policies.

Because the managers and agents can interact and cooperate with other agents and managers flexibly and efficiently at any geographical location on the network, they enable distributed enterprise management.

The Manager/Agent Approach

Unicenter TNG's architecture allows for a distributed management approach. In the manager/ agent architecture, the functions that use management information, control management actions, and delegate management authority are architecturally separate from the functions that produce management data and act on behalf of managers.

Many managers can monitor a single agent, and vice versa. Similarly, multiple Real World Interfaces can use a repository, and multiple managers can update a repository. It is a truly many-to-many relationship.

Consequently, an enterprise can deploy management functionality according to business requirements. Without disrupting or redesigning its network and the people who rely upon it, a company can introduce the management and agent software into a dynamic IT environment, at any level.

Managers: The Bosses A manager is one of many software bosses in an enterprise management system. Managers issue requests to agents for data. They perform analyses on the data received about their management environment.

In order to make the best decision from a high-level perspective, managers correlate the data they get from one or more agents with information received from other data sources.

Managers are functional specialists. Unicenter TNG has, for example, a workload manager, storage manager, asset manager, problem manager, software distribution manager, configuration manager, file manager, calendar manager, report manager, user/security manager, and more. There is also a special manager called a Distributed State Machine, which manages groups of agents that instrument resources. See Appendix B, "Reference to Unicenter TNG's Agents," for a complete listing of Unicenter TNG agents.

Agents: Administrative Assistants Agents are "gofers." Their job is to go where a software manager needs them, follow instructions, and work quietly in the background. Agents primarily monitor information about one or more resources (by gathering and recording) and relay that information to a manager under specific circumstances or criteria.

Agents work on networked devices and monitor their environments. They report on the condition and status of the environment to their manager.

In addition to monitoring, some agents can alter their environment. Agents have small footprints making them scalable so that the system can apply a number of different types of agents to a single resource.

Most agents periodically report to their managers. The primary reason for that reporting is to communicate information about changes in the monitored resource's status. However, managers can also ask (*poll*) for information from agents.

Agents reside at the lowest level of the Unicenter TNG architecture and can manage any networked non-computing devices. The term *instrumentation* refers to the configuration of an agent and its control of a resource.

Instrumenting a Resource   The capability to instrument a resource so that specific information about that resource can be gathered and the resource managed is an important agent-offered feature. For example, suppose that a database administrator (DBA) is interested in a few specific values in a large database maintained by a manufacturing application. She could write an agent to monitor those values and alert her when the values meet certain criteria; see Figure 1.8.

FIGURE 1.8

Unicenter TNG agents can instrument file systems, database applications, and other software applications, significantly increasing the ability to monitor and control such software processes.

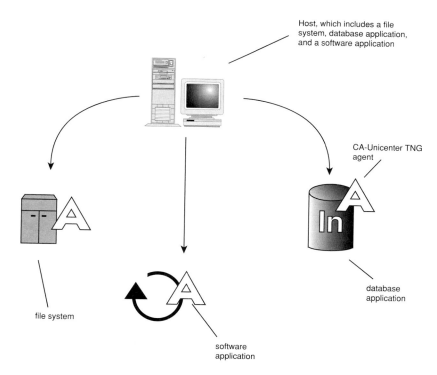

Host, which includes a file system, database application, and a software application

CA-Unicenter TNG agent

database application

file system

software application

The practice of instrumenting network devices has been in place for several years. Many network devices—servers, printers, or routers—have agents built into them by the manufacturer. Whether vendors implement them as hardware, firmware, or software, agents have the job of gathering information about a device.

Unicenter TNG's sophisticated agent technology takes the idea of instrumenting a device to a higher level. With Unicenter TNG, it is possible to instrument practically any resource in an IT infrastructure.

Unicenter TNG includes several useful agents right out of the box, and provides the facilities for creating robust custom agents. In addition, Unicenter TNG has an open architecture and supports agents created by other software vendors who have followed the Unicenter TNG agent specifications.

Tools for Working with and Viewing Agent Information   Unicenter TNG's agent technology facilitates the management of the IT infrastructure. Agents are programs that automatically gather information about the resources in the IT infrastructure. A repository called Object Store keeps data related to agents. (For more detailed information related to agents, refer to Chapter 4, "Server Management.")

Unicenter TNG provides a useful set of tools for viewing agents and their information:

- MIB Browser
- Node View
- DSM View
- Event Browser

Chapter 2, "The Unicenter TNG Framework," provides a detailed discussion of these tools.

Unicenter TNG Base Management Functions

The Unicenter TNG Base Management model for distributed systems management is a flexible client/server–based solution for addressing the systems management challenges in today's environments. Agent technology further enhances the model, adding the manager/agent dimension.

Unicenter TNG Base Management Functions are scaleable, enabling systematic simplification, automation, and a solution that an enterprise can adjust to its specific needs.

Administrators can customize each systems management workstation to reflect their particular needs. For example, one workstation can manage backup and archiving of several disks used networkwide, while several security workstations can be placed throughout the network, bringing control of user administration closer to each business unit.

The following are just a few of the tasks that Unicenter TNG Base Management Functions can perform:

- Direct important system, network, and application event messages to a centralized location, and (optionally) respond automatically to messages that would otherwise require human intervention
- Automatically record, access, track, and resolve problems related to the system and end-user requirements
- Automate repetitive and calendar-based processing in order to reduce errors and free more time for developing new processes and applications that improve an organization's competitive position

■ Improve the integrity and reliability of critical computing resources, especially the information stored on external media

■ Effectively secure the computing environment without disrupting valuable work time

Unicenter TNG Base Management Functions

The following sections address these Unicenter TNG functions:

■ Event Management

■ Workload Management

■ Automated Storage Management

■ Security Management

■ Problem Management

■ Performance Management

Event Management   The Event Management function enables users to do the following:

■ Define policies that identify important activities, such as messages, log entries, and network events

■ Respond to these events automatically

■ Take immediate action as appropriate

The Event Management Console, an advanced tool for systems management, serves as the interface to the Event Management function. The console is a special window in the Unicenter TNG Enterprise Management GUI that enables the user to monitor system events as they occur. As a master console, it provides a complete view of the ongoing event processing across a network of systems.

Event Management lets the user identify events to which a response is desired and specify one or more actions that should be initiated automatically. This means that once a user defines a message and an associated action, the system will automatically perform the specified action whenever Unicenter TNG encounters the related event.

Workload Management   Workload Management enables cross-platform job scheduling. An operator using Unicenter TNG on a Windows NT platform can coordinate jobs between the mainframe schedulers and UNIX or other TNG-enabled platforms. The system can operate upon and track a task once it's defined.

Unicenter TNG Workload Management controls crucial operations, such as scheduling jobs, monitoring job sequence, monitoring job failure, adhering to time requirements, and matching jobs to the machines where there are sufficient resources for them to run most efficiently.

Workload Management automatically selects, schedules, and submits jobs and job sets on the right day(s), at the right time, and in the right order based on the policies stored in the Workload Management database.

Job Tracking   Workload Management also provides the user with a real-time display of scheduling activity. The Job Status and Jobset Status list and the Job Flow GUI provide a current display of active job and jobset status and information on jobs and jobsets that have recently completed.

Automated Storage Management (ASM)

Unicenter TNG's Automated Storage Management provides extensive facilities for coordinating and monitoring storage. It provides the same robust functionality for storage management taken for granted on mainframes today, but does so across platforms and networks. ASM provides management of tapes, diskettes, CD-ROMs, and the like, can employ parallelism, and can take advantage of RAID (Redundant Array of Inexpensive Disks).

The Automated Storage Management (ASM) function includes a complete file backup and archiving system, which tracks the movement of files between online and backup media.

ASM tracks all backup and archive activity in a common database, making it possible to quickly locate backup files in the backup and archival system. This makes for greater efficiency in backup, archive, and most importantly, restore operations.

Backup Facility   The backup process creates a duplicate copy of a file on a backup media while retaining the original version of the file online. When ASM creates a backup version of a file, it also stores summarized information about that version of the file in the ASM database.

Archive Facility   Backup and archive are closely related functions. Logically, archiving differs from backup only in that the system removes an archived file from the active file system after it is copied to backup media, while it does not remove a backed up file after copying.

Restore Facility   The restore facility allows an administrator or an end user to restore files that have been backed up or archived to an active file system. The restore process automatically determines which media are required to perform the restore and calls for the necessary tapes, or restores, transparently from disk save sets as needed.

Security Management

The Security Management function provides a policy-based facility that protects the IT infrastructure.

All of the logon and asset access control policies supported by Unicenter TNG Enterprise Management are maintained through specialized security policies. Once set, the system enforces these policies until the security administrator changes them.

The security provided is in addition to that of the operating system. Unicenter TNG implements security at three logical levels:

Authentication—The system will determine whether this user is valid for accreditation to access the system. Unicenter TNG augments the operating system's logon ID and password facility with policy—rules determining how often, and to what, a password must (or can) be changed, for example.

Authorization—Users are limited in the functions they can carry out and in the files they can use. Unicenter TNG's security takes effect before that of the operating system and it takes effect first. It is possible to group users and create policy for those groups. Unicenter TNG can control all accounts, including UNIX's Super User and Windows NT's Administrator. It can also restrict access to the network operating system.

Audit trails—The system creates audit trails based on user ID or file access.

You may already enforce physical security by restricting access to your data center or computer areas, but you also need to secure the integrity, accuracy, privacy, and confidentiality of the data and programs that reside within the computer system.

Problem Management   Problem Management automates the process of defining, tracking, and resolving problems, and allows identification of the components for which an organization wants problem statistics maintained.

Problem Management allows the inclusion of several types of information as part of a problem definition:

- Categories—Define the general area or type of problem
- Status codes—Denote the current state of the problem
- Responsibility areas—Define the individuals, groups, departments, or others responsible for correcting a problem

As the priority of a problem escalates, the responsibility area can change with it.

Component definitions define the system's configuration, including hardware, software, non-computer–related equipment (such as air conditioning or heating), telecommunications components, security systems, and any other components an organization wants to track.

Problem definitions are entered into Problem Management manually by the Help Desk staff, and automatically by the Machine-Generated Problem Tracking facility.

Machine-Generated Problem Tracking (MGPT) provides for the automatic opening of problem tickets (records) based on activity monitored by the Unicenter TNG Event Management function.

Performance Management   Organizations are finding an increasing need for tools that allow them to effectively and efficiently manage system performance within their enterprises as they implement distributed information systems.

In order to achieve an effective performance management strategy, it is important to address two fundamental requirements:

- The day-to-day management of unexpected performance problems across the enterprise
- The ability to perform long-term planning and trend analysis

These GUI-based applications allow for visualization, management, and configuration of performance and resource usage data collected from distributed systems by the Unicenter TNG Performance Agents. Moreover, they provide an online, real-time window into the performance of the systems across the enterprise. They also make it possible to examine the historical performance of systems over long periods, so users can spot performance bottlenecks, problematical trends, and so on.

Unicenter TNG Performance Management is tightly integrated into the Unicenter TNG Real World Interface map and enables viewing and managing performance data in a context-sensitive fashion by pointing and clicking the managed objects on the 2D and 3D maps.

Performance Scope   Based on the Windows NT platform and fully integrated into the Unicenter TNG Real World Interface component, Performance Scope assists the systems administration and support roles. It provides a real-time view of component performance on managed systems.

Performance Trend   Unicenter TNG Performance Trend supports the System Manager and/or Capacity Planner. Performance Trend (see Figure 1.9) displays historical performance and usage information in a spreadsheet, where users can analyze it.

FIGURE 1.9
Performance Trend graphs network usage information.

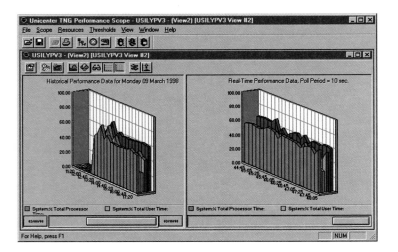

Performance Configuration   The essence of any client/server application is that it has a number of distributed components that execute on many remote and disparate systems. Unicenter TNG's configuration structure performance makes it possible to configure components from a central point of control via intuitive GUIs that provide a common look and feel across disparate platforms.

Chargeback   The Unicenter TNG Chargeback component provides a method for attributing resource accounting data obtained from heterogeneous platforms across the enterprise to "real world" charge groups. This enables the administrator to identify the use being made of each distributed system; this allows charges to be allocated, bills to be generated, accurate budgets to be developed, and various reports to be produced. ●

The Unicenter TNG Framework

In this chapter

What Is a Framework?

Distributed applications are best served by distributed management. This means that distributed management applications themselves are client/server based. All client/server applications are, by nature, partitioned into two or more processes. In practice this also usually means that the client and server portions of the program are distributed across multiple nodes and thus rely on a network to communicate between the application's various components. Partitioning a program into client and server modules running on separate nodes raises complex management issues. A management framework provides the plumbing that standardizes the way these issues are addressed. A framework can tie together applications from the framework provider, independent third parties, and the end customer to increase operational, maintenance, and development efficiencies.

■ **Scalability.** Application scalability has always been a concern, but is especially challenging when managing client/server environments. An ideal framework would work equally well in an environment with 20,000 computers and on a network of 10 computers. It would also completely offset its management overhead by improving the throughput and response time of applications. More tangibly, a well-designed framework will reduce network traffic, limiting expense and service degradation at the size extremes of the environment.

■ **Reliability.** Likewise, reliability has been a constant management concern. This concern is far more difficult to address in a client/server setting. What happens when a file server crashes, a database locks up, or the network link fails? Indeed, dependence upon network components adds an entire dimension that must be integrated into the management paradigm. At a minimum, a distributed environment yields many more potential points of failure. Good frameworks make it possible to address the issues of correct, error-free operation and of application availability, assuring that the client/server system can always function.

■ **Heterogeneity.** This is another management issue peculiar to client/server systems. Heterogeneity demands that, as much as possible, different computing architectures (hardware, software, data, and network protocols) be hidden from operators, administrators, and developers. By providing a higher level of abstraction for systems of all types (legacy, LAN, or UNIX), a framework enables enhanced interoperability closer to the ideal of plug compatibility, or better yet, plug-and-play mode.

■ **Central control.** A framework should also create a single-system image of the total enterprise infrastructure while simultaneously enabling multiple, virtual views in support of more specific business requirements. It should be easy for administrators (ideally, non-technical management personnel) to behave as if they are on a single large computer or, at management discretion, focus on only the resources relevant to their jobs. Another important aspect of dealing with diversity is being able to log on at any workstation, NC, or terminal and have the same management functions, permissions, and authorities. A truly heterogeneous framework enables the management of anything from anywhere.

A basic assumption of the framework paradigm, inherited from the open systems movement, is that most organizations over time choose hardware and operating systems that are best suited to the tasks at hand and create a distributed, heterogeneous computing environment. A management framework is layered on top of this hodgepodge of systems and networks in order to provide core integration services. The customer plugs in some combination of management applications (meaning the most appropriate subset) that applies to the specific mix of elements requiring management. The existence of a standard framework, with open APIs and a shared user interface, allows the customer to build a cooperative yet customizable environment.

The Unicenter TNG Approach

Unicenter TNG Framework is an out-of-the-box enterprise management framework that encapsulates the support infrastructure from Unicenter TNG. This tool embodies all of the essential distributed services required for enterprise management, and it adds supplemental management functions.

Computer Associates (CA) spent hundreds of person-years developing and enhancing an enterprise management platform across every major computing system. The functionality of that product is distilled and condensed in Unicenter TNG Framework.

The original impetus for the development of a management framework came from system and network managers who wanted to acquire management platforms independently of hardware and operating system providers. It quickly became evident, however, that cross-platform application availability was required for widespread acceptance. After all, functionality is not resident in the framework itself, but in the management applications that inhabit it, which are performing all the genuine work.

Unicenter TNG Framework has achieved wide distribution and acceptance. With Unicenter TNG, CA is providing a stable of functionally rich applications, a wide array of distribution partners, a robust infrastructure, and an API set derived from extensive customer implementation. Framework development's original goal was to encourage a vibrant market in management applications, but CA needed to extract Framework from Unicenter TNG in order to achieve rapid, truly widespread acceptance.

Between the enterprise GUI—the Real World Interface—and the Distributed Services layer is where the actual management applications reside. The Unicenter TNG Framework (see Figure 2.1) helps those applications automatically translate machine-level data into business management information.

The goal of Unicenter TNG Framework is to accelerate enterprises' realization of the benefits provided by integrating management of all IT resources via a common, object-oriented infrastructure across all lines of business. Case studies of specific customer decision processes revealed that while adopters of the Framework approach to integrated management highly valued the ability to customize their management environment, significant inhibitors often impeded organizational progress. Lack of properly trained programming personnel is the most commonly cited problem. Moreover, a much larger segment of the market, while fully acknowledging the utility of full-scale enterprise management, could not allocate the resources for a pilot project, let alone supply the business justification for a multi-year implementation effort. Likewise, management software vendors recognized the potential for framework-oriented products, but sales volume indicated limited market penetration even by the "leading" frameworks.

FIGURE 2.1
An illustration of Unicenter TNG's Framework.

Computer Associates determined that extracting Framework from Unicenter TNG would be only a partial solution to the industry requirement for a ubiquitous solution. The Unicenter Software Development Kit (SDK) was available free, and the Real World Interface, Object Repository, and Distributed Services were readily extractable. Still, CA realized that it should package a next-generation framework to deliver management value at installation time. Accordingly, the Unicenter TNG Framework design criteria was to install automatically from a single CD-ROM and return immediate value.

Components of the Unicenter TNG Framework

The Unicenter TNG Framework includes several features. The remainder of this chapter discusses these features.

- Auto Discovery
- Object Repository
- Real World Interface
- Event management
- Calendar management
- Reporting
- Virus detection
- Desktop support

Auto Discovery

The Auto Discovery service automatically finds networked objects and resources within the enterprise and visually displays them for subsequent inspection via an appropriate topology. The Auto Discovery service supports TCP/IP and Novell NetWare IPX networks, discovering elements on these heterogeneous networks and automatically populating the Unicenter TNG Object Repository. Auto Discovery enables users to do many things:

■ Run multiple instances of Discovery simultaneously to balance the network workload

■ Discover all resources in an enterprise, or limit discovery to a specific subnetwork

■ Specify which types of resources Unicenter TNG should discover

■ Discover IPX and TCP/IP networks

■ Determine the topology of the network automatically

■ Initiate discovery manually or schedule periodic automatic updates

Discovery does not drill down inside the systems and identify all the subcomponents within them. For example, if there is a Windows NT server on the network, the discovery process will discover the system, its name and IP address, the operating system it is running, and so on. However, it will not discover the amount of memory the system may have or the disks and their utilization. To discover those details, either a Unicenter TNG Windows NT Agent or a DMI Agent is required.

The automated facilities provided by the Discovery service significantly reduce time spent on network database setup and recurrent maintenance. The reason is that without automation, someone would have to enter all of the data manually. This automation reduces operating costs and provides increased reliability.

Object Repository

A multi-user object repository is at the core of Unicenter TNG Framework, supporting all the management functions and the Real World Interface. The system registers, in the object repository, all networked system nodes and instrumented program entities (such as the elements located by Auto Discovery) that participate in the enterprise. The repository stores the characteristics, status information, and the management methods available for each of its managed objects. It also contains the user interface elements associated with the classes, including 2D icons and 3D representations, menu definitions, and object associations (such as containment, dependencies, and the like). The repository is fully extensible and customizable, which provides the pivotal underpinning that enables the tightest integration between management applications at all levels. In addition, the object repository makes Business Process Views possible, which are unique to Unicenter TNG.

Real World Interface

Unicenter TNG Framework provides a real-time, graphical, 2D, 3D, and Web-based view of all the assets in a network. Its Real World Interface simplifies the management of distributed resources by allowing visual representation of tangible and abstract objects. The GUI rendering engine, which uses the information in the repository to display objects and their menus, builds the objects in the user interface dynamically. Management application developers do not have to write any code to display their objects in Unicenter TNG, nor do they have to worry about cross-platform GUI issues. They get automatic GUI integration across heterogeneous environments just by defining their objects in the repository.

Depicting tangible and abstract computing resources via a common visual metaphor enables the creation of business-specific points of view called *Business Process Views*. Business Process Views help define, organize, and present technical information in a business context by integrating it meaningfully for specific business roles and managers. Business Process Views also better leverage human capabilities and intuitive navigation tools, which resolves enterprise management problems quickly.

Event Management

Managing events is a central capability of the Unicenter TNG Framework. Event management is the critical function; it's essential for enterprise management because it enables proactive and reactive responses to changes in object status. The hub of event management is the enterprise's central control console. Potentially, the system may send so many messages to this enterprise network's central status window that a human operator would be overwhelmed. Unicenter TNG Framework addresses this challenge in multiple, sophisticated ways. It can filter out unimportant messages and forward warnings to other specialized operators, and critical events can trigger automated response, without requiring manual intervention. This flexibility reduces errors and improves overall management efficiencies.

Unicenter TNG Framework's event management capabilities include, besides the Event Console itself, the capability to send and receive SNMP traps, filtering, correlation, escalation, automated actions, and event forwarding to other consoles. In a heterogeneous environment, systems that have the framework installed on them can act as event agents to other systems, enabling cross-platform manager/agent event management. This provides the robust event management features essential for the tight integration of the management applications.

Desktop Support

Managing desktop systems requires a capability to view asset configuration data. The Unicenter TNG Framework includes two standards-based management browsers that make it possible for an operator to connect with remote desktops and network elements. There is an MIB browser for network elements and systems running an SNMP agent, as well as an MIF browser for DMI 2.0–compliant PCs. These built-in components allow a Unicenter TNG Framework operator to remotely inspect and modify configuration parameters in order to resolve deployment or operational errors.

Calendar Management

Most people use calendars to track appointments, special occasions, or other events that depart from the realm of routine. Computers have no natural routine per se, but programs can instruct them to perform as though they were using calendars to define special occasions and daily, weekly, monthly, or yearly routines.

Calendar management in the Unicenter TNG Framework lets users define calendar objects that any management function built on the Framework can use. These shared objects provide flexibility, ease-of-use, and coordination of changes that affect the business policies of an organization. By using shared calendars, all management applications can deliver a much higher level of integration and enforce the same business policies across the enterprise.

For example, calendar objects combined with event management provide a way to set dates and times when different event management policies will be in effect. An organization might decide that during main business hours, a disk full warning should be channeled to the operator's Event Console, but after 6:00 p.m., on the weekends, or holidays, it should be escalated to page a beeper. The Security Management application could use the same calendar to apply different security policies during and after working hours.

Reports

Ch
2

The Unicenter TNG Framework reporting function creates a variety of canned and customized reports concerning the enterprise infrastructure, based on information contained in the database. It categorizes reports by component type and presents them in an easy-to-use Explorer-like fashion. Operators can review the reports online, print them, or export them from the desktop.

Virus Detection

Viruses are a serious and growing problem in today's computing environments. The spread of viruses has become extremely easy because of the increasing use of email and groupware. A single email containing a virus can contaminate the organization's entire computing environment. The Unicenter TNG Framework (see Figure 2.2) provides state of the art virus detection today and is constantly evolving. Market requirements will drive integration of additional functionality into the base infrastructure on an ongoing basis. Scanning can be manual or scheduled through the Framework Calendar service. Virus detection unmasks both predefined and unregistered virus signatures.

FIGURE 2.2
A framework can tie together applications from the vendor, independent third-party applications, and custom-built applications to increase management, maintenance, and development efficiencies.

Working View of the Unicenter TNG Framework

One of the biggest challenges facing enterprise management users is the lack of integration between various tools from different sources. The reason for this lack of integration has been the absence of an enterprise management framework that was technically capable and widely available across heterogeneous platforms. To address this industrywide issue, CA created the Unicenter TNG Framework, which enables platform providers and ISVs to integrate their management applications.

Viewing the Enterprise

As mentioned, simply comprehending (even without attempting to manage) today's business infrastructure is tremendously challenging. It is a dilemma that bedevils even the most sophisticated IT professional. Unicenter TNG provides visualization tools that abstract and simplify the infrastructure in order to cope with this challenge. After Discovery is finished gathering information about the network and systems in a business environment, it stores that data in a single repository. This consolidation alone is very helpful for users. It essentially builds a model of the business environment within the repository, but because the world remains complex, the model itself cannot be simple.

Accordingly, users need tools that help them examine and explain the environment they are planning to manage. Tools that present the environment in easily understood ways are required. The tools have to summarize and analyze the environment and warn of problems or facts not previously grasped.

Unicenter TNG provides tools for visualizing the environment. These tools leverage the model of the environment in the repository. Those tools include the following:

- Real World Interface 3D Map—A 3D virtual reality browser of the environment.
- Real World Interface 2D Map—A 2D dimensional map browser showing the network topology.
- Topology Browser—A tree-structured browser that shows containment.
- Control Panel—An aid for navigating the environment.
- Business Process Views—A way of organizing objects around your processes, not the underlying technology.
- Managed Object Notebook—An object property viewer that also provides property modification capabilities.
- Object Browser—A tree-structured browser that shows objects by their class.

These are by no means all the viewers and browsers in Unicenter TNG. The product includes viewers for specific enterprise management functions as well as specific objects and their agents.

TNG also includes numerous command-line operations. Any function you can accomplish using a GUI is one you can accomplish via the command line. The most frequent use of the command line is writing scripts, customizing features, or integrating Unicenter TNG with other tools. While this is an interesting and important topic, it is for another book.

Being There: Real World Interface 3D and 2D GUIs   The Real World Interface 3D GUI is the most visually striking TNG feature. Its virtual reality (VR) presentation of the environment allows you to be there in all but fact. The user can "walk" through a building and see the systems in their proper relationship to the building or view a geographic area, like Massachu-setts, and see the sites in their proper locations. This presentation takes full advantage of innate human instincts to see and navigate in a 3D world. While it is valuable for modeling the physi-cal world, you can exploit this third dimension in ways that were impossible before.

As striking as 3D virtual reality is, sometimes a 2D GUI is more appropriate. For example, a 2D representation, particularly a 2D map, uses fewer resources and runs faster for when you're filling out a form. Today, a virtual reality display requires a good graphics accelerator to achieve optimal performance. Fortunately, prices of powerful graphics accelerators are falling quickly.

The topology of a network describes the connections between the many components that make up the network. A topology is one of the most difficult to understand parts of any network, or any distributed system. A map is really the only way to view a topology that makes sense. A map is fundamentally a 2D representation. Unicenter TNG includes a 2D map. Behind the scenes, the 2D map drives what you see in the 3D map.

How to View Your Environment

The browsers and viewers described in this chapter all show the objects represented in the repository. They let the user manipulate the repository. The browsers serve as a launching point for performing specific management tasks. They form a common shell from which you can launch all of Unicenter TNG's functions (and more). They allow the user to find and select an object, as well as to invoke the appropriate function on that object. The specific tools and viewers drill deeper and accomplish more.

Common Concepts and Operations   While each browser has its own unique way of present-ing the objects, they share common concepts, and all present some common operations in the same way.

Connecting to a Repository   The environment can have more than one repository in it. The browsers and viewers allow the user to connect to any of the repositories and work with it. There are three steps in selecting a repository:

1. Log on to the Windows NT server where the repository lives.
2. Select the repository.
3. Log on to the repository itself (often an SQL Server).

Logging On to the Windows NT Server   If the repository resides on the same system as the GUI, you have already logged on to the server. Assuming the repository is located on a Windows NT server in the same domain and you are logged in to the domain, you are already logged on to that server. Nevertheless, you must first log on to that server if you want to connect to a repository elsewhere in your network. You can log on to the server three ways:

- You could arrange to have the identical usernames and passwords set up on both your GUI system and the repository server. This is not recommended.

- You can map a network drive on the repository system. You will log on to the server as part of mapping the drive.

■ You can log on directly to the server using the Windows NT `net use` command. The syntax for that command is as follows:

```
net use \\server * /user:domain\username /persistent:yes
```

Selecting a Repository   To select a repository, enter the name of the repository server in the Select Repository window (see Figure 2.3) and press the OK button. The Find button will locate all the servers in your domain. Simply type in the server name if the repository is in another domain.

FIGURE 2.3

The Select Repository window.

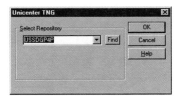

Signing On to the Repository   You need to sign on (see Figure 2.4) after selecting a repository. Enter the password for the SA account. If you are already using another viewer, you may find that you are signed on to the repository. In this case, you may skip this step.

FIGURE 2.4

The Unicenter TNG Repository Sign On window.

Left-Click to Open   As noted in Chapter 1, "The Architecture of Unicenter TNG," any object in the repository can contain other objects through inclusion. The 3D map, the 2D map, and the topology browser can each show you what each object contains. You can open an object as a folder to show what it contains by left-clicking an object in the 3D GUI, or double-clicking in the 2D map or topology viewer.

Right-Click for a Pop-Up Menu   In all of the browsers, right-clicking an object will summon a pop-up menu of commands (see Figure 2.5). Selecting a menu item and clicking it launches that tool. The object's class determines the menu of commands offered. The same menu item for different classes of objects may perform very different functions. For example, the Test menu item for a modem might invoke a "loopback" test, while the Test menu item for a disk might run a thorough scan of the disk for bad files and disk blocks.

Severity Level   The viewers show each object's status, usually by a change in color. Each managed object has a property called Severity, which the viewers use to determine how the object should look. Unicenter TNG, by default, supports seven *severity levels*, as shown in Table 2.1.

FIGURE 2.5

The pop-up menu.

N O T E Three additional severity levels (In Service, Remove, and Future) are defined, but never used.

Table 2.1   The Unicenter TNG Severity Levels

Name	Value	Description
NORMAL	0	No problem
UNKNOWN	1	Status is unknown or uncertain
WARNING	2	Something that has gone wrong may lead to a more serious problem
MINOR	3	A minor problem has occurred; this is generally used when the object is still functioning
MAJOR	4	A major problem has occurred
CRITICAL	5	An even bigger problem has occurred; this demands immediate attention
DOWN	6	The object is not functioning at all

What does a color really mean? The correct response is "Whatever you want it to mean." The precise meaning of any given severity level is determined by the user and is intended to be set according to an organization's policies. For those objects that include other objects, a *policy* can determine how to derive the folder's severity level as a whole from the individual severity levels in the folder's objects. Normally, the severity level of a folder is the worst (maximum) severity level of any included object.

Viewing in 3D   The 3D map gives a very realistic presentation of the environment. You can navigate within that environment using the mouse by clicking, by flying with the mouse, or by using a Spaceball, a special 3D input device.

Running the 3D Map   To run the 3D map, select Start, Programs, CA-Unicenter TNG WorldView, 3D Map from the Windows NT taskbar's Start menu; alternatively, you can click the 3D Map icon in the WorldView folder.

Two windows, one showing the 3D map (see Figure 2.6) and one showing the 2D map, will appear. The process of loading data into the map takes some time, and the system displays messages showing the progress. The 3D map will initially show a spinning globe, like that in Figure 2.6. This is your starting point.

FIGURE 2.6

Unicenter TNG's 3D world.

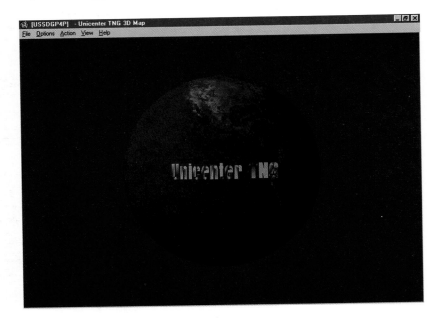

Navigating in 3D   What you see in the 3D map is a scene. The scene shows a number of objects, set against a *backdrop*, that are contained in the particular folder you are viewing. A 3D icon, a three-dimensional model of the object, represents each object.

You view the scene as if looking through a camera. You can *fly* the camera around the scene to various *viewpoints*. You can move the camera through all three dimensions, forward, back, left, right, up, and down. You can also change the direction in which the camera is pointing, turning it left or right, up or down, or by rolling it left or right.

The 3D map has some predefined viewpoints for any scene. There is a *panorama* viewpoint, which shows the entire scene. There is a *close-up* viewpoint for each object.

There are a number of ways to navigate and fly through the 3D map:

- Point and click
- Keyboard shortcuts
- The Spaceball
- Flying with the mouse
- Topology Browser
- Control Panel

Point and Click   The simplest way to navigate in 3D—and the first you are likely to use—is the point-and-click interface. Point at any object with the mouse and single-click. The user interface will fly the camera into a close-up of the object. Click again, and you will fly into the object; a scene will open and display the folder's contents. When you reach an object that does not include any others, TNG will beep and not allow you to fly into the object.

 TIP   Do not double-click objects in the 3D map. The first click will start the 3D user interface flying into the object, but the second is interpreted to mean stop or cancel the action just selected. In other words, it will seem like nothing happened!

When you click the initial globe, you will see the map of the world laid out flat (see Figure 2.7), with all of the objects in the global folder (called ManagedObjects) in the map. You should see one object in this folder if you have just run Network Discovery; the object represents the entire TCP/IP network (as shown in Figure 2.8).

FIGURE 2.7
The Unicenter TNG world laid flat.

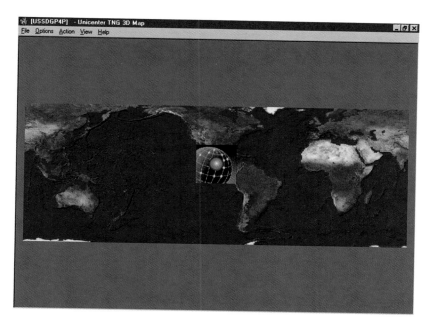

You will end up with other icons in this folder as you customize the map and add other Unicenter functions.

Figure 2.8 shows a typical 3D view of a network, with routers and subnets within the IP network. The lines between the systems represent the links between them.

Backspace to Leave   Press the Backspace key when you no longer want to view a folder and want to return to the next highest level. This returns you to a panoramic view of the entire folder. If you press Backspace at that point, the camera will leave the scene and return you to a close-up of the object you just left in the next highest folder. Again, if you press the Backspace key while the 3D view is flying "back," it will cancel the current operation and you will return to where you were. Patience is a virtue.

FIGURE 2.8
A network folder viewed in Unicenter TNG.

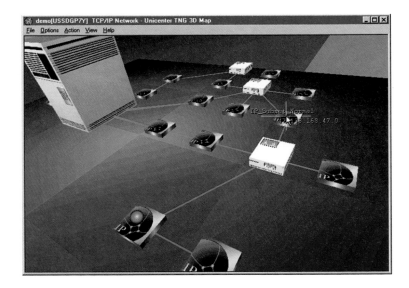

Severity in the "Red Ball"   The color of a ball that floats over the object shows the object's severity level in the 3D map. If the object's severity level is NORMAL, there will not be any ball at all. If the object's severity level is WARNING, the ball will be yellow; if it is CRITICAL, the ball will be red.

The nearest Windows NT workstation in Figure 2.9 has a yellow ball over it, while another resource has a red ball over it.

Lingering Cross Hairs   A cross hair appears, centered on the cursor, as the mouse pointer moves over the objects in the 3D map. The cross hair displays information about the object in each of its four quadrants. For example, the cursor in Figure 2.9 is over the subnet on the right, and the cross hair shows the object's class (IP_Subnet) in the upper-left quadrant. The upper-right quadrant of the cross hair shows the object's severity (Normal). The cross hair also shows the object's label (107) in the lower left and the object's name (141.202.107.0) in the lower right. The exact data displayed in the cross hairs depends on the class of the object and is something you can customize.

Wireframe and Texture Mapping   Presenting a realistic scene in the 3D map is an intensive task for the computer, especially while your viewpoint is flying around the objects. The 3D map lets you trade realism for compute cycles by selecting the Viewing option. You select Viewing via a number of check items under the Options menu. Table 2.2 describes the options that affect the realism of the 3D scene. Each check item is toggled on and off. You can also toggle one of these options by pressing the Ctrl key listed with each option.

FIGURE 2.9
The severity level of an object as displayed in the 3D map.

Table 2.2   3D Realism Options

Option	Key	Initial Value	Effect when Checked	Effect when Unchecked
Wireframe	Ctrl+W		You see the scene as a wireframe without surfaces.	Objects appear with surfaces. Whether those surfaces have textures depends on the other check items.
Texturing Off	Ctrl+T	✓	You see the objects as shapes with textures applied to the surfaces.	You see the objects as shapes without textures.
Perspective-Correct Textures	Ctrl+P	✓	Unicenter TNG corrects the textures for the effect of perspective.	Unicenter TNG does not correct the textures for perspective, so the scene is slightly less realistic.
Auto-Texture mode	Ctrl+U		You see textures applied to objects viewed when flying.	When flying, objects appear as simple shapes without textures.

Figure 2.10 shows the scene with texturing. Figure 2.11 shows the scene without textures, but with surfaces. Figure 2.12 shows the scene as a wireframe model.

FIGURE 2.10

The 3D scene with textures.

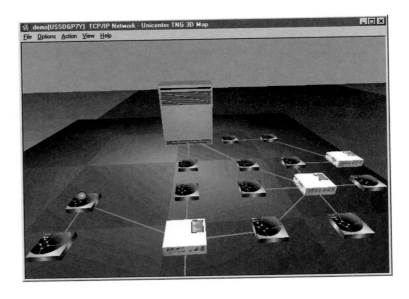

FIGURE 2.11

The 3D scene without textures.

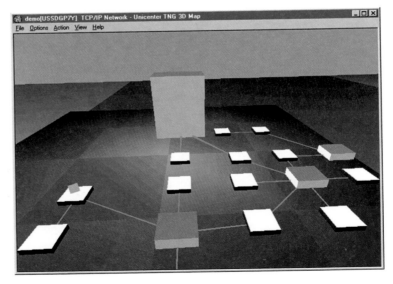

FIGURE 2.12
The 3D scene in
wireframe.

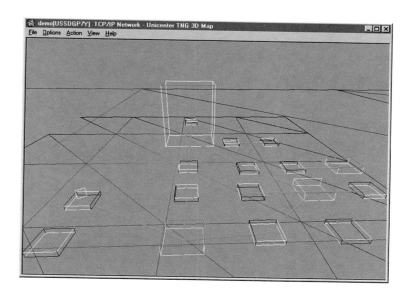

In terms of processor utilization, the wireframe model is the most efficient representation. It is more demanding to show the objects as simple surfaces, without texture. Slower yet is to show the objects with textures, but with textures turned off while flying; this is the default setting. The slowest but most realistic keeps the texture when flying through the scene—a very compute-intensive operation. To set this degree of realism, check Texturing Off, Perspective-Correct Textures, and Auto-Texture mode. Using this level of realism demands a hardware accelerator.

Flying in 3D   Using the mouse for navigating only allows stepping from one predefined viewpoint to another. However, the 3D map allows flying to any point and seeing from any perspective. You can fly through the 3D map using either a Spaceball or your mouse.

To enter an object, just fly into (or collide with) it. Your perspective will change to display the interior of that folder. As you withdraw (or pull away) from the object, you will eventually back out of the folder and return to a scene that shows the object you just left as a 3D icon.

Viewing in 2D   To run the 2D map, select Start, Programs, CA-Unicenter TNG WorldView, 2D Map from the Windows NT taskbar's Start menu; you can instead click the 2D Map icon in the WorldView folder.

Modes   The 2D map (see Figure 2.13) operates in one of two modes: Run mode or Design mode. Normally you will be in Run mode while managing the environment. Design mode is mostly for 2D and 3D map customization, repositioning icons, including objects in one folder or another, and the like.

FIGURE 2.13
Unicenter TNG's 2D
map.

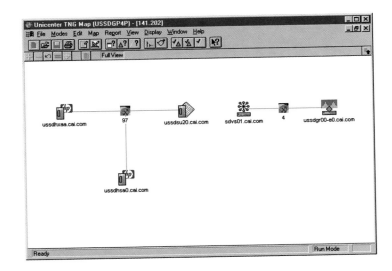

Folders and Icons   As described in Chapter 1, the object repository is capable of representing one object being included in another. For example, a system includes one or more disk drives, and itself is included within a LAN segment. The 2D map represents inclusion with folders and icons. Each object has both. When you open a folder, a window within the larger 2D map window represents the folder containing an object. All the objects that are contained within that folder's window appear as icons; see Figure 2.14.

FIGURE 2.14
Opening folders in the
2D map.

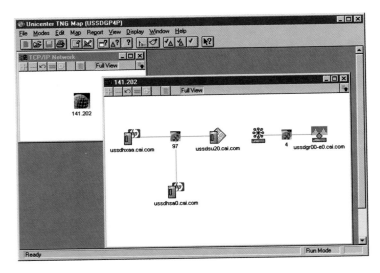

Links and Connectors   The map indicates associations between the objects as links between them (the green lines in Figure 2.13). These links represent the association objects in the repository, as well as some computed links based on IP addresses. If the other end of a link is not in the folder, the other end is symbolically represented by an offscreen connector (a small square).

Navigation in Run Mode   Navigating with the 2D map involves opening and closing folders. TNG provides a number of techniques for navigating through the 2D map.

Double-clicking an icon in the 2D map (while in Run mode) opens the folder associated with that icon as long as it includes at least one other object. Double-clicking the icon shown in Figure 2.14 for the 141.202 network (upper left) opens the larger folder (lower right). Ctrl+F4 closes the current folder.

Ch

2

 The Up Folder tool opens the folder that contains this folder.

Double-clicking an offscreen connector will open a folder that shows the other end of the link.

A single click will select the icon and bring up cross hairs that show some information about the object.

Zoom In, Zoom Out   Sometimes a folder will include many icons and the window will grow crowded. The 2D map allows you to zoom in to a section of the map and focus on a portion of the folder. The controls for *scaling* (zooming) the map are in each folder window's toolbar.

 Click the button with the plus (+) sign to zoom in. Your cursor will change to a magnifying glass with centering cross hairs. Move the cursor to one corner of the area you want to focus on, click the left mouse button, and drag the cursor to the other corner. This highlights the area, as shown in Figure 2.15. Click the mouse button again and the window will zoom in, as shown in Figure 2.16.

FIGURE 2.15
Zooming in on a
selected area.

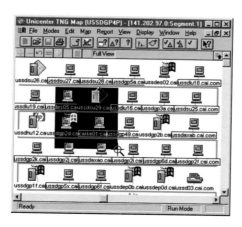

When you zoom in on a small portion of the map, you can pan the window to see different parts of the map. You can use the scrollbars at the bottom and right side of the folder window.

FIGURE 2.16
The enlarged portion of
the folder that is
zoomed in on.

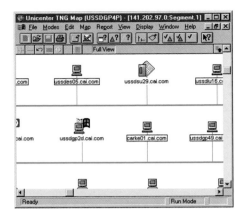

You can use the Centering tool to reposition the window on the map. The cursor will change to a centering cross hair when you click the button.

Move the cursor to the spot in the folder that you want to appear in the center of the window and left-click.

The Zoom Out tool shrinks the map by a factor of 2, so you will see four times as much of the map in the window folder.

The Undo tool reverses the last zoom in or out command. If used repeatedly, it will step you back through the series of magnifications.

The Restore tool returns the window to its initial magnification, showing the entire folder.

Severity in Icon Color   The color of the icon indicates the severity level of the object.

The Managed Objects Folder   The Managed Objects folder is the top-level folder in the 2D and 3D maps. It includes any objects that are not included in any others. The map identifies these orphan objects when it starts and loads objects from the repository.

The Managed Objects folder in the 2D map is the map opened when you first run the 2D map. A picture of a globe in the 3D map represents the Managed Objects folder.

Topology Browser   The Topology browser shows a Microsoft Explorer-style view of the inclusion tree; this is shown in Figure 2.17.

Running the Topology Browser   You run the Topology browser from within either the 2D or 3D maps. Select the Topology Browser menu item from the View menu.

Inclusion Tree   The Topology browser's left pane shows objects arranged as an inclusion tree, with subordinate objects listed below and to the right of their parent. Clicking the small box with a plus or minus sign will, respectively, show and hide the list of children.

FIGURE 2.17
The Unicenter TNG
Topology browser.

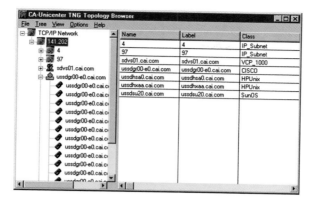

Right Pane Object Details List   The right pane shows all the objects included in the selected object as a table. The columns in the table list object attributes, such as name, label, class, address, and status. Clicking on an object's icon or name in the left pane will select that object and display the associated attributes of the child objects in the right pane.

Double-Click to Go There   The Topology browser is linked to the 2D or 3D map from which it was launched. Double-clicking an object in the Topology browser tells the map to go there. In the case of the 3D map, the viewpoint being displayed will alter to show the indicated object. In the case of the 2D map, the selected object's folder will open, assuming the selected object has a folder.

Control Panel   The Control Panel keeps track of which folders you opened to get where you are. Like the Topology browser, its primary utility is to help you navigate through the 2D and 3D maps. To view the Control Panel, select Control Panel from the View menu. You will see a window, as shown in Figure 2.18. The combo box shows the currently open folder. The list below shows the folders that contain your current folder. Double-clicking any of these names will go there, navigating to the corresponding folder on the map.

FIGURE 2.18
Unicenter TNG's Control
Panel.

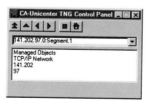

The Control Panel also remembers the folders you have opened recently. Pressing the Backward button moves you to the previous object. Pressing the Forward button moves you ahead in the list.

Screen Layout   The Topology browser is the easiest way to navigate directly to where you want to look in the 2D and 3D maps. The Control Panel allows you to step forward and back through windows you have recently viewed. Looking at two parts of a problem you are trying to diagnose is an example. You'll find that an arrangement of the screen similar to that shown in Figure 2.19 works well. All the tools for navigating through the map are close at hand.

FIGURE 2.19
Customize the screen layout to make navigation easy.

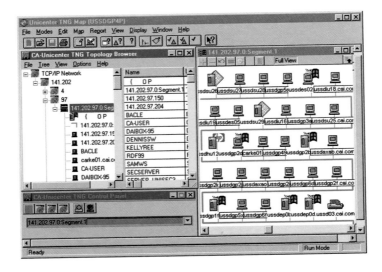

Object Browser   The Object browser presents a Microsoft Explorer-style tree of all the objects in the repository; this is shown in Figure 2.20. The Object browser is a standalone application, like the 2D map.

To run the Object browser, select Start, Programs, CA-Unicenter TNG WorldView, Object Browser from the Windows NT taskbar's Start menu; alternatively, you can click the Object Browser icon in the WorldView folder.

FIGURE 2.20
Object browser.

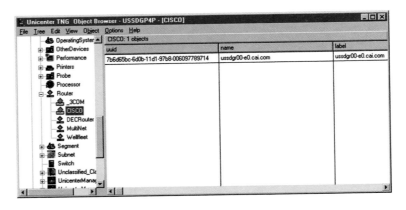

Inheritance Tree The Object browser's left pane lists all the object classes defined in the TNG repository in an inheritance tree. Subclasses are listed below and to the right of their superclasses.

Object List The Object browser's right pane lists all the objects of the selected class in a table and shows all the instances' properties in the columns. The Object browser shows you all the objects of a particular kind, and in Figure 2.20 you see all of the Cisco routers—but it does not show any of the environment's structure. The maps and the Topology browser better serve that purpose.

Class Browser The Class browser displays a tree view of the class definitions in the repository. You use it in conjunction with the Class Editor to create and modify object classes. This topic is beyond the scope of this book.

Managed Object Notebook The Managed Object Notebook (see Figure 2.21) shows a managed object's properties. You generally launch it from one of the browsers—the 2D or 3D maps, the Object browser, the Control Panel, or the Topology browser. Right-click the object in any of these browsers and select Open Details from the pop-up menu.

FIGURE 2.21
The Managed Object
Notebook's Main page.

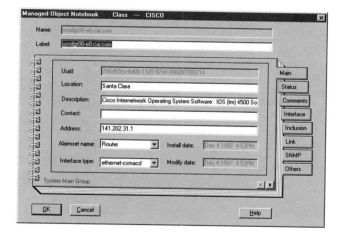

Unicenter TNG uses notebooks as a consistent user interface to view and manipulate data. Notebooks have pages; clicking the tabs (which are generally on the right side of the notebook) moves you to the selected page.

An object's class defines the specific pages and properties for that object. The Managed Object class defines pages and properties inherited by any subclass. The pages are Main, Status, and Others; the Status and Others pages are shown in Figure 2.22 and Figure 2.23, respectively. The Inclusion and Link pages show inclusion associations and links that relate managed objects to other managed objects. Many systems have SNMP pages and Comments (see Figure 2.24) pages as well.

FIGURE 2.22
The Managed Object
Notebook's Status page.

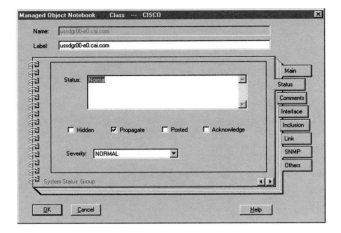

FIGURE 2.23
The Managed Object
Notebook's Others page.

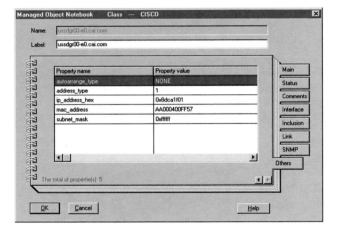

Changing Property Values   You can change the values of most of the properties of objects in
the repository with the Managed Object Notebook. You can change any property with a white
background. The specific technique depends on the type of data the property represents;
normal Windows conventions apply to most. In cases where data is displayed as name value
tables, such as in Figure 2.24, you can simply double-click the property value; a small window
will open in which you can edit the value (see Figure 2.25).

Reporting   You can print a few simple reports from the Real World Interface browsers. These
reports help document either the state and topology of the network or the contents of the repository.

Maps   To print a folder from the 2D map, simply select it and select Print from the File menu.

FIGURE 2.24

The Managed Object Notebook's Comments page.

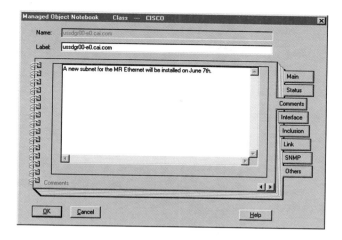

FIGURE 2.25

Changing properties in the Property dialog box.

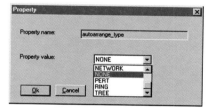

You can also capture the map displayed in a folder to the Clipboard or to a file. From there you can either paste the map from the Clipboard or link it into a document or presentation. Figure 2.26 shows a map copied through the Clipboard from the 2D map into this book as a Windows metafile (.wmf). To capture a map, simply select it and select Export Picture from the File menu. The window shown in Figure 2.27 lets you select whether the map will be stored as a bitmap or Windows metafile and whether to copy it to a file or the Clipboard.

FIGURE 2.26

The map copied as a Windows metafile via the Clipboard.

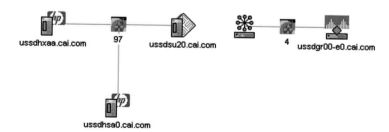

Object Reports From the 2D map you can also generate textual reports of objects and links using the commands under the Report menu. This requires adjusting print settings and fonts. The following procedure works:

1. Select the print font size with the Print Fonts item in the 2D map's Display menu. You will see the Set Print Fonts window (see Figure 2.28).

Ch

2

FIGURE 2.27
The Copy Picture
window.

FIGURE 2.28
The Set Print Fonts
window.

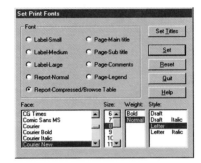

2. Choose to set the Report-Compressed/Browse Table font. This controls the fonts used in the printed reports.

3. Choose the font size and face. A fixed-width font like Courier New (with a font size of 9) works well.

4. Click the Set button to change the setting, and then click Quit to close the window.

The 2D map can generate a summary network report. Landscape mode printing is necessary because this report is 132 columns wide. The following steps instruct you on how to print a summary report:

1. In Windows NT's Printers Setup window, select the printer you want to use and choose Document Defaults from the File menu. Choose Landscape Orientation.

2. In the 2D Map, select Print Setup from the File menu and choose the printer you want to use. Click Setup and then choose Landscape Orientation.

3. Select Network Summary from the Report menu in the 2D map. Click Report to Printer, and then click the Report button (see Figure 2.29).

Other reports from the 2D map are set up to print in 80 columns and in portrait orientation. A 9-point Courier New font with the printer set in portrait orientation as the Document Default works well.

FIGURE 2.29
The Network Summary Report window.

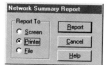

The other reports generate information on objects and links. They allow you to select, by a number of criteria, exactly which objects appear on reports:

- The Object Details report lists all of the objects or LANs.
- Object by Name lets you select objects by their names.
- Object by Folder allows you to select certain folders and report on all the objects within them. This is useful for reporting on certain portions of the network.
- Object by Class allows you to select certain classes and report on all the objects of that class. This is useful for seeing how all your HP-UX servers are doing as one example.

Object by Class and Object by Folder allow you to select the severity levels of the objects that appear on reports. For example, if you want a report of all Windows NT systems with a Major problem (or worse), you would select Object by Class and set up the report as shown in Figure 2.30.

FIGURE 2.30
The Object Report by Class window illustrates the setup for a report of Windows NT systems with Major problems.

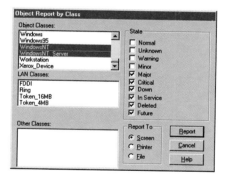

Printing Tables and Trees   The Topology browser, Object browser, and Class browser each allow printing a report on their respective contents.

The Topology browser's Print Objects Tree command in the File menu allows you to print a tree showing what objects are include in which folders. Its Print Objects List command in the File menu lets you print a table of all the objects included within the selected folder, as well as some of their properties.

The Object browser's Print Class Tree command in the File menu allows you to print a tree showing all the object classes. Its Print Objects List command in the File menu allows you to print a table of all the objects of a particular class as well as all of its properties.

The Print Class Tree command in the File menu of the Class browser allows you to print a tree showing all the object classes. The Print Class Level Properties and Print Instance Level Properties commands in the File menu allow you to print a table of class and instance level property definitions.

By default, the table reports show only the first few columns of the table. As with any report utility however, printing in Landscape mode, adjusting the column width, and reordering the table's columns allows for formatting the report to suit your needs.

Adjusting Table Column Width and Order   To adjust the table column width, right-click the bar between the table headings and drag the separator to the left or right.

To change the order of the columns, click any column's heading and drag the column heading to the left or right and drop it in the position desired.

Understanding Events: Logs and Consoles

Operators are responsible for solving a variety of problems as they arise. As such, they are mostly concerned with handling events generated by the operating system, or by applications leveraging the operating system's built-in event logging and reporting capabilities. Unicenter TNG provides event management functions to handle these events. The two main tools for this are TNG's Event Console and status displays (like the 2D and 3D maps). The status displays provide an overview of the "situation"—what's up, what's down, and so on. However, most operators cannot spend their time idly staring at a display until something "breaks" or otherwise goes awry. At the minimum, they need recent problems and changes organized into a prioritized list of events in order to determine which issue needs to be handled next. The TNG Event Console performs exactly that function. The Event Console gets its data from a log, which is simply a file that records messages. The log contains two types of messages: event messages and commands. The current log file is closed and a new one created every day. Each system with an event agent or manager installed has its own set of daily logs.

Using the Event Console

The Event Console can be started in three ways: through the Enterprise Management function GUI, from within the 2D or 3D map, or through a command line.

Launching the Event Console from the Real World Interface   To launch the Event Console from the TNG GUI, open the system where the log file resides, open Unispace object (as shown in Figure 2.31), and right-click the Events object. A pop-up menu appears. Choose Console Log to open an Event Console (see Figure 2.35).

Launching the Event Console from the Enterprise Management Browser   To invoke the local Event Console via the Enterprise Management browser, select Enterprise Managers from the Unicenter TNG Enterprise Management pull-down menu.

To do this, click on the Windows NT Start button and select Unicenter TNG Enterprise Management. From the resulting menu, select Enterprise Managers.

FIGURE 2.31

Unispace with the management functions.

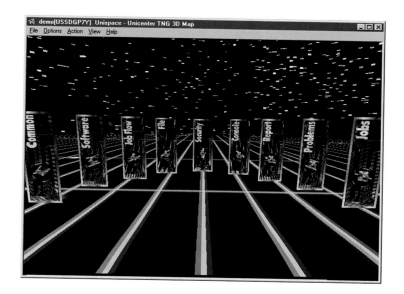

You see a window like that in Figure 2.32.

FIGURE 2.32

The Enterprise Managers main window.

Double-clicking the Windows NT icon opens the window shown in Figure 2.33. This window shows the various Enterprise Management functions installed on that system.

FIGURE 2.33

The Enterprise Managers - Functions window.

Double-click the icon labeled Event; this opens the window shown in Figure 2.34.

Double-click the icon labeled Console Logs; an Event Console window appears. It's shown in Figure 2.35.

FIGURE 2.34
The Event window.

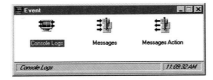

FIGURE 2.35
The Console window.

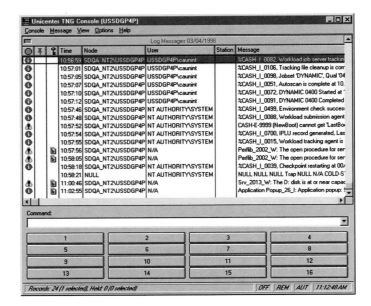

The Event Console Display   Figure 2.36 depicts a typical console's window.

The console has the normal title bar, pull-down menu, and toolbar typical of any window. The main part of the display is the Log Messages area, which displays all the messages in the log. The Held Messages area is above it. *Held messages* are those that are important (as determined by policy) and need to be replied to or acknowledged. You can adjust the space given to each of these areas by dragging the bar between them up or down. The Held Message area closes when there are no held messages. Both the Log Messages area and the Held Messages area display the events in a table, and each row is a single message. The window shows the messages sorted by time with the latest message at the bottom of the list. You can select which columns to display and can filter the display to show only relevant messages. For instance, you can show only messages from 1 to 2 p.m.

The Event Console window, which is below these two areas, has an area where you can enter commands; 16 command buttons that can be configured to invoke common commands are below that.

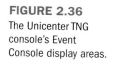

FIGURE 2.36

The Unicenter TNG console's Event Console display areas.

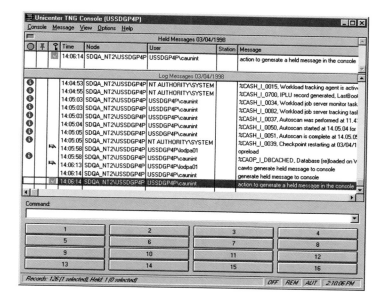

At the bottom of the window there is a status bar that shows how many messages are in the log and how many the system has marked as held. It also shows whether the Log Message area is displaying filtered messages or all messages. The status bar additionally indicates whether the system will execute commands remotely or locally, whether scrolling is automatic or manual, and the current time. Near the upper left, an indicator light shows the state of the currently displayed log.

Symbols indicate a message's severity and flags. To see a legend describing these fields, select View, Legend in the pull-down menu.

Annotating Messages   You can add an annotation to any message. An *annotation* is essentially a note, or additional information. This is a convenient place to mark information or progress made in attempting to diagnose a problem. One manager might write an annotation describing the progress made so far, so that a manager who takes over later will know where to begin. You can have a number of annotations on a message. The page displays the name of the user who entered the annotation, the node used, the time of the annotation, and the body of the text (see Figure 2.37).

Click New to add an annotation. A window will pop up; type the message. In this example you can just type the note in as shown in Figure 2.38.

Held Messages   Held messages require a reply or an acknowledgment. They will remain in the Held Messages area of the window until you acknowledge them or reply to them. Holding messages for acknowledgment is a good way to avoid missing particularly important information.

FIGURE 2.37
The Message Detail
window's Annotations
tab.

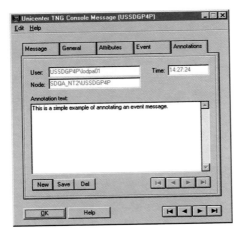

FIGURE 2.38
A New Annotation
message window.

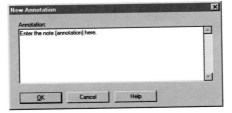

Select the message with a single-click and select Message, Acknowledge from the pull-down menu to acknowledge a held message.

To reply to a held message, select the message with a single-click and select Message, Reply from the pull-down menu. The user program that has been waiting for the reply will receive the text you enter. Take a look at Figure 2.39.

FIGURE 2.39
Replying to a message.

Commands   The Event Console's command area allows you to enter a command just as you would in a command-line window or at the DOS prompt. Commands will execute in either a local or a remote context.

Local commands execute on the user's desktop, in the context of the user who is logged on, and using the Event Console. Local commands are useful in launching a GUI that will place its output on the local screen. The log does not track local commands. For example, entering the local command `notepad todo.txt` would run the Notepad text editor on the file todo.txt in your default directory.

Remote commands execute under the control of the Event Agent for the machine whose log you are viewing. The log tracks remote commands and any output they produce. Remote commands generally run tests on a system or control a system. For example, you might stop and restart the print spooler with a remote command if you found that the printer appeared to be hung.

```
net stop service Spooler

net start service Spooler
```

The log shows the output of those commands as messages. Figure 2.40 shows the result of issuing these two commands.

FIGURE 2.40

The result of the remote commands.

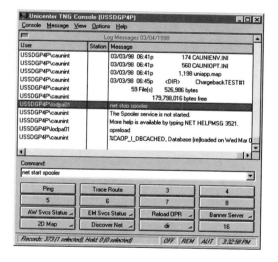

To select whether a command is executed locally or remotely, select Options, Command, Local, or try Options, Command, Remote from the pull-down menu. The one with a check mark is currently in effect.

Command Buttons   You can assign commonly used commands to one of 16 command buttons. Clicking a button enters the command just as if you had typed it in the command area.

Customizing Buttons   To assign a command to one of the buttons, choose Options, Settings from the Event Console's pull-down menu; you then select the Buttons tab—you'll see what's shown in Figure 2.41. Enter the label for each button and the actual command in the appropriate field. There are two check boxes, Local and Auto, with each button.

Checking Local instructs the system to execute the command locally, while leaving it unchecked causes the system to execute the command remotely (on the agent machine).

FIGURE 2.41
The Console Settings
window's Buttons tab.

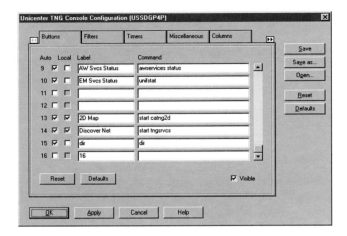

Checking Auto means the button will automatically execute the command immediately after
the button is pressed. Leaving it clear tells the system to enter the command, but not to invoke
it until you have had a chance to edit the command. These *manual command buttons* allow you
to finish the command and to fill out details. For example, you could assign a button to the
trace route command without the destination. As another example, you might enter the syntax for a command you use infrequently. Whenever you press the button, it will show the syntax of the command as an aide.

Left-click the button, complete the command, and press Enter to execute a manual command
button.

Filtering Messages   Because event logs can get rather large, it is often helpful to view only
events related to the current problem. The Event Console allows you to filter the log and shows
only those events that fit a specific criterion. Filtering selects a subset of the log for viewing; it
does not change the content of the log. To filter the Console log, choose Options, Settings from
the Event Console pull-down menu and then select the Filters tab (see Figure 2.42).

You would use a filter such as that shown in Figure 2.43 to show the messages after a particular
time.

You can select very particular groups of messages by combining filters. For example, you
might select those messages where Node is the name of a router, Time is between 8 a.m. and
12 noon, and Severity is not Informational (I). You could then view only events that may indicate a problem for that router during the specified time.

FIGURE 2.42
Filtering the Console log to show only messages since noon.

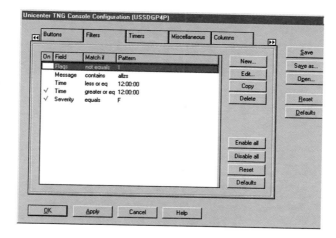

FIGURE 2.43
Editing the message filter.

Automated Actions—The Event Message/Action Engine

The Event Console enables operators to see the events captured by Unicenter TNG and manually react to them. Nevertheless, as mentioned earlier, automation is essential for responding to events—and therefore problems—quickly. No human can react as fast as a computer. Unicenter TNG has always supported a simple form of automation in its event message/action engine. The event message/action engine is part of every Event Agent, as well as part of the Event Manager. There is little difference between the two.

The event message/action engine examines each event message and compares it against defined patterns before placing it in the Event log. If the event matches one of the patterns, the engine executes any actions defined for that message pattern. Those actions allow message filtering, forwarding to other managers, modification of the message, defining how the message is to be displayed, and most importantly, invoking any command, including those that may repair the problem.

The process of setting up this automatic processing of events is relatively straightforward. First, you identify message patterns requiring action. Second, you define the response (one or more actions) the system will undertake for each of those patterns. While it is easy to implement a policy this way, deciding what constitutes good policy is anything but simple. This is where operational knowledge and organizational goals intersect. Experience shows that defining policy is a much greater challenge than applying it, but bridging this chasm is the key to successful operations.

As an example, turn to the problem of managing a network printer spooled from a Windows NT server. This printer is old and prone to frequent paper jams. If possible, someone should notify Operations before users complain. Building a policy to address this requirement means considering the following issues:

1. Does the system generate events when the problem arises? In the printer jam example, the printer reports the jam over the network to the server, and the printer driver logs the event in the Windows NT system Event log. The availability of this event is a big help in fixing the problem and makes it a good candidate for automated response.

2. Review a complete list to determine which events the system should discard or mask. Filtering messages simplifies problem resolution by reducing clutter and focusing attention. In the printer example, the driver reports an event every time a file is printed. This is irrelevant to your needs, and so you decide to hide this event. You will not discard it, as it might be useful in problem analysis or for recovery to know the last job printed before an error.

3. You must determine which events indicate a problem, and just as importantly, what events indicate the problem is resolved. Events are logged when a paper jam occurs, when the printer is out of paper, or when the cover of the printer is open. Each of these indicates a problem. It also reports when the printer is ready to run. The latter is logged whenever a jam gets cleared or paper is added to the printer. Ready indicates that the problem has been resolved.

4. Now you should consider what to do in response to each event. The actions can be thought of as a simple To Do list, or in technical terms, a *script* written for the message/action engine. You can do the following within that script:

   a. Manipulate the message and its appearance in the log.

   b. Display messages on the console and change the status of objects in the repository.

   c. Issue either local or remote commands.

   d. Control the script's execution flow (*branching*), building in appropriate logic.

5. Next, in terms of the printer example, you need to display a message when the printer goes down and another when it comes back up. You also want to change the status of the printer in the repository to display when the printer is having a problem.

6. Finally, you need to deploy and implement the policy. The policy can be initially implemented entirely through the Unicenter GUI, but after local testing it can be stored as a *cautil* script file. That way it can be distributed at any time to other systems. The Message Record – Detail window shown in Figure 2.44 is the starting point in the Unicenter TNG GUI for implementing a policy.

FIGURE 2.44
The Criteria page of the Message Record - Detail window.

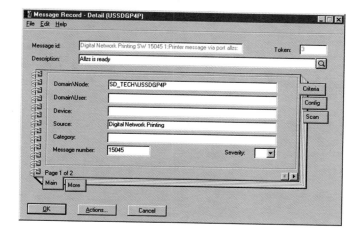

Pattern Fields   The only field you must enter is the Message ID; the other fields further refine the pattern. You should enter * into Token; this will assign the next unused token to this pattern. Choose Message Save from the menu when you have finished defining the pattern. This will store the pattern and allow you to add actions for it. When you have defined all the actions, click OK to close the window.

The message/action engine will not start checking messages against the pattern or acting on any of the message actions you define until you restart or reload it.

Pattern Token   A number entered into the Token field identifies each message pattern. Each message pattern must have a unique number assigned to it. The system automatically assigns tokens.

Description   This is where this pattern's purpose is described. It takes no part in pattern matching.

Pattern Matching   A *message pattern* defines the values that must appear in a message in order for it to "match" the pattern. The previous section discusses the fields in a message. Table 2.3 explains the various fields in a message pattern, the page of the Message Record – Detail window on which they appear, and how they match against log messages. All of the filled-in pattern fields must match their message fields in order for a message to match the pattern.

Table 2.3   Pattern Matching Fields

Pattern Field	Detail Page	Message Field	Notes
Message ID	All	Message Text	See "Message Text Matching"
Scan Text, From, To	Scan	Message Text	See "Message Text Matching"
Source	Criteria, Main	Facility or Source	See "Message Facility and ID Number (Type) Matching"
Message Number	Criteria, Main	Message ID	See "Message Facility and ID Number (Type) Matching"
Domain\Node	Criteria, Main	Node	
Domain\User	Criteria, Main	User	
Device	Criteria, Main	Device	
Workstation	Criteria, More	Workstation	
Program	Criteria, More	?Process?	
Category	Criteria, Main	Category	
Severity	Criteria, Main	Severity	Failure, Error, Warning, Informational, or Success
Job Set, Job Name, Job Number, Job Qualifier	Criteria, More	Workload	Fields identifying the workload job where the message originated, see "Matching Other Message Fields"
User Data	Criteria, More	User Data	

Pattern Field	Detail Page	Message Field	Notes
Message Type	Config	Command Flag	Message or command, see "Matching Commands Versus Messages"
Calendar	Config	Date/Time Written	See "Matching Message Time Against a Calendar"

Message Text Matching

Most pattern matching is done against the message text using the pattern's message ID. You must enter data in this field. You could enter the exact text of the message you want to match in the Message ID field, but in most cases the text varies with specific data in specific places in the message. You can enter wildcards into the message ID to deal with those variable parts of a message.

When matching the text of a message against the pattern, the message's text and the pattern's message ID are split into a sequence of words (or tokens) separated by spaces or tabs. The program then compares each word of the pattern message ID to the corresponding word in the message text. If each word matches, the pattern's message ID matches the message text. This means that if the pattern ID is shorter than the message text, only the initial few words of the message are checked. The pattern ID a b c matches the message text a b c d e f.

Words in the pattern ID can contain the wildcard characters *, which matches zero or more characters, or ?, which matches any single character. For example, the pattern ID word Print* matches the corresponding message text word if it is Printer, or if it is Printing. Indeed, the whole word can be just *, which matches any word. The pattern ID * matches any message text and is used very often. Matching based on words occasionally surprises users familiar with wildcards in file specifications. For example, the pattern ID Print* Down would not match the message text Print Queue Down. Instead, you would need to specify this as Print * Down.

You can choose which characters the system treats as wildcard characters when comparing the pattern's text with the message. This is useful in the rare case where the default wildcard characters are important parts of the message text. In that case other characters like @, #, $, %, ~, &, or J could be used as wildcards.

You can also match against the message text by scanning it for particular text strings. You set this up on the Scan page shown in Figure 2.45.

Enter the text you want to search for in the Text field, and then enter the starting and ending character positions you want to scan in the From and To fields. For example, set the Scan Text to allzs to match any message text that contains the string allzs (the name of a printer). A message text's maximum size is 254 characters, so scanning from 1 to 254 searches the entire text. A pattern ID of * results in such a scan.

FIGURE 2.45
The Scan page of the
Message Record - Detail
window.

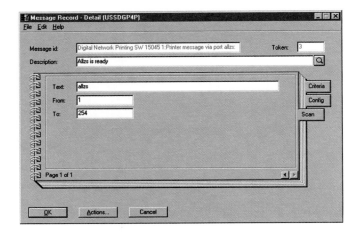

While word-based pattern matching is easy to understand, you can also compare the message
text to the pattern ID via regular expression matching, which is more powerful. UNIX shell
scripts commonly use regular expressions.

Message Facility and ID Number (Type) Matching

As described in the previous section, the message facility and message ID number fields often
identify the message type independently of the text. Text can vary as developers produce
different versions of software and will vary depending on language. Ideally, developers should
keep the facility the same and leave the ID number fixed as long as the meaning of the
message remains the same. To match a particular message type, you would set the pattern ID
to *, the pattern source to the facility name, and the pattern message number to the message
ID number. These pattern fields are set on the main criteria page.

Matching Message Time Against a Calendar

You can compare the timestamp of a message to a calendar to determine whether the pattern
matches a message. Calendars control message handling. For example, an operator may not
want to worry about the printer during the times he is not there. The system may handle any
printer jams while he is on vacation differently, or not at all.

Unicenter TNG uses calendars throughout to control everything from login to backups. Calendars most naturally arise in discussions of production, which you find in Chapter 4, "Server
Management." Simply stated, each calendar has a name (for example, OperatorIsIn). By
entering a calendar name in this pattern field, the match succeeds if the system logged the
message at a date and time within the range set for the calendar.

Matching Commands Versus Messages

The log records both event messages and command inputs and outputs. You can choose what
sort of message a pattern will check by selecting a message type. Use Message for event
messages and Command for command inputs and outputs.

Matching Other Message Fields

You can also match a pattern against other message fields as listed in the *Unicenter TNG Administrator's Guide*. You can match against fields that identify where the message came from (Node, User, Device, and Process), the batch job the message is about (Workload and Workstation), or optional information about the message (Severity, Category, and User Data). These are straightforward matches. The pattern fields can contain wildcards (except Severity, of course). If left blank in the pattern, these will match any value in the message. Fields such as Workstation that do not appear on the Message Record Detail window's Main page can be found on the More page as shown in Figure 2.46.

Ch
2

FIGURE 2.46
The Message Record - Detail window's More page.

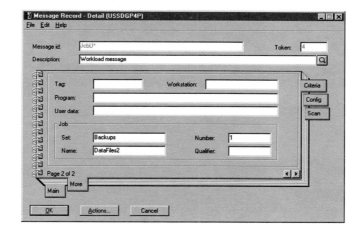

Matching Frequent Messages

Sometimes, when something in a system goes wrong, a component will start logging the same (or similar) event messages repeatedly. For example, if a database fills a disk but continually attempts to write a record, it might generate hundreds of these messages in a short time. While the first event message is important, all subsequent warnings just clutter the log. In other cases, however, otherwise routine event messages suddenly generated in a short period might point to a real problem. For example, the system logs an event when a user fails to log in because he enters the wrong password. A few such events likely indicate nothing more serious than misspellings or absent-minded users. However, many such events over a short period might indicate an attempt to break in.

A message pattern can detect frequent messages of the same type using Frequency Count and Frequency Interval. The engine counts the number of event messages that match the pattern. If the number of messages counted exceeds the number of expected messages in a given Frequency Interval, then the message pattern executes its actions.

Defining Message Actions

Message actions tell the message/action engine what to do when it finds a message that matches the pattern. The actions might be as simple as modifying how the message is displayed, or as complex as running a complex series of actions to diagnose and repair a problem. The actions are much like a simple scripting language. You can control the order in which actions are taken, manipulate the messages, display information, and execute commands and programs from action steps.

Take the following steps to define the actions for a message pattern while you are defining the pattern. After you have filled in the pattern fields, choose Message, Save, and then click the Actions button at the bottom of the window shown in Figure 2.46. If the pattern already exists, select the message pattern from the Message Action Summary window (see Figure 2.47), and then choose File, Open from the menu. Click the Actions button.

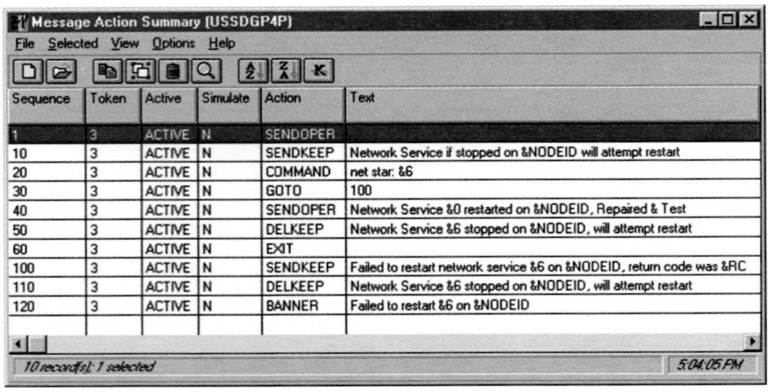

FIGURE 2.47

Action Summary window for a message pattern.

FIGURE 2.48

The Message Record Action window's Action page.

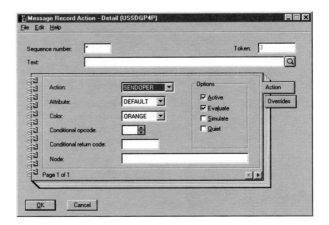

Either way, you will see a list of actions defined for this pattern like that in Figure 2.48. To create a new action, select Action, New from the pull-down menu; you will see the window in Figure 2.49. The Action selection defines the action the system will take, and the remaining fields modify and control how the system runs that action. The following sections describe all of them. However, you should plan the actions that you want taken before you actually define an action.

FIGURE 2.49
The Message Record Action window's Overrides page.

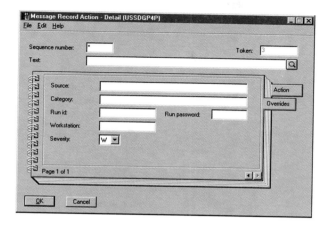

Action Sequences You can instruct Unicenter TNG to run a number of actions for any pattern. You order the actions by defining a sequence number for each message. The system processes message actions in sequence order. You can control the flow of execution within that sequence using the techniques described in this section.

As you add actions, you can let the system choose the sequence number for the new action by entering an asterisk in the Sequence field. As in BASIC, the system will assign a number 10 digits higher than the highest sequence number currently in use.

If you are entering a series of actions, it is generally easier to choose File, Save, and New from the Action window menu, rather than clicking OK and then choosing Selected, New from the List window.

Many of the actions are similar to commands executed by the COMMAND action, which is either entered by a user at the command line or executed in a batch script.

Overriding Message Fields

Table 2.4 shows the various fields in a message you can override.

Table 2.4   Overriden

Action Field	Page	Message Field Overridden	Notes
Message Text	All	Message Text	Refer to "Message Text Matching"

continues

Table 2.4   Continued

Action Field	Page	Message Field Overridden	Notes
Source	Overrides	Facility or Source	Refer to "Message Facility and ID Number (Type) Matching"
Category	Overrides	Category	
Run ID?	Overrides	Message ID	This is either the message ID (unlikely) or Workload (or some fraction of it)
Workstation	Overrides	Workstation	
Severity	Overrides	Severity	**F**ailure, **E**rror, **W**arning, **I**nformational, or **S**uccess
Run ID?	Overrides	Workload	Fields identifying the Workload job where the message originated; refer to "Matching Other Message Fields" above
Attribute	Action	Attribute	
Color	Action	Color	

Overriding Display Attributes and Color

You can draw attention to a message in the console by setting its Color and Display attributes. The values for Color are Red, Orange, Yellow, Green, Blue, Purple, and the default Black. The values for the Display attribute are Default (colored text on a white background), Reverse (white text on a colored background), and Blink (colored, blinking text on a white background).

It is a good idea to avoid using blinking text except in extreme cases. Various studies have shown that blinking text can't be ignored, which means that while it is on the screen, the operator won't be able to see much else, such as the information needed to fix the problem. It is also annoying, which should be sufficient reason to employ it judiciously.

A similar problem occurs with sending a beep to the console.

Finally, a significant number of people (primarily males) are colorblind and cannot distinguish between certain colors or shades. Thus, it is always a good idea to check with the operators and find out what colors and shading work well for them.

DISCARD   The DISCARD action prevents the system from writing the message in the log. Therefore, DISCARD can filter out unwanted or unneeded messages. Define a message pattern that matches the message and then set the only action to DISCARD.

Other actions can be included after the DISCARD action has been in order to write other messages to the log or even write the same message again. This can replace the original message with a different one. In this case the first action is DISCARD and the second is SENDOPER, with the desired text.

While the DISCARD action prevents this pattern from writing a message to the log, it does not prevent other patterns that match the message from writing the message to the log.

HILITE   The HILITE action writes a message to the log, just like SENDOPER does with the Highlight flag set. The Highlight flag causes a box to appear around the message. Otherwise, the action operates the same as SENDOPER.

SUPPRESS   The SUPPRESS action writes a message to the log, just like SENDOPER, but with the Invisible flag set. That actually does nothing. The system displays invisible messages by default. Nevertheless, it is quite easy to set a filter on the console display so that invisible messages do not clutter the display.

SENDKEEP   The SENDKEEP action writes a message to the log with the Keep flag set. This causes the system to display the message in the Held Messages area of the console until the operator acknowledges it.

EVALUATE   The EVALUATE action generates a new message and sends it to the Pattern Matcher. The Pattern Matcher, and indeed the whole message-action engine, will treat this as a brand-new message. The system handles that new message like any other, except that it disables the current pattern while evaluating the new message. This prevents the engine from looping forever if you send the message in without change.

EVALUATE generates a return code that can be tested. The return code will be 0 if the message matched a pattern and 1 if it did not match any.

For example, assume that you have several messages with different texts but essentially the same meaning; you would like to take the same action for all of them. You could define a message pattern for each with an action that resulted in the same new message for all. You would then define a pattern for that new message and run in that message the action you wanted all of the messages to perform.

The EVALUATE action can also send a message to the Pattern Matcher on another system via the action's Node field. That system will evaluate the message against the patterns defined for its engine. The SENDOPER action (as well as the rest of the actions) write directly to the log file on that system.

Communicating with the User and Operator

These actions allow the action sequencer to interact with the operator and users beyond simply sending messages to the log.

DELKEEP   The DELKEEP action searches the log for held messages that match the text in the action's Text field and acknowledges them. DELKEEP's most common use is to clear messages from the Held Messages area when the underlying fault has been fixed. The following section gives an example of this. Note that this only sets the Acknowledged flag for the message—it does not actually delete any message.

DELKEEP acknowledges any kind of help message, whether the message is waiting for an acknowledgment or for a reply. However, it does not send a reply to a user waiting for it, and the user will still be waiting for that reply message. Use AUTORPLY for messages waiting for a reply, and use DELKEEP for messages waiting for a simple acknowledgment.

AUTORPLY   The AUTORPLY action returns a reply to the user who issued the message. This only makes sense as an action defined for a message issued with the Reply flag set (one issued by cawtor or the equivalent API call to the software, for example).

AUTORPLY works well in situations when no operator is present and a batch job issues a message that needs some reply. Because the job is generally waiting for the reply before proceeding, it does not make sense to force it to wait until an operator is around.

AUTORPLY also works well if you have previously defined criteria that permit the software to determine what corrective action the system should take. For example, a program might need to know the name of the directory in which it should build a kit. The developer may have written the program in anticipation that an operator would provide the directory name. If you later found a way to generate the directory automatically, you could build a message pattern with an AUTORPLY action that returns the directory rather than change the program.

The first word in the action's Text field should contain the reply ID. The reply ID is always the first word of the message, so you can fill it in by supplying &1 as the first word in the reply text.

WAITOPER   The WAITOPER action writes a message to the log and waits for a reply. This is the same as issuing a cawtor command. Unlike the other variations on SENDOPER, WAITOPER does not copy other message fields, like Source and User, from the message that matched the pattern.

WAITOPER can give the operator control over the timing of various automatic actions. For example, you could build actions that shut down and restart a database if an event message indicates that it has a particular problem—but you might want to send a message to the operator before the database is shut down so he or she can warn users and make sure no critical work is going on.

BANNER (TSBCLNT)   Operators might not have the console up on their screens when an important event happens. The BANNER action lets you draw their attention to the message by displaying a text message in a scrolling window (much like a ticker tape), which appears at the top of the operator's screen. The action's text is what appears.

SENDUSER   The SENDUSER action sends a text message to the user identified in the event message the engine is handling. The action's Text field supplies the actual message. Only UNIX systems support SENDUSER.

An Example of Printer Problems

Here is a simple example of how you can use the message action engine to track a problem. The same network printer mentioned previously (called allzs) is preprogrammed to write event records to the Windows NT system log file when the printer jams, runs out of paper, is ready, or prints a job. The system logs the following message text:

```
Digital Network Printing SW_15101_W: Printer message via port allzs: Upper paper
➥tray is missing or not aligned
Digital Network Printing SW_15123_W: Printer message via port allzs: Please clear
➥paper jam caused by main transport station

Digital Network Printing SW_15045_I: Printer message via port allzs: Print Engine
➥ready
```

The printer also supplies a Facility (*source*) of Digital Network Printing and a Message Number of 15101. Either the text or the source/number can be used to match the message. You match the source and message number in the following patterns.

There are several things you need to do for any problem: display a held message on the console, display a banner across the screen, and reset the status of the network printer in the repository so that the 2D and 3D maps display its correct status. Undo all of these actions when the printer is repaired.

There are a number of messages that indicate a problem. You need to perform the same basic tasks for each problem. In order to accomplish that, you send a message back to the Pattern Matcher that reads as follows:

```
Allzs problem: Upper paper tray missing

Allzs problem: Paper jam

Allzs problem: Out of paper
```

Ch
2

This can be matched on the first two words of text, and all the actions can be run there.

Examples of the message patterns and actions you would define are shown in Table 2.5.

Table 2.5   Pattern and Actions for a Printer Problem

Pattern: Upper paper tray missing

Pattern Field	Value to Match
Text	*
Source	Digital Network Printing
Message Number	15101

Actions:

Seq	IF rc	Action	Fields	Value
10		SENDOPER	Color	RED
20		EVALUATE	Text	Allzs problem: Upper paper tray missing

The actions first write the message to the log and display it in red and then re-enter an edited and clearer message for common handling (see Table 2.6).

Table 2.6   Common Pattern and Actions for a Printer Problem

Pattern: Allzs problem

Pattern Field	Value to Match
Text	Allzs problem: *

Actions:

Seq	IF rc	Action	Fields	Value
10		SENDKEEP	Color	RED
20		BANNER	Text	&text
30		COMMAND	Text	setstat -C Printserver20 -N allzs.cai.com &text

This matches a number of problem messages (see Table 2.7). Action 10 sends the message to the console's held area as a kept message waiting for acknowledgment. Action 20 displays the message in a banner. Action 30 sets the status of the object in the repository.

Table 2.7 Common Pattern and Actions for a Printer Problem

Pattern: `Allzs ready`

Pattern Field	Value to Match
Text	`Digital Network Printing`
	`SW_15045_I: Printer message via`
	`port allzs: Print Engine ready`

Actions:

Seq	IF rc	Action	Fields	Value
10		SENDOPER	Color	`GREEN`
20		DELKEEP	Text	`Allzs problem: *`
30		BANNER	Text	`Allzs Ready`
40		COMMAND	Text	`setstat -C Printserver20 -N allzs.cai.com Normal`

This message, `Print Engine ready`, indicates that the printer is up and online. Action 20 removes all of the held messages awaiting acknowledgment because they have been fixed. Action 40 sets the status of the object in the repository back to `NORMAL`.

Example: Keeping Services Alive

This example sets up a pattern and actions to restart various services should they stop running. To accomplish this, we use the Windows NT System Agent (described in Chapter 4) to detect whether any important service has failed. If the service does go down, the actions display a message indicating the problem and then attempt to restart the service. If the restart succeeds, it acknowledges the held message; if it fails to fix the problem, it presents another message (see Table 2.8).

Table 2.8 Pattern and Actions to Detect and Restart a Stopped Service

Pattern: Service fails

Pattern Field	Value to Match
Text	`NT Agent reports Service ( * ) Critical ( ClassName = ntServiceInst oldState = * newState = Critical )`

continues

Table 2.8 Continued

Actions:

Seq	IF rc	Action	Fields	Value
10		SENDOPER	Color Severity	RED Warning
20		SENDKEEP	Text Color Severity	Network Service &6 stopped on &NODEID, will attempt restart RED Warning
30		COMMAND	Text Color	net start &6 Blue
40	> 0	GOTO	Text	100
50		SENDOPER	Text Color Severity	Repaired &text Green Success
60		DELKEEP	Text	Network Service &6 stopped on &NODEID, will attempt restart
70		EXIT		
100		SENDKEEP	Text Color Attribute Severity	Failed to restart network service &6 on &NODEID, return code was &RC RED Reverse Fatal
110		DELKEEP	Text	Network Service &6 stopped on &NODEID, will attempt restart
120		BANNER	Text	Failed to restart network service &6

The important action here is 30, which issues the command to restart the service. If it suc-ceeds, it will return a code of 0. Anything else indicates a problem of some kind. Action 40 tests the return code, and jumps to action 100 when it is greater than 0. Actions 60 and 110 remove the held message issued in action 20, which indicates that a restart is in progress. Actions 60 and 100 display additional appropriate messages. ●

Basic Network Management

In this chapter

Challenges

Network managers face many challenges. Networks often consist of thousands of heterogeneous devices connected by token ring, Ethernet, or X.25 and separated by wide expanses of geography. The size and scope of today's networks make them difficult to manage effectively.

Given the size and geographic dispersion of the typical network, it is extremely difficult for the person charged with network management to even know all of the devices that are in the network, much less the location of those devices. However, it is impossible to effectively manage networks without being aware of all of the components that must be managed. The basic maxim applied to other areas of management is valid here as well: "You can't manage it if you don't know it exists."

Knowing that a managed object exists essentially consists of trying to keep an accurate and updated inventory—a challenge in itself when considering all of the additions, changes, and deletions from the network that may occur daily. Problem determination is more difficult, if not impossible, when the inventory of network assets is inaccurate or does not contain enough information about the failing network component.

The network manager is confronted by a myriad of devices supplied by a variety of vendors, diverse communications protocols, and complex network topologies, which adds to the difficulty. The permutations of platforms, communications protocols, application software, servers, mainframes, desktops, and databases that could be connected to the network are infinite. Attempting to sort out this tangled web can be an overwhelming task.

The complexities of the IT environments lead to another challenge for the network manager. There is an avalanche of data to sift through in order to find information that is useful for the task at hand, be it problem determination, adding a new device to an existing network, or dealing with performance issues. At times, it may seem like searching for a needle in a haystack.

It is simply impossible to manage the network environment effectively without using a sophisticated management tool. Unicenter TNG includes extensive management capabilities to address the problem. This chapter will address some of the key questions that must be answered in order to take advantage of this management resource.

Where to Begin?

The first question all new enterprise managers should ask is "What systems am I responsible for?" If they can't answer that most basic question, they ought to find the answer as the first order of business. Ignorance is not bliss for a network manager. Rogue systems are vulnerable back doors for hackers. Less dramatically, these hidden or camouflaged assets drain productivity because they are unknown quantities. Something as simple as missing important upgrades makes problems more likely to occur, diagnosis more time consuming, and remedies more difficult to administer. This degrades productivity in the long run.

Each management task described in this book starts with a good inventory of the systems and a good topology of the network. A manager needs the inventory to understand which systems should be backed up. What systems require an upgrade to Windows NT 5.0? What servers should be assigned new user accounts? Topology is necessary to figure out why all of a sudden Human Resources isn't getting email from Accounting, or where it would be best to install a faster link for improving performance.

Slipping Through the Net

The following transpired years ago in the network development group at a major New England computer company: This company once built network equipment (one of the first Ethernets ran through the building) and designed networking software. They knew they had at least one of every kind of major network software and hardware that existed at the time, save one. SNA, TCP/IP, DECnet, Netware, NetBios, and XNS were all present—but not Appletalk. They were positive that there were not any Macintoshes on the company network. It was the punchline of many jokes. When they actually looked at the results of a discovery, however, they found that a dozen Macintoshes had been happily running on their intranet for over a year.

Another company experienced an unexpected benefit of Auto-Discovery when the enterprise IT map, generated via Auto-Discovery, showed a connected network emanating from a division that the company had sold two years before.

The fact that this sold company still had a connection to the parent company's network constituted a security breach. A manual inventory of networks and networked devices would not have revealed this security breach because the resident experts were certain this network had been disconnected. This rogue network would only have been found by accident, an undue and impractical amount of checking, or a computer-driven Auto-Discovery service. The discovery of this security breach was an unexpected use and benefit of Unicenter TNG's Auto-Discovery service.

Ch
3

The Brave New World of Unicenter TNG Discovery

The Discovery service included with Unicenter TNG automatically detects devices on your network and populates the Unicenter TNG Common Object Repository with objects that represent your network devices and their relationships. Once created, these objects can be displayed by Unicenter TNG's GUI and monitored and controlled by the applications in the Enterprise Management layer of Unicenter TNG, such as the Security and Event Managers, as well as by third-party manager applications.

Unicenter TNG Discovery provides significant advantages over other network discovery applications. Unicenter TNG Discovery allows you to do the following:

- Run multiple instances of Discovery on multiple machines at the same time.
- Run Discovery as a service, allowing you to perform other work on your machine.
- Define granularity. You can discover all devices in a subnet or specific elements connected to a specific segment.
- Start Discovery automatically or manually.

The automated facilities provided by Discovery reduce time spent on manual network database maintenance, entry validation, network map creation, and routine network maintenance activities. This reduction lowers operating costs and provides increased network reliability.

Prerequisites for Running Discovery

Besides installing Unicenter TNG itself, there are four primary prerequisites that must be met before running Discovery:

■ There must be a Common Object Repository (CORE). You don't have to worry about this because the CORE is created as a result of the installation process so that Discovery can be run automatically.

■ The Real World Interface should be installed. This also occurs automatically during Unicenter TNG's initial installation, although technically the Real World Interface is not a prerequisite to run Discovery. (See Chapter 2, "The Unicenter TNG Framework," for information about installing this component.)

■ The machine from which Discovery is run must be connected to the network and have valid IP and gateway addresses, as well as subnet masks. It is possible to discover from any network connection all of the other devices and subnets that are connected to the network on which it is located. However, there are more time-efficient ways to discover large networks. Multiple instances of Auto-Discovery can be run simultaneously, populating a single common repository. For example, in a one-router network connecting four geographic regions (North, South, East, and West), it would make sense to run Discovery in each of the locations simultaneously in order to save time and (by reducing cross-router traffic) bandwidth. Running multiple threads per Discovery instance will also speed execution.

 TIP   Depending upon server size, it is typically impractical to run more than nine simultaneous discoveries against a single repository.

■ Both TCP/IP and SNMP service must be installed and configured properly on target devices, whether they are network, computing, or non-IT devices.

Loading Factors

Many network managers worry that the load imposed by Discovery will bring the network to its knees. A little arithmetic can calm this fear. With ARP cache, the traffic is all in SNMP Gets. Getting a MIB variable takes about 200 bytes of network traffic. For a 100 host subnet with two routers attached to each subnet and each router having eight interfaces and five addresses, you can estimate the number of variables retrieved; assume that many interfaces are disabled. The total data for ARP cache turns out to be less than 450KB, less than 300KB for fast ARP, and less than 225KB for a Ping sweep. Furthermore, studies have found that that normal management traffic for most organizations (polling, traps, and so on) represents only 1–2 percent of available bandwidth—not considered a major impact.

Discovering a Network

Unicenter TNG gives you lots of options for discovering your network, but there are really two basic approaches: the Discovery Wizard and Advanced Discovery. In the wizard-based approach, Unicenter TNG explores the network to its heart's content. Unless you purposely limit it to your subnet, the Discovery Wizard finds everything on your network at once. You don't need to know, plan, or do much. Just start it and go get a beverage. When you come back, there will be plenty to observe.

In the Advanced Discovery method, you carefully control what has been discovered and decide for yourself where to look and what to find next. The Advanced Discovery method can obviously exercise more discretion, but it also asks for a bit more input.

The Discovery Wizard

The Discovery Wizard executes (initially) at the time of installation and is the easiest way to find all of the devices on the network and its subnets. Of course, if specified, the exploration can be limited to particular segments or subnets. It is wise to determine whether the network is connected to external networks, such as the Internet, before using the global discovery approach. If it is, it's strongly suggested that you isolate it from the external network via appropriately configured firewalls, gateways, or routers before running Discovery.

The reason it is important for the network to be isolated from the Internet is that Unicenter TNG's Discovery process is very thorough. It will discover every device on every network and subnetwork that it can reach. While this thoroughness is generally desirable and produces very interesting results on a properly configured college or corporate campus, it can also deliver surprising results. For example, if a dial-up connection (circumventing a firewall) to the Internet (via an ISP) is active during Discovery, Unicenter TNG will continue its process beyond campus boundaries and potentially map all the ISP's assets as well. That can produce a real "world view," but it may take hours to run to conclusion. However much fun this sounds, the ISP owners may not be amused due to privacy and bandwidth issues. Of course, if the ISP owners had Unicenter TNG installed, they would have the security mechanisms to prevent such unanticipated inspections!

Running Network Discovery   A network's presence must be recognized before it can be managed. Discovery is the process by which Unicenter TNG actually probes the network and finds components to be managed. Unicenter TNG Discovery not only inventories network elements (such as routers, hubs, and NICs), it also detects systems and depicts the relationship between them in order to help you visualize the network.

 T I P   Your results may be more complete if you run Discovery during the day. Devices are often powered down during the off hours; if so, a late-night Discovery can miss them. Also, the ARP cache mechanism uses temporary storage in the routers, so a system that has not sent or received traffic lately will be discarded from the cache. As a consequence, if a device is not found in the ARP cache, it will not be targeted for the confirming Ping that actually locates devices at their addresses.

Ch
3

To run Network Discovery, click the Start menu, Programs, TNG WorldView, Auto Discovery; alternatively, you can double-click the Auto-Discovery icon in the TNG WorldView folder.

The first window you see is Discovery's Distributed Services window, shown in Figure 3.1. This lists the servers where copies of Discovery are running. You will see only your machine listed immediately after initial installation. Of course, additional servers could be introduced. Jot down at this point the name of your local server and repository for later reference.

FIGURE 3.1
Discovery's Distributed Services window.

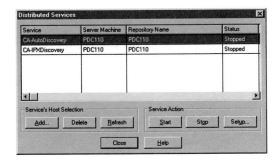

From this window you can see the status of the Discovery servers, start and stop the servers, or begin configuring the servers. Notice that Discovery can be run on both TCP/IP and IPX-based networks. The default selection will be for discovery of an IP network. If you are running on Novell NetWare, it might be appropriate to select CA-IPXDiscovery by clicking that server instead. For this example you accept the default selection TCP/IP.

Next, click the Setup button (shown at the bottom of the screen in Figure 3.1) to start customizing the Discovery Wizard. Figure 3.2 displays the Discovery Wizard's opening screen.

FIGURE 3.2
The Unicenter TNG Discovery Wizard.

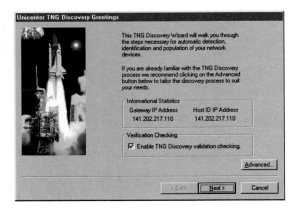

Note that the Unicenter TNG Discovery Wizard automatically retrieves your gateway and host IP addresses. Discovery always starts with the subnet your server is in. It figures out the host IP address and the address of a router in the subnet (the gateway address) from the system.

Now allow the wizard to walk you through the steps required for launching Auto-Discovery.

You can tune the discovery parameters more precisely by selecting the Advanced button on the bottom right of the Unicenter TNG Discovery Greetings window. Experienced network administrators may want to jump ahead to the "Advanced Discovery" section in this chapter if parts of the network have already been mapped. In the vast majority of circumstances, however, the Unicenter TNG Discovery Wizard will suit the purposes at hand. If there's any doubt, readers should choose Next, which brings up the Unicenter TNG Repository Selection window (see Figure 3.3).

FIGURE 3.3
The Discovery Wizard's Repository Selection window.

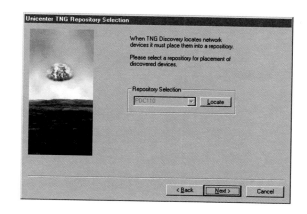

Repository Page   The repository is the central storehouse for all your managed objects. Stored information about each of those objects is in this repository. There are many classes of objects attached to your network (routers, servers, databases, applications, and so on). Within each class, there will normally be many individual objects. Information about each class and each object within it is stored in Unicenter TNG's central repository. It is the discovery process that populates the repository with information about your enterprise's managed objects.

The Discovery setup's Repository Selection window (shown in Figure 3.3) allows you to change the repository where Discovery will store the objects that it finds. The Repository Selection panel allows you to send the results of the search to any repository, including remote repositories. This is useful for accelerating the discovery of large networks. Multiple discovery engines can run simultaneously and the information consolidated to a central point. Assuming this is your first discovery, you should select a new repository name for population.

Selecting the Next button will take you to Discovery Wizard's Scope window (see Figure 3.4).

The Unicenter TNG Discovery Scope window allows you to choose between two search modes. You indicate how much of the network will be discovered. It is possible to limit yourself to the immediate subnet, of course, but in the interest of simplicity, the default is accepted here and the entire network is canvassed. Select the Next button to get to the Methodology window (see Figure 3.5).

Ch

3

FIGURE 3.4
The Discovery Wizard's
Scope window.

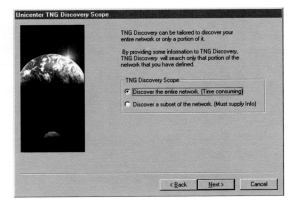

FIGURE 3.5
The Discovery Wizard's
Methodology window.

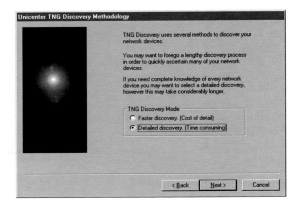

Most network elements can be located quickly and efficiently by inspecting data contained in devices' ARP cache. However, thoroughness requires an exhaustive Ping sweep, which tests all the network addresses in a given range by querying them each at least once. Here you accept the default setting again (Detailed Discovery) and simply click the Next button to reach the Unicenter TNG Discovery DHCP Configuration window (see Figure 3.6).

Dynamic Host Configuration Protocol (DHCP) is a dynamic IP address assignment protocol. DHCP specifies the use of pooled addresses that are assigned to systems on an as-needed basis and includes recommendations for guaranteeing unique IP addresses among nodes in local and wide area networks. It is particularly useful for handling mobile devices such as laptops. Unicenter TNG's Discovery simplifies network management in a DHCP environment:

- Providing screens for system managers to identify IP address ranges for DHCP subnets (see Figure 3.6).
- Enabling periodic reruns for subnets and devices identified as DHCP based.
- Automatically updates the object information for DHCP devices.

FIGURE 3.6
Discovery Wizard's
DHCP Configuration
window.

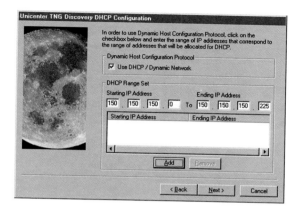

- If a device's subnet or address within a subnet has changed, Discovery moves the objects into the correct subnets and switches IP addresses to keep the subnet as static as possible, making management easier.
- Deletes unclassified DHCP devices if other devices are using their IP addresses.
- Updates the status of a classified device if its IP address conflicts with others.

This is a binary selection, depending upon whether your network addresses are assigned dynamically or statically. If your network uses DHCP, simply check that option and assign one or more address ranges to be searched in the DHCP Range Set area. An address range has been entered for a subnet that does employ DHCP. Some networks in an organization may be using DHCP, while others are not; check with your network administrator if you're uncertain. Click the Next button to reach the Unicenter TNG Discovery Multiple Instances window (see Figure 3.7).

FIGURE 3.7
The Discovery Wizard's
Multiple Instances
window allows you to
set speed adjustments.

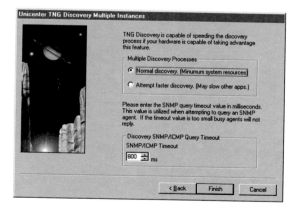

The Unicenter TNG Discovery Multiple Instances window provides two parameters that can impact the speed of the discovery process, although with potential tradeoffs. Starting multiple instances of the discovery engine will leverage additional memory, network bandwidth, and (on SMP machines) processors. This may come at the expense of other processes or applications running on the Discovery host machine.

Likewise, reducing the SNMP/ICMP query time-out value offers a potential tradeoff that hastens the discovery process. The lower the time-out value is set, the more likely that a busy agent will not have the opportunity to respond while the discovery engine is listening and therefore remain (temporarily) anonymous. The discovery process will commence when you click the Finish button. You don't have to be a networking guru to discover a network with the Unicenter TNG Discovery Wizard.

This raises the question "How long will it take to discover my network?" This is difficult to estimate. The time required is dependent upon several factors:

- Speed of the system on which Unicenter TNG is running
- Speed of the networks across which the discovery traffic must travel
- Number of devices to be discovered
- Number of discovery engines simultaneously executing
- Number of threads running per discovery engine

However, the main limiting factor is the speed with which the engines can write their results to the repository. A secondary factor is the network bandwidth available to carry the discovery traffic (although a large or dense network could slow Discovery). Discovery of just one subnet, especially if it is a small subnet, is typically measured in minutes. Watching the Discovery Monitor is reassuring because it helps meter the rate of progress.

 Discovery Monitor   The Discovery Monitor lets you watch over Network Discovery's shoulder as it searches the network. Observing its progress is usually fun. To run it, either click the Discovery Monitor icon or select the Start menu, Programs, Unicenter TNG WorldView, Discovery Monitor.

You will see the CA-TNG Discovery Monitor window (see Figure 3.8). The counts will increase as objects are added to the repository. The counts will move in fits because Discovery, in the interest of efficiency, waits awhile before writing them to the repository.

FIGURE 3.8
The Discovery Monitor window.

Click the OK button and then start the Discovery Monitor.

Advanced Discovery

Advanced Discovery gives you more control by letting you limit how far the discovery process explores. The basic plan is to run through multiple passes of Discovery. Each pass searches through a few subnets at a time. This way, you slowly build a picture of the network outward from your local network.

Subnet Management   You can display the results of your discovery when the Discovery Monitor or trace console indicates that Discovery is complete. There are two display methods: the Discovery Subnet Management window and the 2D map.

The Discovery Subnet Management window (see Figure 3.9) displays all of the subnets that were discovered. The window displays two panes. The right pane displays subnets that will be discovered on the next pass, while the left pane lists subnets that have already been discovered or were bypassed. The left pane subnets will not need to be rediscovered on the next pass.

FIGURE 3.9
The Discovery Subnet Management window.

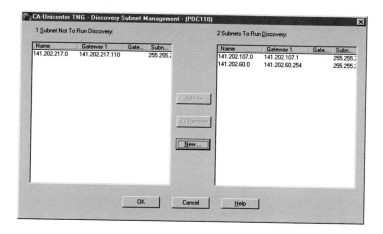

Click the subnet and then click the Add or Remove button (whichever is active) to move the subnet from one side to the other. You can see more information about a subnet by double-clicking it in either pane. You will see the Modify Subnet window, as is shown in Figure 3.10.

FIGURE 3.10
The Modify Subnet window.

TIP   You can see more information about a listed subnet by double-clicking it.

The subnets you choose to discover determine the direction in which Discovery proceeds. Before running an Advanced Discovery pass, be sure the subnets that have already been discovered, as well as those subnets you do not want to discover, are displayed in the left panel of the Subnet Management window. The right panel of the Subnet Management window should list all the subnets that you want to discover. Discovery will only discover the subnets listed on the right panel of the screen.

What if Something Isn't Found?

It is quite possible that the first pass of Discovery will not find all of the devices on your network. There are a number of factors that can account for this. Portions of the network may be down, devices may not respond to SNMP queries (if so, check on the community name), ARP caches may be stale, or devices may be turned off or disconnected from the network. This does not reflect a problem with Unicenter TNG. Instead, it is simply the result of the limitations of an automated discovery process. A management system can no more discover devices attached to a network that is down than a person could manually inventory supplies in a warehouse without entering it. If you do encounter this situation, you will want to make additional Discovery passes on your network. It is also wise to run Discovery periodically to ensure that any changes have been detected and reflected in the repository. Rediscovery incrementally adds new systems, new networks, and new subnets to your existing repository.

Periodic Rediscovery

It is inevitable that over time the network will change. New systems and new networks will be added. Old ones will be removed. The first discovery is unlikely to find everything. You will want to rediscover your network a few times at the start using different methods, and periodically thereafter.

Removing old systems is a more difficult task. It's hard to tell the difference between a system that has been removed from the network and one that is down right now. The removal of systems and networks is best accomplished in conjunction with event and fault-management policies.

Backing It Up: TNG Repository Import/Export Exchange Facility (TRIX)

After putting this much effort into building a repository, it would be a shame to lose it all. Like any database, it's important that you back up the repository. The repository can be backed up using the underlying database's backup services (such as Microsoft SQL), an enterprise backup solution like the Unicenter TNG Advanced Storage option (also known as ARCserve), or the Save Demo utility provided on the TNG CD-ROM. However, there is a backup utility specifically designed for the repository; it's known as TRIX (Unicenter TNG Repository Import/Export Exchange).

TRIX takes the contents of the repository and turns them into a TRIX script—a text file that can be easily backed up and exported for safe storage. TRIX can also be used to transfer objects from one repository to another. You export them from one repository, copy the script to the other system, edit it, and import the script again later. TRIX has many other uses in customizing Unicenter TNG, but most of those are beyond the scope of this book.

Technically Speaking: How Discovery Works

Discovery starts at the local Discovery server and explores outward from there. It proceeds through the network in steps, looking for hosts, routers, and subnets. Discovery starts with just one subnet: the subnet local to the Discovery server. The steps it follows for each subnet are as follows:

1. Discovery for network devices does its work based on the method selected in the Discovery Setup window. It searches a subnet for assigned addresses in the subnet using one of three techniques: ARP cache, fast ARP, or Ping sweep.

   - ARP cache—The ARP cache method starts at the gateway address (the nearest router's address) for the current subnet and uses the gateway's ARP cache to discover information about the devices. An SNMP request (GET) is initiated for each device found in the ARP cache. If the device does not respond, it is a TCP device; otherwise, the information on the device is added to the CORE.

   - Fast ARP—The fast ARP method saves time by checking only the ARP cache of routers. Fast ARP is the best choice when updating the database between the more intensive services initiated by Ping sweep and ARP cache.

   - Ping sweep—The Ping sweep method sends ICMP pings to all of the devices on the network based on the subnet mask. The discovery engine then retrieves SNMP information. If there's no SNMP information available, it is assumed that the device is a non-SNMP device. Discovery then receives the attributes from the device's MIB and adds the information to the Common Object Repository.

   Each of the discovery methods has advantages and disadvantages. The Ping sweep option gives you more complete quantitative information—meaning it finds more devices—because every address in the range selected (potentially the entire network) is pinged. Even if a device type is not recognized, its presence will be known. The same device quite possibly would not be discovered at all through the ARP cache method.

   On the other hand, ARP cache provides the MAC address information on all the devices that are found in the ARP cache in the router. Ping sweep, however, generates additional network traffic and is thus more time consuming than ARP cache. A combination of Ping sweep and ARP cache is sometimes required to discover every device in the network.

2. For each address it finds, Discovery tries to figure out what type of system it is (host, router, and the like) using SNMP and DNS. If it is a new system, it creates an object in the repository for it.

   - Classified objects—Objects having an SNMP-compliant agent and a matching Unicenter TNG class definition are *classified objects*. Typical examples are a UNIX workstation or Windows NT server. By default, any classified object is visible on the 2D and 3D maps.

   - Unclassified objects—Non-SNMP devices might have IP or MAC address conflicts, or they might be of a model that does not match any Unicenter TNG class. Unclassified objects are placed in the Unclassified_TCP class, which is a subclass of unclassified objects. Unclassified objects is a subclass of the Managed Objects class.

Ch
3

3. SNMP is used to find out what interfaces and addresses are in each system, and they're added to the repository. Each address is checked to see what subnet it resides in. If the device is found in a new subnet (that matches the subnet filter), it too is added to the repository.

Classifying an IP System

Once Discovery finds a new IP address, it uses SNMP to get information from MIB-II to classify the system in the repository. MIB-II (Management Information Base II) provides basic information about TCP/IP and is supported by nearly all TCP/IP implementations. MIB-II provides a description of the system, a contact person, the location of the system, and the system's vendor and equipment type.

Discovery can find the name of the system in one of two ways. It looks in DNS to find the name corresponding to the address. If that fails, it uses SNMP to ask the system what it thinks its name is.

Finding New Interfaces and Subnets

Information in the SNMP MIB (MIB-II) tells Discovery what interfaces are in the system, what IP addresses are assigned to those interfaces, and what subnet masks are used for those addresses. From all that, Discovery adds interfaces to the repository for the systems and figures out what subnets are attached to the system. Discovery classifies the interface based on its type and uses that to create LAN segments in the subnets. If any new subnets show up, they are compared with the subnet mask to see if they should be added to the repository and discovered.

Armed with a list of new subnets, Discovery can now go on and discover what they contain. Discovery rolls outward like the ripples on a still pond until it finds everything.

Maps

Network Discovery generates a map of the network, but that map is driven by the topology of the IP network. Much of TNG's power comes from your ability to customize its display. The maps can be customized in two main ways. You can also customize TNG to reflect more closely the physical structure of your environment. You can customize TNG to reflect the logical structure of your environment through Business Process Views, but that is covered later in this chapter.

Customizing Topological Representation (Maps)

Maps are topological representations. Customizing your maps is accomplished through the Real World Interface 2D map (see Figure 3.11). Chapter 2 discusses navigating through the 2D view in more detail. If you have not already read Chapter 2 or are not already familiar with navigating through the 2D view, you may want to review that section before proceeding with this chapter.

FIGURE 3.11
A 2D map.

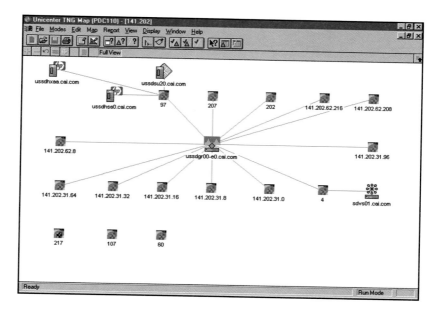

You can change the location of an icon on a 2D map with the following steps:

1. In the WorldView folder, double-click the 2D Map icon.
2. Click OK in the Unicenter TNG dialog box. The information from the repository will be loaded and the 2D window should appear.
3. Click Modes on the menu bar located at the top of the 2D window.
4. Select Design to bring up Design mode. You must be in Design mode to create new objects, define new relationships between objects, and do any detailed customization of the 2D map. The Toolbox menu will appear when you select Design mode. The Toolbox menu displays all of the managed object class definitions, as well as the classes for the map-only objects. The Toolbox menu displays in icon format, a hierarchical list format, or a tree format. You are now ready to customize your display.

To move, copy, or rearrange any managed object (devices and systems, for instance) on your topology map, do the following in Design mode:

1. Open the source and destination folders on the 2D map.
2. Select the object that you want to copy or move in the source folder, left-click it, and drag it to a blank section in the destination folder.

 TIP The shortcut for copying and moving multiple objects simultaneously is to click the first object and then hold down the Shift key while clicking the second and each additional object. Once all objects are selected, release the Shift key (without releasing the mouse button) and drag the dotted-lined rectangle to the destination folder.

3. The Select Operation dialog box will appear after you drag and drop the object.

4. Select one of the following options:

- Create New Parent—Creates a copy of the object in the destination folder without changing the original object in the source folder. The links in the source folder are not retained automatically (a basic copy function).
- Move Selected Devices—Deletes the object from the source folder and moves it to the destination folder (a basic move function).
- Keep Links—All of the links between objects except for the link to the parent folder are retained when they are moved into the destination folder. (This displays when Move Selected Devices is specified.)

Once you have moved and copied all of the objects to their proper places, you have finished customizing your topological representation.

Adding a Background Map

It is very common for users to want to add a background to the maps in their Unicenter TNG displays. The most common background is a map of the geographic area where the network is located. For example, a company with locations scattered around the United States might want to have a map of the United States for the background of the highest level display. Unicenter TNG provides a selection of commonly requested geographical maps to use as backgrounds for folders. The TRIX feature, which enables objects to be moved in and out of the repository for external customization, creation, or backup, is also available.

You must be in Design mode and perform the following steps in order to add a special background:

1. Click Map on the menu bar at the top of the 2D window.

2. Select the appropriate map type from the Map menu. The choices are Continents, Countries, Regions, Sub-Regions, and Groups. (Select Countries if you want to overlay a map of the U.S.)

3. Scroll through the selections on the dialog box and select the map that you want by highlighting it. Then click OK. The map that you have selected will now appear on your screen beneath your network layout.

4. You can drag and drop your Network icon onto the map and place it near its location. Unicenter TNG can automatically place an object on the map based upon user-supplied telephone area codes or latitude and longitude coordinates.

5. To use this automatic positioning feature, right-click the object that you are positioning in Design mode. Select the Edit option from the pop-up menu. The Edit Folder dialog box will now appear (see Figure 3.12).

N O T E   If the Edit Folder dialog box does not contain the positioning fields, click Cancel and drag the object slightly onto the geographic map. This will reset the object to register the geographic map as its background. Select Edit again and the Edit folder should contain the positioning fields. ▪

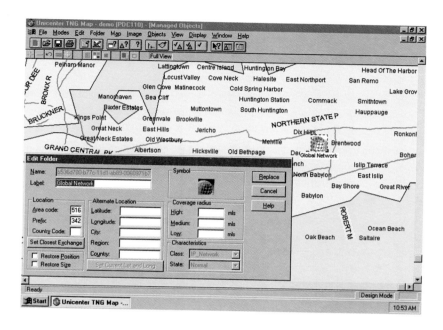

FIGURE 3.12
Background map.

You can now enter the information that will position the network. Enter the area code and prefix (exchange) for U.S. and Canadian locations. Include the country code for international locations. You may enter the latitude and longitude coordinates in the Alternate Location group box instead of the telephone information. Click the Replace button when you are done. Your network will appear in the correct location if you have entered the correct information.

6. Do the following if you want more information overlaid on the map (place names, roads, and the like): Click Map on the menu bar. Select Map Overlays from the pop-up menu. You can customize the level of detail that will be displayed on your map on the Set Overlays dialog box. The folder automatically brings in levels of detail if you select the Auto option. The other options are On and Off.

Your map is now customized. Through the use of this feature, it is possible to transfer more information to the operators in less time.

The Business Process View (BPV)

The previously described tools are visual versions of traditional system management tools. Such traditional management methods and tools, however, allow system managers to track the status of resources (individual servers, clients, routers, printers, operating systems, databases, applications, and so on), but only in isolation from other contexts.

If a problem with a critical business process develops, it is incumbent on the system manager to figure out which of the enterprise's computers, software, and network devices support the impacted business process. Then the system manager extracts the data applicable to the problem at hand from the torrent of (mostly irrelevant) information received from devices throughout the entire network. This complicated process must be repeated every time the system manager needs to determine status.

IT professionals tend to focus their attention using a horizontal, resource-centric perspective. For example, there are traditionally separate system management groups for application support, database administration, systems programming, and network management.

This horizontal view is limiting when IT organizations are called upon to answer business-relevant questions. Answering business-relevant questions requires cutting across different resource technologies and seeing the bigger picture.

Business people tend to organize themselves and focus their attention using a vertical perspective. A typical business-oriented question is "When can I get my Accounts Receivable reports?" To answer this question, an enterprise manager must, at the very least, know the status of the Accounts Receivable application, its database(s), whether other applications on which the Accounts Receivable application depends are working, and whether the underlying systems, network, and printers are functioning well. Business Process Views provide this vertical perspective. Figure 3.13 shows the relationship between Business Process Views and the underlying information system.

FIGURE 3.13
The Business Process View.

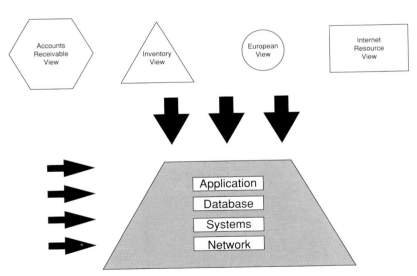

Unicenter TNG's Business Process Views invert an IT infrastructure's traditional resource-centric view. It organizes its Business Process Views by application (Accounts Receivable, Building Management, and so on), functional role (financial, security, maintenance), geography (Europe, physical plant 185), organization (the XB97 License Group), and so on. These Business Process Views, however, cross all the horizontal views for that business process. This allows system managers to deal with both applications and resources simultaneously and to filter and map IT resource information to business problems.

Figure 3.14 shows an example of a real Business Process View for a Payroll application in a medium sized, networked company. The Payroll application requires a database server, a database, a Payroll application server, the Payroll application, the operating systems for the two servers, a workstation for data entry, a printer, and a network router and hub all working together.

FIGURE 3.14

A typical Business Process View for a Payroll application.

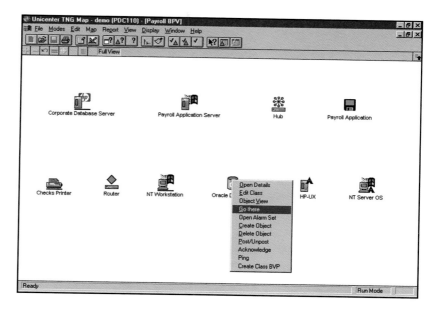

Maintaining a list of Business Process Views in one place is a good idea. Suppose some payroll checks have not been printed. If you always display this list, as shown in Figure 3.15, the manager can see when the problem occurs in Payroll because the Payroll Business Process turns red, indicating a Critical status.

FIGURE 3.15

Displayed list of Business Process Views.

Double-clicking the problematic Business Process View brings up the Payroll Business Process View (see Figure 3.14). This view shows all the IT resources involved in the payroll process. At a glance, the system manager can determine that the router, hub, servers, workstation, printer, operating systems, and Payroll application are running properly. However, the Oracle database icon is red, indicating that it has a problem. A database problem could cause the application to run erratically and skip the printing of some checks.

Right-clicking the Oracle icon brings up a pop-up menu. Selecting Go There brings the system manager to the 2D map in which the errant Oracle database is located. From here, the system manager can double-click the corporate database server on which Oracle runs in order to drill down into the server components, then right-click the Oracle icon in order to bring up the Oracle Agent. The agent might show that the database is currently overloaded. Bouncing some users will cause the database to run properly again, thereby solving the skipped-checks problem.

In this way, system managers can focus only on the Payroll process. The Business Process View filters out all extraneous or irrelevant information, but provides a vertical view that cuts across all the relevant horizontal resource technologies (applications, databases, systems, and networks).

The following formal methodology provides an example (a subset) of developing a sophisticated Business Process View for a distribution application. The company, a large distributor, began its Business Process View development by first drawing a paper diagram that showed the applications that are part of their distribution system and the interactions between these applications. Then the company's architecture, IT, and systems and network management groups performed the following steps using Unicenter TNG:

1. Start Unicenter TNG's 2D map facility. When the Managed Objects folder comes up, switch to Design mode. Drag the icon for the Business Process View object from the Design Mode toolbox that appears in the Managed Objects folder. Then click the Business Process View icon to open its folder.

2. Still in Design mode and in the Business Process View folder, draw the application interaction diagram using Unicenter TNG's shapes and text icons, as shown in Figure 3.16. Of course, drawing an application interaction diagram and using it as the basis for a Business Process View is not technically necessary to define a Business Process View. It is a simple method, however, for ensuring that nothing is inadvertently omitted from the Business Process View created.

3. Open the 2D maps of the enterprise in which the hardware and software involved in the distribution application are located. Drag the platforms, devices, databases, applications, and other software involved in the distribution application from these maps to the application interaction diagram you created. Choosing Create New Parent from the pop-up menu causes the platform to be copied, rather than deleted, from the original map (see Figure 3.17).

4. Remove the ovals used to create the application interaction diagram. This will result in a folder containing all the platforms, devices, and software involved in the Business Process View. Right-clicking anywhere in the folder and selecting Arrange, Bus from the pop-up menu causes Unicenter TNG to arrange the computer icons on the bus (see Figure 3.18).

FIGURE 3.16
Application interactions in a distribution application.

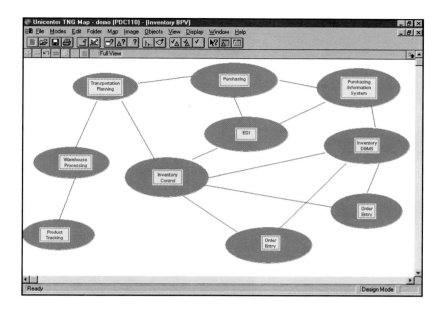

FIGURE 3.17
Computers involved in the application interactions.

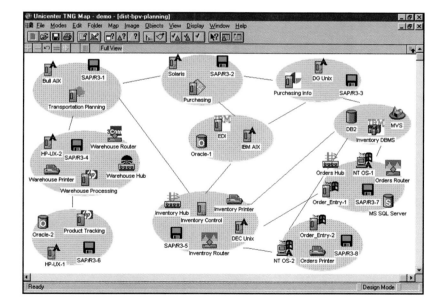

FIGURE 3.18
Creating the final distribution Business Process View.

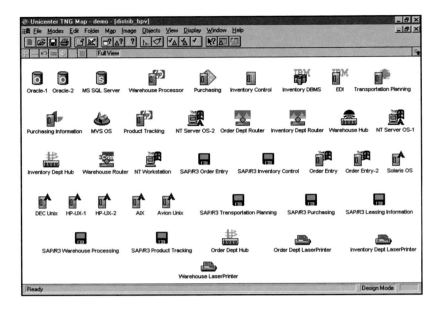

5. Save the Business Process View. In the future, this Distribution Business Process View will be displayed in the list of Business Process Views. Should a problem be indicated (by a change in color or any other method), a single-click on the desired Business Process View opens it for viewing.

A Business Process View is itself a managed object. As such, it is stored in the Common Object Repository and is accessible using either Unicenter TNG 2D or 3D maps. Business Process Views are visually represented as separate folders in the 2D map; they are represented as specific views on the 3D map.

The greatest value of Business Process Views is that they show, at a glance, not only the status of different computers, devices, networks, and software, but also the dependencies between component devices. Although an application may not appear to be working properly, the problem may really be on an interconnected computer. This is easier to figure out using Business Process Views than with traditional tools.

See Chapter 10, "Application Management," for step-by-step instructions on two ways to create Business Process Views.

Network Performance Management

Unicenter TNG will allow you not only to monitor the managed objects in your network, but also to manage the performance of those objects.

Leveraging ObjectView is the best way to gauge responsiveness of individual network components in real-time. ObjectView allows for instrumentation of network components and the creation of formulas behind these performance gauges, making their data meaningful for non-technical personnel. Unicenter TNG's Response Management Option (RMO) should be installed, however, for actual end-to-end network performance monitoring, including analysis of historical data.

ObjectView

ObjectView is primarily a performance tool. It provides performance statistics on a device based on the agent's monitoring of the device. Additionally, it provides device configuration information based on the device's MIB.

ObjectView is commonly used for monitoring network performance (see Figure 3.19). Examples of ObjectView-provided information are the number of devices connected, which interfaces are down, and the number of packets coming in compared with the number going out. This information makes ObjectView a good troubleshooting tool and performance monitor.

FIGURE 3.19
Monitoring network performance with ObjectView.

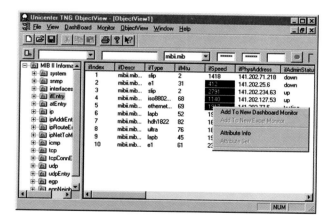

ObjectView also allows system managers to visually display the monitored attributes in various types of graphs, meters, and tables. System managers select the attributes they want to monitor and add them to Excel or to the ObjectView DashBoard (see Figure 3.20).

Response Management Option (RMO)

Unicenter TNG Response Manager Option is a client/server performance manager for the distributed network. It measures service levels, capacity utilization, and errors for LAN segments and server machines. It also provides information on Ethernet segments, WAN links, and Cisco routers.

The Response Manager Option's historical database shares object identifiers with the repository, enabling the Response Manager Option to use Unicenter TNG's discovery of the environment while enhancing it with non-IP network resources. Performance alerts are sent directly to Unicenter TNG's repository, displayed on the map, and accessible through the Unicenter TNG Event browser.

FIGURE 3.20
Visually monitoring performance with the DashBoard: dial gauge (a) and line graphs (b).

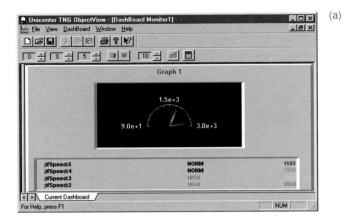

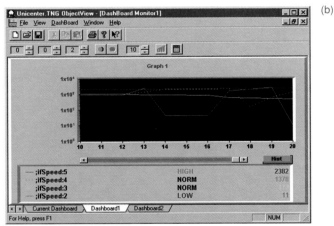

Unicenter TNG RMO is able to manage very large environments by having separate servers collect data from different regional areas of the network. The data is then presented in an integrated fashion. Response Manager Option's historical database contains interval data and data summarized by the day, week, month, and year. Historical and real-time reports are available.

RMO works by monitoring client/server applications and network hardware and software and then comparing them against established service-level agreements. Response Manager Option also reports a problem when the predefined performance objectives are not met. It does this by collecting network performance statistics from Response Manager probes or from SNMP agents (using RMON and MIB II data), which are already deployed in your environment.

RMO can also be used to help with capacity planning for your enterprise network. Using Response Manager Option's data, you determine when and how to move workstations, split over-utilized resources, expand or add file servers, or provide more efficient communication gateways.

Creating Reports on Network Assets

Asset identification is the first step in asset management. With Unicenter TNG, the inventory of assets is created through the discovery process. Once the inventory has been created, the next step is to analyze it and make decisions. Unicenter TNG's report facilities are well suited for this task. The bundled reporting facilities are intuitive and easy to use and provide a sophisticated level of reporting.

Reports can be generated from several locations:

- 2D map
- Object Browser
- Class Browser
- Topology Browser
- Common Object Repository

The views presented by these browsers organize and display complicated information and allow a simplified, yet comprehensive, look at your IT assets and infrastructure.

Many reports are designed to provide specific details about subsets of objects, object classes, folders, critical events, and topology. There are two options for creating reports on managed objects or the assets listed in the Common Object Repository:

- The 2D map provides an object detail report using the Report menu.
- The Object Browser provides object-specific information using the Print Objects List option in the File menu.

Generating Reports from the 2D Map

This dialog is accessible in Run mode from the Report Object Details menu command. You simply do the following when you need a report on all critical segments in the network:

1. Select Report option.
2. Select By Object Detail.
3. Select LANS.
4. Select Critical.
5. Select Report.

This simple five-step process produces a detailed report on the critical segments. In addition to Class of Objects, other choices include Severity States and Output Destination.

The 2D browser provides the following in addition to the object detail report:

- *Summary report of the network.* This is a high-level report providing summary information about the network components.
- *Object by name.* This is a report that lets you select the objects for the report by their name.

Ch
3

■ *Object by folder.* This report allows you to select certain folders and report on all the objects within them. This is useful for reporting on certain portions of the network.

■ *Object by class.* For this report you need to select certain classes of objects. The result is a report for all of the objects in that class. For example, you might want to review the information about all of the Cisco routers in the network.

These reports allow you to select exactly which objects are reported on by a number of criteria so you can examine network subsets.

In a similar way, Unicenter TNG can produce reports based on the Object, Class, or Topology Browsers, as well as from the Common Object Repository.

Distributed State Machine

A *distributed state machine* (DSM) tracks the status of objects across a network. One such object might be a shared laser printer. The printer can be in different *states*. It might be out of paper or toner. It might be jammed or offline. It might have too many jobs waiting to be printed, or it may be running fine. The DSM's job is to collect information from this printer, its brethren, and all the workstations under its surveillance in order to track their status.

The DSM pulls information from agents and from the repository. The repository is used to determine which systems are in a DSM's *domain*, as well as the class of those systems. Object classification was performed during Network Discovery.

The DSM talks to software *agents* (see Chapter 4, "Server Management") to collect information about the monitored resource. It periodically asks (or *polls*) the agent to get data. The DSM can retrieve information like the number of jobs queued for printing. It can also accept unsolicited events, in particular SNMP *traps*, sent from the agent.

The DSM even has its own discovery process. In the same way that Network Discovery finds the elements on a network, the DSM discovers what resources exist inside monitored systems. This discovery process provides greater detail on what software and hardware resources reside on a system. For example, it would identify the Microsoft SQL Server database and Exchange application on a groupware server. DSM's reason for finding these objects is to keep their status up to date via its state machine. In summary, the DSM knows an object's state, remembers how it has changed, and stores the object's current state in the repository.

In the repository, the status of the object is mapped to a severity using alarm sets. *Alarm sets* are simple tables mapping status to severity. They can be applied to specific objects, which allows operators or users to apply whatever *policy* they desire to a given severity level. In some situations, you can simply remove certain status values from consideration if they aren't relevant.

A DSM policy can be thought of as a collection of rules. A policy tells the DSM what objects should be watched, how to find them, what their potential states are, what data to poll for, how often to poll, what events to accept (*collect*), and most importantly, how to make state changes as various things happen.

Basically, rules are distilled from knowledge about how an object works. However, they can also be customized to reflect desires about how things ought to work. For example, a rule can set polling frequency. Polling more often detects problems faster, while polling less often keeps network traffic down. You can change the threshold level on a print queue to reflect exactly what you mean by too many jobs queued. Whoever sets policy determines what really matters. If operators are not responsible for refilling supplies, they can alter policy so that a printer doesn't enter into a problem status when the paper runs out.

DSM policies are defined on classes of objects and then applied to instances. What this means is that we only have to develop a policy once, and then the DSM automatically applies it to all the objects of that class within the DSM's domain. Potentially, this saves tremendous amounts of work. For example, if your domain contains 1,000 NetPCs, you need only develop policy for one and apply it to them all.

Writing DSM policy from scratch takes some practice, so Unicenter TNG includes a policy generator and wizards to help develop new policies. In practice, however, most customers modify or supplement policies supplied by CA or by the vendor of the managed object.

Once the DSM has been set up and is operating, it is largely invisible. That's good, since it is only meant to mind the store while you do something more interesting. The best tools stay out of the way.

How to Set Up a Distributed State Machine

Setting up a DSM on a system is very easy. There are only three steps required: install the DSM software, identify the systems for which the DSM is responsible, and turn it on.

The DSM is installed as a part of the overall Agent Technology installation. The components that make up the DSM are shown in Figure 3.21. Focus here on the Domain Manager, which keeps track of what the DSM watches, the network state machine, which actually watches the state of objects, and the repository gateway, which interacts with the repository and sets the status of objects there. The SNMP gateway, SNMP Admin, Object Store, and Object Request Broker are components used in SNMP Agents, which are covered in Chapter 4.

Configuring the Domain

Edit the configuration file TNGAWS\Services\AWS_WVGATE\gwipflt.dat to set up the domain that the DSM will watch.

Each line of the file identifies a system, or collection of systems, that is to be monitored. The systems are identified by their IP addresses. Addresses are used so the DSM can operate even if a large part of the network is down. You can either list each system or include a collection of addresses using wildcard syntax. For example, 141.202.15.* tells the DSM to monitor all the systems from 141.202.15.0 to 141.202.15.255.

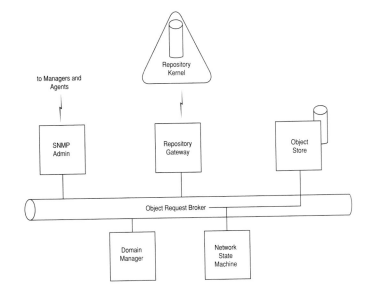

FIGURE 3.21
The components of the
distributed state
machine.

Initially, the DSM configuration file tells the DSM to monitor every system in the repository (via *.*.*.*). Depending upon the size of your network, you might want to divide the network among multiple DSMs.

Listing 3.1 shows a configuration file for monitoring a single subnet and a few routers. Note that the address of the routers is the address associated with the router in the repository.

Listing 3.1   *gwipflt.dat*—DSM Domain Configuration File

```
141.202.15.*
141.202.39.1
141.202.2.1
141.202.35.1
141.202.92.1
```

Viewing Status with Node View

The DSM stores the status of objects in the repository for the use of Real World Interface browsers and other programs. More importantly, the DSM also maintains the internal state of the objects. This is usually more granular (detailed) than the status stored in the repository. For example, when the Windows NT System Agent watches a file system (or even an individual file), the DSM tracks that information too, while the repository remains ignorant.

The Node View viewer included with the TNG Agent technologies allows you to see the detailed state information kept by the DSM for a particular system. To run it, select an icon for one of the agents in the node, right-click it, and choose View Node from the pop-up menu. You will see the Node View window, as it's shown in Figure 3.22.

FIGURE 3.22
The Node View window.

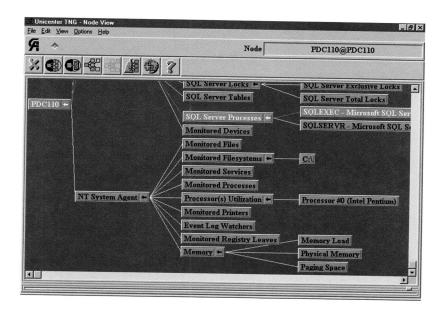

The Node View display contains a number of panes, as shown in Figure 3.23. Starting from the top, there is a standard window title and menu bar. Below that is a status bar. It displays the update status on the left, and when the status is being updated the indicator turns red. On the right is the address of the node being displayed, along with the name of the DSM watching it. In Figure 3.23 the system being viewed has the address 141.202.4.78, and the DSM is the one on PDC110. Below the status line is a toolbar.

The main part of the window is given to a tree of objects in the node that the DSM is monitoring. Each object shows its status (at least as far as the DSM knows it). The status is color-coded. The meaning of the various colors is given in Table 3.1. The status is propagated up the tree, so the top object, the node, shows the worst status of any object it contains.

Table 3.1   Node View Colors

Color	Description
Dark Green	The object is OK.
Light Green	The object has returned to OK from a problem state; acknowledge the object to return it to OK.
Red	The object has a problem.
Orange	The object has a problem, but it has been acknowledged.
Blue	The status of the object is unknown (either because the Node View can't communicate with the DSM, or because the DSM hasn't yet determined the state of the object).

FIGURE 3.23
The Node View window
panes.

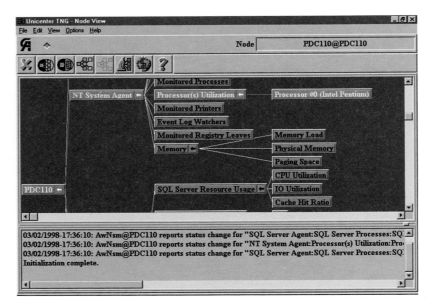

A guidance window is at the bottom of the Node View display. This area echoes any commands that are invoked through Node View. These commands could be entered into a command line via an application.

Mini Tree Navigation Window

The number of objects in a node can be quite large. Node View provides a mini tree, which helps you navigate the objects by providing an overview. Choose View, Show Mini Tree to display it, or View, Hide Mini Tree to close it.

If you click any object in the mini tree, the main object tree will be changed to show the corresponding icon.

Object Description

Node View maintains quite a bit of information about the objects. View, Show Object Description in the menu brings up the Object Description window (shown in Figure 3.24) for whatever object is selected in the tree. View, Hide Object Description closes the window.

FIGURE 3.24
The Object Description window.

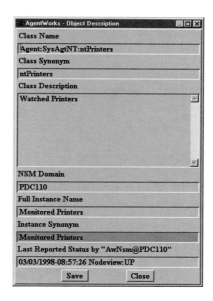

Ch

3

Customizing the Node View Display

The Node View display can be customized to show more or less information in the icons. By default, window panes can be displayed or hidden. To control these preferences, choose View, Display Preferences from the menu. You will see the Display Preferences window (see Figure 3.25).

FIGURE 3.25
The Display Preferences window.

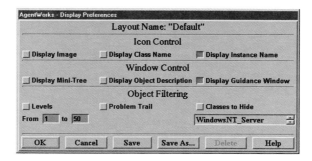

You can launch the Agent View from the Node View display to see more detailed information about the specific object. You can also acknowledge any status change or view a history of recent events collected by the DSM about the object.

To invoke any of these, right-click the object and select the appropriate function from the pop-up menu. View Agent brings up the Agent View; Acknowledge acknowledges the status.

DSM Event Viewer

Right-clicking an object and choosing View Events from the pop-up menu displays a list of events for the object and its children, as shown in Figure 3.26. These events are sent to the event log, which is described in Chapter 4. The display shows what the DSM remembers sending (which is not always identical to events the event log receives). The DSM remembers these events temporarily. When the DSM is restarted, all of the events are cleared.

FIGURE 3.26

The Event Browser window.

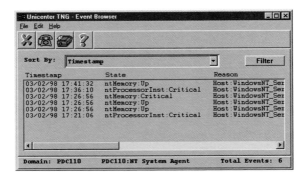

Each event is displayed as a single line. You can select the information displayed about an event by clicking the Filter button. It will open the Filter window (shown in Figure 3.27), where fields can be added or removed. The fields are Timestamp, State, Reported By (the DSM detecting the event), Reason, Host, Object, Class, and Domain.

FIGURE 3.27

The Filter window.

There is a status line at the bottom of the window that displays a number of facts. On the left it shows the domain (the DSM that is supplying the events, for example). In the middle it shows the specific object for which the events apply.

Setting Status

As the DSM determines the status of various objects, it reports that to the Real World Interface browsers by setting the status of the object in the Object Repository. You can also set the status through the SETSTAT command. This command can be used in scripts or invoked by the message/action engine as a way to reflect the status of some object in the repository. The command's syntax is available in the *Unicenter TNG Administrator's Guide*.

Mapping Status to Severity

The Real World Interface browsers display an object's severity. The severity is determined from the status of the object (by the DSM itself or by the SETSTAT command) and the status of the objects included within it.

Status is converted into severity by an *alarm set*, which is a table that maps the many possible status values into the few severity values.

The severity of objects *propagates* up to their parent in the display, allowing operators and even casual users to track down a problem by following the red ball (in 3D) or tracking the red icons (in 2D). The severity of the PDC110-Unispace object is determined by the combined severity of all the objects it contains. In turn, the PDC110-Unispace object's status propagates up to the PDC110 object, on to the 141.202.4.78 Segment.1 object, and so on, all the way to the top of the inclusion tree.

Viewing Status and Severity

From any of the Real World Interface browsers, you can see the status and severity of an object by opening its notebook and turning to the Status page, shown in Figure 3.28. To open the notebook, right-click the object and choose Object Details from the pop-up menu.

FIGURE 3.28

The Status page of the Managed Object Notebook.

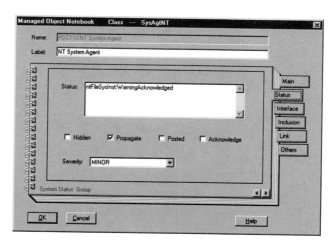

AlarmSet

An alarmset is a table that maps status values into severity. Each managed object has an alarmset associated with it. This information is listed on the Main page of the object's notebook. Many objects share alarmsets. All objects of the same class generally use the same alarmset. This makes managing status and severity easier, since the policy can then be shared for all objects of a class. To handle exceptions, or to handle new classes of objects, you can create new alarmsets and assign specific alarmsets to specific objects.

You can view and edit an alarmset by right-clicking an object in one of the Real World Interface browsers and choosing Open AlarmSet from the pop-up menu. You will see a window like that in Figure 3.29; it shows the entries in the table. You can double-click an entry to change it or click the New button to add a new entry, using the window in Figure 3.30.

FIGURE 3.29
The AlarmSet Dialog box.

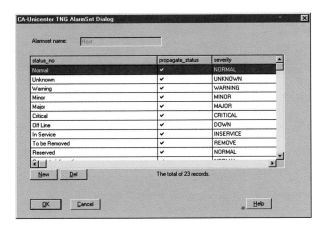

FIGURE 3.30
Adding an Alarmset entry.

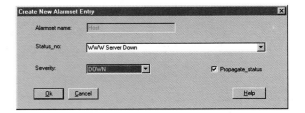

Propagating Status and Severity

By default, the status of an object propagates up to its parent. Sometimes that is not appropriate. If a particular service is always down, or its status does not matter because it is a test system, then you can ignore its status by turning propagation off for that object. To turn propagation off, uncheck the Propagate box on the Status page of the managed object's notebook.

You can also turn off propagation of specific status values in an alarmset entry. That way, you can arrange it so that critical problems are propagated, but warnings are not. To turn off propagation of a specific status value, uncheck the Propagate Status box on the alarmset entry previously shown in Figure 3.29.

Technically Speaking: Polling and Event Notification

In enterprise management, polling is a request-response interaction between a manager and an agent. The manager discovers information about a managed resource by periodically querying an agent and requesting that certain values be provided. The agent responds by gathering the information from the target resource and sending it to the manager. The two top arrows in Figure 3.31 show this kind of request-response scenario.

Periodic polling stands in contrast to event notification whereby agents automatically and autonomously notify managers of events of interest. This notification is asynchronous and is not based on any request that a manager issues. The bottom arrow in the figure shows such a notification scenario.

FIGURE 3.31
Manager/agent communications infrastructure.

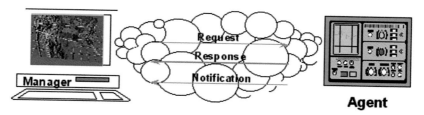

Ch
3

Polling and event notification complement one another. Polling is a simple and robust method. However, because there must be time intervals between the polling of any given device, there can be a delay between the occurrence of a problem and its detection. Event notification can provide immediate notification when events occur. On the other hand, event notification limits the information an agent provides to a network or systems manager.

Some products in the marketplace support either polling or event notification, but not both. You might hear about the advantages of not having to poll for information, or vice versa. Do not get the idea that polling and event notification is an either/or situation. The reality is that there are situations where polling is efficient and event notification is informative. Neither polling nor event notification (SNMP traps, for example) provides a complete management solution. The two methodologies are complementary and together provide a reasonably accurate and timely view of each device without incurring unnecessary overhead.

For example, it is inefficient to monitor a router by polling that router's agent every five seconds to find out if the router's bit error rate exceeds a threshold. This is like asking somebody every few moments if they feel sick. Having to respond 10,000 times that you feel fine is a heavy price to pay just to let somebody know on question 10,001 that you are getting a headache. It is much more efficient for the agent to *raise an alarm* (send an alert event) when the router exceeds the pre-specified bit error rate threshold, or for you to ask for aspirin when you need it.

On the other hand, the manager might need more information to fix the problem after receiving the notification that the router's bit error rate is too high. Is the bit error rate a problem on the input side or on the output side? A manager really has to poll agents to get additional specific information.

The most important reason for polling, however, is to clear up the situation when a manager hasn't heard from its agent for a while. There are two reasons for an agent not sending out any notification for awhile. First, lack of notification may mean that the resource is functioning properly and there is no reason to communicate. Second, no notification may mean that the agent or resource is down. The management system does not know the difference for certain. If the manager cannot poll the agent to find out that it is still responding to events, it has no way of telling, on its own initiative, whether the managed resource is up or down! ●

Server Management

In this chapter

Servers are the heart and soul of today's computing environment. Many people think of servers as very big computers, often running the UNIX operating system. However, this is a dated perspective. It is not hardware or an operating system that defines a system as a server, but rather its role of providing services to client systems. A computer, whether running UNIX, Windows NT, MVS, or any of a plethora of other operating systems, is classified as a server if it is providing application, file, print, database, or other services to dependent systems. The inherent complexity of heterogeneous, distributed environments, along with the diversity of tasks performed, makes managing servers both essential and challenging.

Server management is comprised of several functions.

> Server Monitoring—This function is the base component of server management. This requires someone or something to keep a constant watch on the status of the managed servers. This is a painfully tedious chore for human beings, much of which, fortunately, Unicenter TNG is easily able to handle. This chapter explains how to set up Unicenter TNG for monitoring servers. Monitoring is essential for detecting problems as soon as they occur, and for gathering data for use in performance management.

> Workload Management—This function consists of scheduling and tracking the jobs that run across one or more servers in a heterogeneous environment. Workload management takes into account calendar requirements (like the time of day, day of the week, or holidays). It also considers dependencies between workloads, (such as whether Job A must be finished before Job B should commence) as well as what to do in the case of a failure.

> Server Performance Management—While monitoring focuses on server availability, the purpose of server performance management is to ensure that servers are working efficiently. The keys to this function are data collection and trend analysis.

> Server Capacity Planning—While performance management focuses on current effectiveness, capacity planning ensures that servers will work efficiently in the future. The keys to this function are historical analysis and forecasting.

This chapter discusses issues relating to each of these essential functions of server management. Unicenter TNG supports many operating platforms, but for illustrative purposes, Windows NT will be used as the example.

Server Monitoring

Server monitoring is a function of Unicenter TNG's Agent Technology component. Operators control their server environments by monitoring and managing software instrumentation. Agents provide this instrumentation. Agents allow management applications to see and understand management information generated by desktops, servers, databases, and applications in support of optimizing the efficiency and effectiveness of business operations.

Agents for various resources come from one of two sources, the vendor of the resource or independent software companies like Computer Associates (CA). The vendor providing a resource, like router hardware, often provides an agent as an integral part of the product. This is usually true for network hardware. Many operating systems now include an SNMP agent. For example, Microsoft includes an agent with both Windows 95 and Windows NT; UNIX vendors include an agent with UNIX, and so on.

The system may not load or run these agents by default. On Windows 95 or Windows NT, the user must install the agent and run it. Operators should install agents on every system because they provide the support needed to manage the system. Among other things, this allows Network Discovery to correctly identify and classify the system, and it enables Unicenter TNG to monitor and manage the system more productively.

Independent software vendors, including CA, tend to provide more information in their agents than is typically found in agents from hardware vendors. These more robust *smart agents* sometimes include intelligent monitoring features. Agents that can intelligently monitor software, such as the Unicenter TNG NT System Agent and the Unicenter TNG Exchange Agent, are rare.

You can look at the data provided by any (SNMP-based) agent directly by using viewers collectively known as *MIB browsers*. Unicenter TNG includes a number of MIB browsers, including ObjectView, MIB Browser, and command line utilities.

In general, MIB browsers display raw data. You really need better tools to be productive. Unicenter TNG includes a family of Agent Viewers that users can customize to display data pertaining to a specific agent more clearly. You must interpret the raw data for it to become information, or better yet, knowledge.

How to Set Up Unicenter's SNMP Agents

When you installed Unicenter TNG, it included installation of agents. To set up the agents on a system, you need only start them. You can configure them to monitor certain resources for you by defining and loading *configuration sets*.

Figure 4.1 shows the basic components of the Unicenter TNG agents. At the heart of the agents is an *object request broker* or *ORB*. This is the darkened cylinder in the illustration, and it provides a communications path between the components. In most cases, the ORB and all the other agent components will be on the same system, but it is possible to use a remote ORB, although none of the examples in this book depends on that. The ORB and the *distributed services bus* are the same thing.

Various components plug in to the ORB. The two above the ORB in Figure 4.1 are shared services used by many sub-agents, for example the NT System and SQL Server Agents shown below the ORB. Almost every component uses the *object store* to file information locally. The *SNMP Admin* component implements the SNMP protocol. Roughly speaking, Admin decides which sub-agent (or object store) can respond to an SNMP request and provides the gateway services that handle protocol details like message encoding. Of course, SNMP is a widely used protocol, but the distributed services bus can support many other gateways as well. All of the components run as NT services or daemons on UNIX.

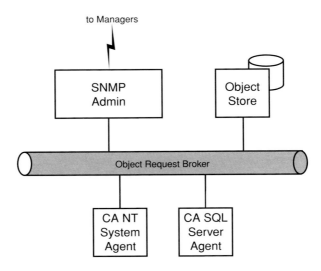

FIGURE 4.1
The SNMP Agent components.

Viewing Agents

Unicenter TNG provides a number of packaged viewers for browsing agent information. *Agent view* provides a high-level view of an agent, with the information presented in an easy-to-understand format. Other viewers (ObjectView and MIB Browser*)* provide a sparser interface closer to the MIB. Finally, a series of commands provides access to the primitive SNMP data. Generally, you should use the highest level viewer you can.

Agent Viewer

Out of the box, all CA agents come equipped with the Agent Viewer. The Agent Viewer presents the information in a streamlined and simplified format called an *agent view*. An agent view provides a number of pages of data showing charts, meters, status, and other useful information about an agent. Generally, it provides a summary page that displays the overall status of all the data provided by the agent.

Each agent view is customized for a particular class of agent. That's good, as it allows the developer to build a view that provides the most important information in the best way. The Agent Viewer is a tool driven by configuration files (abrowser files) that allow the developer to select and display specific information from the MIB for a particular application or hardware component (see Figure 4.2). Two different resources (a printer and an application, for example) will have two different abrowser files associated with them, and therefore, there will be different agent views for each class of object.

To see an agent view from one of the Real World Interface browsers like the 3D map, right-click an agent's icon and select View Agent from the pop-up menu.

To change the page and resources, select View from the menu and then you can choose from all the pages available in the agent view.

FIGURE 4.2

The System Agent for NT View - Summary window.

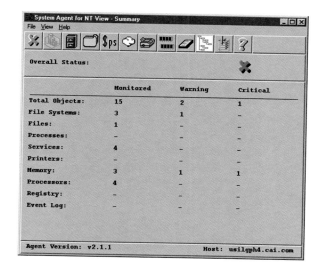

Things to Do with Agents

Each agent instruments certain resources and provides information about them. Therefore, agents allow you to look at and control many things. The number and types of agents, as well as the kinds of information each provides, could fill an encyclopedia. This section gives just a taste of the capabilities supplied by Unicenter TNG agents.

The NT System Agent

The NT System Agent instruments both versions of the Windows NT operating system: Microsoft NT Workstation and Microsoft NT Server. It monitors a number of resources, in the operating system. The NT System Agent monitors some resources for every system, but for other resources, users should direct it specifically. For example, the NT System Agent can monitor the size of files, but you have to tell it which files to watch. The resources that the NT System Agent monitors are:

- Processors: Always monitors CPU utilization
- Memory: Always monitors physical and swap space used
- File Systems: As directed, monitors usage and relative growth
- Files: As directed, monitors existence, time last modified, usage, and relative growth
- Printers: As directed, monitors status and queue length
- Processes: As directed, monitors existence
- Services: As directed, monitors status (running or not)
- Registry Entries: As directed, monitors the value of a Registry entry for change
- Event Log records: As directed, monitors the event log to see if it contains records of a particular type

Ch 4

NT Memory   The NT System Agent monitors the memory used on the system. It watches three numbers: the *memory load, physical memory utilization,* and *swap space utilization.* Windows NT is a virtual-memory system. Besides the physical memory chips, it uses a portion of its disk space (called a paging file) to store data that would otherwise have to be in memory. The NT System Agent monitors both the percentage of physical (chip) memory used and the percentage of paging file (swap) space used.

The NT System Agent also monitors *memory load,* a measure of the number of memory pages available for running processes to use. If the number of available pages is greater than or equal to 1100 (about 4MB), memory load is zero. If the number of available pages falls to 100 or fewer, the memory load is 100. The formula for memory load is

```
Memory-load = 100 - (Available Pages - 100)/10
```

Figure 4.3 shows the NT System Agent View Memory page. At the top are three gauges displaying the current values of memory load, physical memory utilization, and swap space utilization. Warning (yellow) and Critical (red) thresholds are displayed as small tick marks (triangles with lines indicating their setting). Below that are three graphs of the values collected over the past 100 polls. The window shows time on a logarithmic scale. It also gives recent polls (on the right) more space than earlier polls (on the left). Below the graphs, the screen displays total and available physical space and swap space. Beneath that is a window showing the Poll Interval.

FIGURE 4.3

The Memory window.

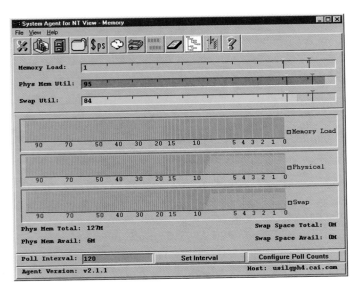

The agent maintains the thresholds and polls. If it sees that the value has exceeded the threshold for more than three sample polls, the agent will send out a trap (message) indicating a problem. If it later falls below the threshold, the agent will send another trap indicating the status has improved. Notice how this smart agent cuts network traffic. The agent locally polls these three values and only reports across the network to a manager (such as a distributed state machine or an event log or console) when something important happens. From this window, you can set threshold parameters such as how often the data is polled and how many times a value may exceed the threshold prior to declaring a problem.

Changing Thresholds and Other Agent Settings   To change a threshold, double-click the meter to display the window in Figure 4.4. Drag the Threshold slider to the left or right to change the value, and then click OK.

FIGURE 4.4

Setting a threshold.

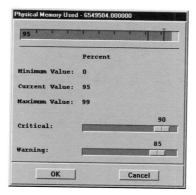

To change the polling interval (the time between two polls), enter a new value and click the Set Interval button in the Memory window shown previously in Figure 4.3.

To change the number of times a value must exceed the threshold in order for the agent to decide a threshold has been crossed and a problem exists, click the Configure Poll Counts button to see the Configure Poll Counts window (see Figure 4.5). Change any of the three values shown and click OK when you are finished.

You can use the same techniques to change settings in all the agent views.

FIGURE 4.5

Configuring poll counts.

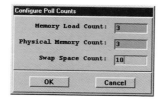

Processor   The Processors page monitors the *CPU utilization* —the percentage of time each CPU is busy. It displays both a meter with thresholds and a graph for each CPU in the system. As with memory, you can set the poll interval at the bottom of the window and set the thresholds by double-clicking the meter. To configure the poll count and other information about a processor, click the button labeled with a "C."

Ch

4

To see the Processors window, choose View, Processors from the menu. You will see a window like that shown in Figure 4.6.

FIGURE 4.6
The System Agent for NT View - Processors window.

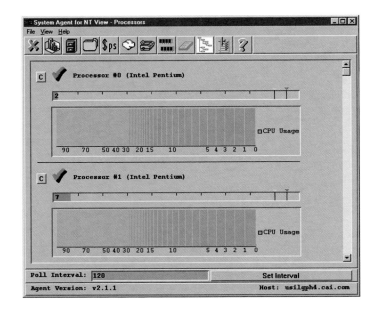

Services Windows NT runs certain programs in the background as *services*. UNIX systems use the term *daemons* to refer to such programs. These programs make distributed systems work and are really the servers referred to in the client/server paradigm. It is very important that these services keep running. The NT System Agent can monitor services to see if they are functioning or not and send traps when the status changes.

To see the Services page of the NT System Agent View, choose View, Services from the menu. You will see the window shown in Figure 4.7. Each line shows a single service being monitored, its name, its state, and so on.

The Alert Level determines what state will trigger a problem. Setting the Alert Level to Inactive means that if the service is not running (inactive), the agent will send a Critical problem alert. In this event, the Services Status will show a problem with a big red X. Services that are running appear as a green check mark.

Listing Available Services NT system administrators are familiar with the Services control panel that displays many services and their status on the local system. Unicenter TNG allows you to see all the services and their status remotely, through the Available Services page of the NT System Agent View. To see that page, choose View, Available Services from the menu. The page in Figure 4.8 shows the names of the services, a description of each service, and the status of each service in a table.

FIGURE 4.7
The System Agent for NT View - Services window.

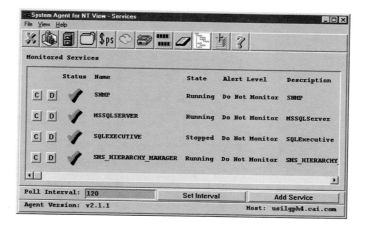

FIGURE 4.8
The System Agent for NT View - Available Services window.

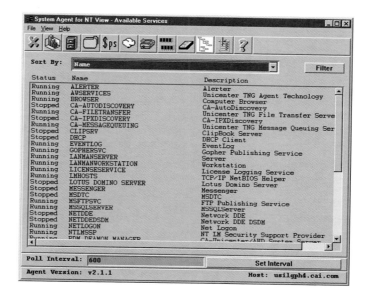

The name of the service is the name used internally by Windows NT and the NT System Agent to refer to the service. The Description is a more meaningful name used in the Services control panel. You can sort the table on any of the three fields by selecting a field from the Sort By selection, and you can filter the fields displayed by clicking the Filter button.

Adding a Service to Monitor   To add a service to those watched by the NT System Agent, click the Add Service button at the bottom of the window shown in Figure 4.7. You will see the window shown in Figure 4.9. Enter the name of the service you want to monitor in the Name field. (As mentioned before, this is the internal name, not the name displayed by the Services control panel.) Next, choose the Monitor Level from the selection.

FIGURE 4.9
Adding a watched service.

The choices are:

- Do Not Monitor, which means the service status changes don't generate any problems, although they will be shown in the agent view.
- Inactive, which raises an alarm if the service is not running.
- Active, which raises an alarm if the service is running.

Then click OK.

Configuring and Deleting Monitored Resources   In general, if an agent view shows a button with a C, clicking it will configure settings for that resource in the agent. If an agent view shows a button labeled with a D, clicking it will delete the resource.

Processes   The NT System Agent can detect if certain processes (programs) are running or not. You can use this knowledge to ensure that certain processes are always running. Using this information, you can also detect rogue processes. For example, the System Agent can detect if the system is currently running a particular application, such as a program that accesses the salary database. It can also detect if multiple copies of a program are running. Multiple copies of some server applications run fine; others do not work well if two copies are competing for resources.

To view the monitored processes, choose View, Processes from the menu. To view the list of processes currently running in the system, choose View, Available Processes from the menu.

Table 4.1 lists the fields in the Monitored Processes table. As with services, you can add a process to monitor by clicking the Add Process button. You will find the button at the bottom of the page. You can configure a monitored process by clicking the C button or delete the watched process by clicking the D button in the table.

Table 4.1   Monitored Processes Fields

Status	One of: Normal (green ✓), Warning (yellow), Critical (red X), or Unknown (blue ?).
Name	The name of the process; usually the name of the program currently running in the process.

Alert Level	The level or importance of any problem detected, one of Critical, Warning, or Do Not Monitor (meaning this process will generate no alerts).
Existence	If set to Alert, an alarm will be generated if the process exists (someone is running this program). If set to Do Not Alert, an alarm will be generated if the process does not exist.
Instance Monitoring (InstMon)	If true, the watcher counts and alerts based on the number of processes running with this name.
Instances	The number of instances of this process that exist.
Instances Warning (Warn)	The threshold number of processes that generates a Warning alert.
Instances Critical (Crit)	The threshold number of process instances that generates a Critical alert.
Thread Monitoring (ThrdMon)	Controls whether the agent watches the number of threads running under this process or processes. If set to Do Not Monitor, the agent does not watch this. If set to Above, the agent generates an alert if more than this number of threads exist. If set to Below, an alert is generated if fewer than the reference number of threads exist.
Thread Reference (ThrdRef)	The number of threads used as a base for thread monitoring.
ThrdMin	The minimum number of threads seen for this process.
ThrdMax	The maximum number of threads seen for this process.
Description	A description of the process. Set by configuring the process.

Ch

4

Monitoring File Systems   The NT System Agent can also monitor the file systems (logical drives) for their utilization. To see the page for Monitored File Systems (see Figure 4.10), choose View, File Systems from the menu.

FIGURE 4.10
The System Agent for NT View - File Systems window.

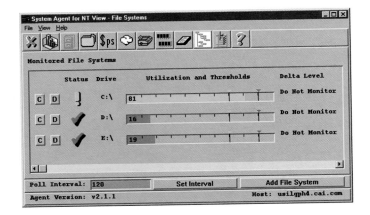

Table 4.2 lists the fields in the Monitored File Systems table.

Table 4.2   File System Fields

Status	One of: Normal (green ✓), Warning (yellow ⚠), Critical (red X), or Unknown (blue ?).
Drive	The drive's name.
Utilization and Threshold	The disk space utilization as a meter with thresholds. Double-click the meter to change the thresholds.
Delta Level	Controls whether the file system watcher looks for changes in disk space utilization. If set to Do Not Monitor, the agent will not watch for changes in utilization. If set to Warning, the agent will watch for sudden changes in utilization. If it detects such a change, it will raise a Warning alert. If set to Critical, the agent will raise a Critical alert.

Delta Threshold	If the agent is watching the disk for large changes in utilization, this value is the size of a change that will trigger an alert. For example, if set to 2% and the disk space utilization changes from 26% to 29%, an alert will be raised.
Util%	The percentage of time the disk drive is busy reading or writing data.
Format	The file system on the disk—FAT, NTFS, and so on.
Label	The label in the disk when it was formatted.
Type	Fixed or Removable.
Description	You can set the description to anything you wish.
Total (KB)	The total space on the disk, as measured in kilobytes.
Used (KB)	The space used on the disk, as measured in kilobytes.
Free (KB)	The free space on the disk, as measured in kilobytes.
AvgUtil	The average value of the utilization since the agent started watching the file system or since the agent last started.
MinUtil	The smallest value of utilization since the agent started.
MaxUtil	The largest value of utilization since the agent started watching.

Ch
4

Adding and Configuring a File System Watcher   To configure the settings for a watched file system, click the C button listed with the file system in the table, and you can set the Delta (change) Level, Delta Threshold, and Description for the file system (see Figure 4.11).

To add a new file system watcher, click the Add File System button at the bottom of the page shown in Figure 4.10. You will see the window shown in Figure 4.12, where you can name the file system you want to monitor and set the thresholds.

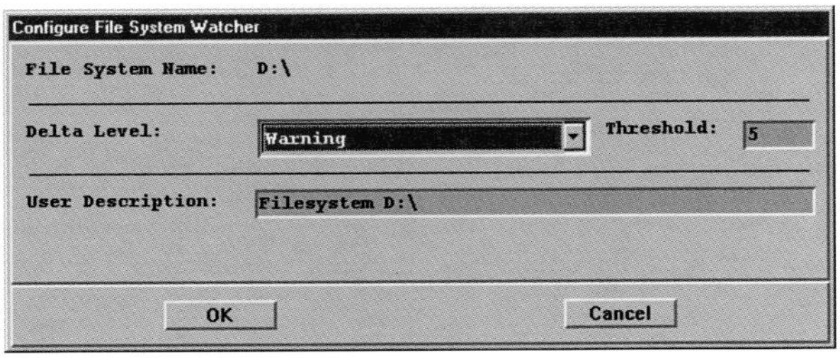

FIGURE 4.11
Configuring a file system watcher.

Configure File System Watcher

File System Name: D:\

Delta Level: Warning ▾   Threshold: 5

User Description: Filesystem D:\

OK   Cancel

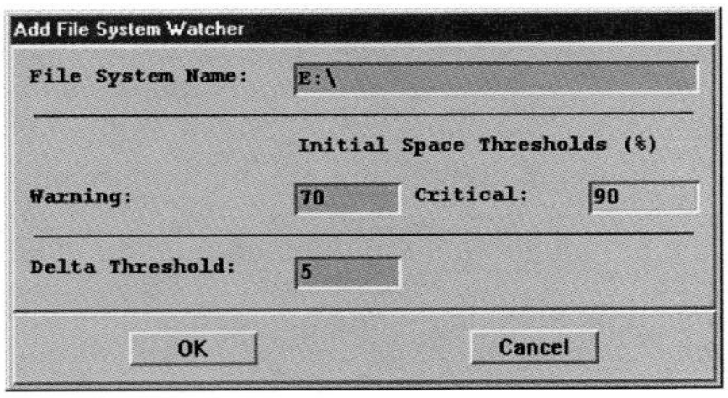

FIGURE 4.12
Adding a file system watcher.

Add File System Watcher

File System Name: E:\

Initial Space Thresholds (%)

Warning: 70   Critical: 90

Delta Threshold: 5

OK   Cancel

Monitoring Files   The NT System Agent can watch individual files as well as entire file systems. It can monitor how much space the files use and when a file was last changed. To view the monitored files, choose View, Files from the menu. You will see the page shown in Figure 4.13. The page shows, in table format, all the files the agent is watching. Table 4.3 lists all the fields in a monitored file and their meanings.

FIGURE 4.13
The monitored files.

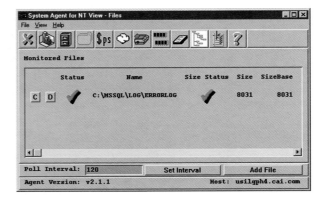

The agent watches three things about a file: the absolute size of the file, the change in the size of the file, and the timestamp indicating when the file was last changed. The agent always watches the absolute size of the file against the Warning and Critical thresholds, but watching for large size changes and timestamp is optional.

To add a file watcher, click the Add File button. Click the C button to configure a file watcher. Click the D button to delete a file watcher.

Table 4.3 Monitored File Fields

Status	The combined status of the file. One of: Normal (green ✓), Warning (yellow), Critical (red X), or Unknown (blue ?).
Name	The name of the file.
Size Status	The status of the file based on its size.
Size	The current size of the file in bytes.
Size Base	The original size of the file. The size the agent compares the size against to see how much it has grown.
Size Warning Threshold (SizeWarn)	Threshold size that will generate a Warning status and alert.
Size Critical Threshold (SizeCrit)	Threshold size that will generate a Critical status and alert.
Size Change Flag and Status	Controls whether the agent changes the status of the file based on changes in its size between two polls. If set to Do Not Monitor, the agent does not watch this. When set to Warning, if the file grows more than the threshold, the agent will send a Warning alert. If set to Critical, the agent will send a Critical alert. The Agent View page also includes a Reset button with the Status and Flag. If you click on the button, it will acknowledge the alert and reset the base file size.
Size Change (Bytes) (SizeChng)	The threshold used for file size changes in bytes.

continues

Ch
4

Table 4.3 Continued

Timestamp	The time of the last file modification.
Timestamp Status	Controls whether the agent changes the status of the file based on the time of the last file modification. If set to Do Not Monitor, the agent does not watch this. When set to Warning, if the file is modified, the agent will send a Warning alert. If set to Critical, it will send a Critical alert. The agent view includes a Reset button with the status.
Size Minimum	The minimum size of the file.
Size Maximum	The maximum size of the file.
Size Average	The average size of the file since the agent started watching it.
Description	A description of the file. Set by configuring the file.

Printers   The NT System Agent can monitor selected printers that the system serves. It can watch the NT event log file for events related to the printer and monitor the printer queue length (see Table 4.4).

Table 4.4 Monitored Printer Fields

Status	The combined status of the printer, one of: Normal (green ✓), Warning (yellow), Critical (red X), or Unknown (blue ?).
Printer	The name of the printer.
Event Status	The status of the printer based on event monitoring.
Event Monitor	This setting controls whether the agent watches for printer events. If set to Critical or Warning, the agent will

	look for events and raise the appropriate level of alert if required. If set to Do Not Monitor, the agent will not watch for printer events.
Queue Status	The status of the printer based on monitoring the queue length.
Queue Monitoring	This setting controls whether the agent watches the length of the print queue. If set to Monitor, the agent will compare the queue length against the thresholds. If set to Do Not Monitor, the agent will not monitor the queue length.
Queue	The length of the print queue.
Queue Warning Threshold	If the queue length is longer than this threshold, the agent will raise a Warning alert.
Queue Critical Threshold	If the queue length is longer than this threshold, the agent will raise a Critical alert.
Printer Description	A description of the printer. Set by configuring the printer.

Registry Leaves   Every operating system has its own way (or, as is most common, dozens of ways) of storing configuration settings and other data that control how it operates. Windows 3.1 uses initialization files (.INI). UNIX systems use environment variables, text configuration files, and many other techniques for storing this data. Windows NT stores much of its configuration information in the *Registry*. The Registry is a tree-structured database of configuration information. Data is stored in *Registry leaves*. Registry leaves are simple data values that the operating system or applications can read and write. A Registry leaf name is comprised of three parts. The first part is a *root* that names the tree that contains the leaf. The second part is a *key* that names the path through the tree to get to the leaf, like a directory name. The third part is the *leaf name* itself. An example of a name for a particular Registry leaf is HKEY_LOCAL_MACHINE (the root), SYSTEM\CurrentControlSet\Services\SNMP\Parameters\RFC1156Agent (the key), and sysContact (the leaf name). That particular Registry leaf stores the contact name for the system reported by the MIB2 agent that comes with NT.

The Registry can store many kinds of data in a leaf, including strings, numbers, and binary data.

Ch
4

Changing a Registry entry to the wrong value can have disastrous consequences and lead to all kinds of problems. The NT System Agent will watch selected Registry leaves and send an alert should they change. As a simple example, a Windows NT system has one name used in TCP/IP (the DNS name) and another used in Windows Networking (the computer or machine name). Operators will want to keep these names the same and make sure that users do not change them. Both names are stored in the Registry. The TCP/IP DNS name is stored in the HKEY_LOCAL_MACHINE tree, under the SYSTEM\CurrentControlSet\Services\Tcpip\Parameters key in the Hostname leaf. The Windows Networking Computer Name is stored in the HKEY_LOCAL_MACHINE tree, under the SYSTEM\CurrentControlSet\Control\ComputerName\ComputerName key in the ComputerName leaf. A cautious operator can set up Registry leaf watchers to monitor both leaves and raise an alert when either changes.

To view the monitored Registry leaves, choose View, Registry. The resulting page shows a table of the Registry leaves the watchers are monitoring. Table 4.5 shows the fields in the table. To add a Registry leaf watcher, click the Add Registry Leaf button at the bottom of the page. Click the C button in the leaf's row to configure a Registry leaf watcher. If the value of the leaf changes, clicking the Reset button in the row will acknowledge the change, reset the status to Normal, and update the Previous Value field to equal the current value.

Table 4.5   Monitored Registry Leaf Fields

Status	The status of the Registry leaf, one of: Normal (green ✓), Warning (yellow), Critical (red X), or Unknown (blue ?).
Reset Button	Click to reset the status of the leaf.
Handle	The root of the tree.
Key	The path to the leaf.
Leaf	The name of the leaf.
Current Value	The current value of the Registry leaf.
Previous Value	The previous value of the Registry leaf.
Type	The kind of data stored, either string or integer.
Monitor Level	This setting controls whether an agent watches for changes and which types of changes to watch. If set to Do Not Monitor, the agent will simply report on the Registry leaf value but not monitor for change. If set to Change, any modification will cause the agent to raise an alert. If set to Thresholds, the Registry leaf must store a number (an integer), and then the agent will

compare the value of the leaf against the
Warning and Critical thresholds.

Warning Threshold   If the value of the leaf is greater than this
threshold, the agent will raise a Warning
alert.

Critical Threshold   If the value of the leaf is greater than this
threshold, the agent will raise a Critical
alert.

MIB II Agents

Most systems that support TCP/IP have MIB II agents. Unicenter TNG includes an agent view
for MIB II, but generally only applies it to routers and other network devices. For network
devices with MIB II icons in Unispace, you can invoke the MIB II agent view. To do this, select
the MIB II icon, right-click it, and choose View Agent from the pop-up menu.

 TIP   The MIB II agent appears as an icon in Unispace only if the DSM has been told by policy to include it.
The default policy for hosts and workstations does not apply the MIB II policy to those systems.

The MIB II agent view includes these pages:

▪ Summary: An overview, presenting information about the system.

▪ Interfaces: A table showing all the interfaces in the system.

▪ Interface Traffic: A table of the interfaces, showing graphs of input and output packets
and packet types. Figure 4.14 shows this window.

Ch

4

FIGURE 4.14
The MIB II View -
Interface Traffic window.

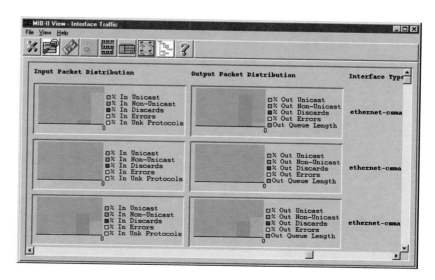

- Internet Protocol: Graphs input and output packets by type.

- Internet Control Message Protocol (ICMP): Graphs input and output ICMP packets by type. This is where you can see the number of Ping packets sent and received by this system, for example.

- TCP Connections: Shows a table of all the TCP connections, their states, and what system and port is at the other (remote) end.

- SNMP: A graph of the amount of SNMP traffic handled by the agent on the system by type of message sent or received.

Via the command line, you can use the Agent Viewer to look at the MIB II agent on any system. See the *Unicenter TNG Administrator's Guide* for full syntax.

Other Agents

There are a huge variety of agents besides the SAP R/3, Oracle, Lotus Notes, Microsoft Exchange, and SQL Server agents. See Appendix B, "Reference to Unicenter TNG's Agents," for a complete listing of available agents.

Job Scheduling and Workload Management

An essential element of server management is the scheduling and shepherding of production workloads in support of essential business functions, such as payroll. This requires making *jobs* (meaning software routines) run according to a schedule and in a proper sequence. Operators typically monitor the execution of these tasks, just as they monitor networks and servers to ensure reliable and efficient service.

Production jobs generally run in the background as *batch* jobs. Although batch jobs are usually run in a low-priority execution environment, or during "off" hours, they are usually important to the business. Most production jobs run on a fixed schedule. *Job scheduling* refers to running background jobs. However, background jobs can be run *on demand*, or when something happens (an event occurs), such as a *job trigger*.

The *Workload Management* facility in Unicenter TNG is useful to operators for automating the execution of these important jobs. This manager provides a sophisticated control environment across platforms and time zones. Not only will Workload Management handle the allocation of work; it can also provide automatic recovery facilities when problems occur.

Jobs and Job Sets

A *job* is the smallest unit of work scheduled. Think of it as a single boxcar in a freight train. Getting real work done means running a number of jobs together. The term *job set* refers to this collection of jobs. Job sets, like freight trains, are the things you schedule and run. Every job is just a step in a larger job set.

A job runs a single batch script or a single program. The system returns a *status code* indicating job success or failure. Jobs are never run alone, they are always part of a larger job set.

Generally, each application is set up as a job set. A job set can include a number of individual jobs.

A jobset name, job name, job number, and a job occurrence qualifier identify each job. The job name normally is the name of the program or batch file that the job runs, or a name that describes what the job does. Including the jobset name in the identifier of a job enables running the same program or batch file in multiple job sets. In fact, the same job might be run more than once in a job set (like Job B in Figure 4.15), but each is given its own job number. In some cases, the system needs to run a job such as a sort utility more than once during the day. These are called *cyclic* jobs, and you can choose how many times and how frequently to run them. Unicenter TNG gives each occurrence of a cyclic job its own qualifier, which tells the day of the month it ran the job. The system can also run on-demand jobs more than once in a day and assigns a unique qualifier to each such job occurrence.

Workload Management describes dependencies by listing the jobs that must *precede* a job. In a distributed environment, jobs running on one system may depend on jobs running on another. TNG provides *distributed job scheduling*. A *scheduling manager* starts and tracks jobs that a *scheduling agent* runs on each system.

Sometimes the order in which two jobs run does not matter, but, because they both use the same resource, they should not run at the same time. For those jobs, you can define a resource and indicate that one job or another should use it exclusively.

Often however, the output of one job serves as the input for another. When the monitor schedules jobs, dependencies between them determine the order in which they run. Operators define dependencies by stating what jobs must precede any given job. More than one job may be a predecessor of a job; for example, in Figure 4.15, Job F has Jobs D, B2, and C as predecessors. Similarly, many jobs can have the same job as a predecessor; for example, Jobs D, B1, and C all list Job A as a predecessor.

Resources

By considering the resource requirements of all the jobs that need to be processed, you can achieve workload balancing. Once you define the system resources, Workload Management considers these resource profiles to

- Ensure that the minimum number of resources required by a job or job set is available before submitting the work.
- Submit work efficiently to make the best use of the available resources, given the currently scheduled workload.

Resources can be hardware, software, or any logical object.

The physical objects defined as resources should match the reality of the system. Printers are serial devices. Only one job can use a given printer at any time. It would be inappropriate to simultaneously submit two jobs requiring the same printer. Defining the physical printer to the two jobs as a resource that can only be used by one job at one time (usage is private) ensures sequential job submission.

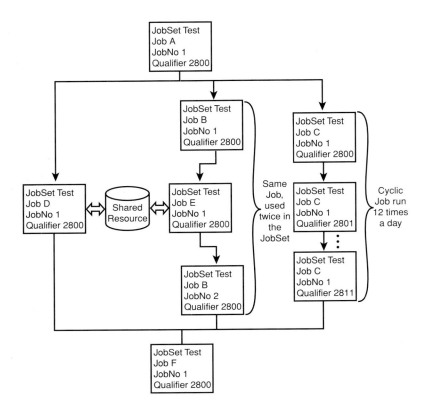

FIGURE 4.15

Jobs and job sets.

Logical objects defined as resources associated with jobs can provide powerful control capabilities. If it is necessary to ensure that two jobs never run at the same time, defining a logical resource to both jobs and defining their usage of the logical resource as private (that is, one job at a time) will ensure that the two jobs never contend.

Before starting each job, Workload Management compares the resources available at a station and the resources required by a job or job set. If the required resources are unavailable at the station, Workload Management will consider the station unable to support the needs of the job or job set and will attempt to find an alternate eligible station.

Stations

In Unicenter TNG, any system where jobs can be run (and hence where a scheduling agent must be running) is deemed a *station*. Think of each station as "the place where work gets done." You can assign logical names to the locations that perform tasks through the definition of station profiles. Which station does the processing does not matter for some jobs. For more efficient resource utilization in this case, you define a *station group* that includes all the machines capable of running the job. This allows you to schedule work on multiple stations or the best available station in a group. Unicenter TNG defines the computer on which the Workload Manager resides as the default station.

Workload Management *balances* the workload among the stations in a group. Some jobs may require a specific type of printer, disk, or tape drive to run. Workload Management allows you to define these as *resources*. It then schedules workloads so no more than one job attempts to access the resource at a time.

A typical production job involves more than just executing a program. There are also job setup and post-processing requirements that the system must perform to ensure the correct processing of jobs. You can schedule tasks to occur in a variety of locations. Defining a station allows that location to execute a task. The three types of stations are:

- PRECPU—For manual tasks performed before running a job on a device (loading a printer with special forms, for example).
- CPU—For automated tasks. This relates CPU stations to their platform (AS/400, MVS, NetWare, Tandem, UNIX, and Windows NT).
- POSTCPU—For manual tasks performed after a device has completed a job (distributing printed reports, for example).

Workload scheduling helps ensure correct job setup and the existence of appropriate manual checks and balances by providing the same level of attention to critical non-CPU tasks as it would to CPU-based processes.

Calendars

A *calendar* controls when a job set runs. Unicenter TNG uses calendars in security, event processing, storage management, capacity planning, and more.

A calendar is simply a collection of days and times. When you define a calendar, each day in the year is either inside the calendar (and *on)* or outside the calendar (and *off)*. TNG's calendar service answers the simple question, "Is this calendar now on or not?" For example, operators might define a calendar called NormalWk that represents normal working hours, which for their organization means 7 a.m. to 7 p.m., Monday through Saturday. There are many ways to use this calendar. In security, it can control access to a file, allowing most users access to the file only during normal working hours. In event processing, it can ensure that the message/action engine does one thing during normal working hours and something else at other times.

How Calendars Work

Unicenter TNG implements the calendar service as a *calendar manager* and a *calendar agent*, as shown in Figure 4.16. An application using calendars would call its local calendar agent asking if the calendar is now on. The calendar agent actually stores a calendar in memory because it checks calendars frequently. When the calendar agent starts, it can either load memory from the database in the manager, or it can copy to disk and load quickly from a *decision support binary* (DSB). A calendar manager administers the database of calendars. This organization allows many calendar agents to share the same calendar definitions. Calendar viewers define calendars, setting the days and times when they are on or off. Operators commit the defined calendars to the agent's DSB.

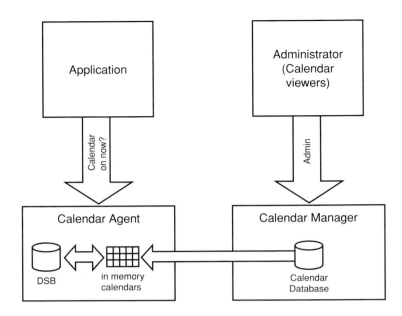

Configuring the Calendar Service

Setting up the calendar service (either manager or agent) is easy because there is little to configure. You can start or stop the calendar service using the following commands:

```
unicntrl stop cal
unicntrl stop cal
```

Creating a New Calendar

To create a calendar from the Real World Interface browser, right click the Common icon for the calendar manager in Unispace and choose Calendars from the pop-up menu. From the Enterprise Management program group, double-click the Calendars icon. In either case, you will see a window listing the defined calendars, as shown in Figure 4.17.

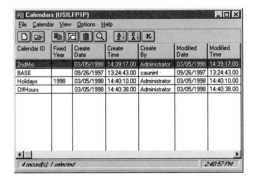

Choose Calendar, New from the menu, and you will see the Calendar window shown in Figure 4.18.

FIGURE 4.18
The Holiday Calendar window.

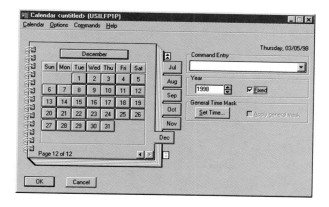

From here, you can turn certain days on or off. Blue numerals show the days that are on, while black numerals indicate those that are off. You can turn days on or off by clicking with the mouse or using commands.

With the mouse, you can click a specific day (like December 25) to change it from on to off or vice versa. Alternatively, you can click a day of the week (like Saturday) to change the state of all Saturdays. You also can click a day and drag the mouse to select a number of dates to change.

You can enter commands from the menu or in the Command Entry field. The menu includes commonly used commands for the days of the week, holidays, and special calendars. A larger collection is available through the Command Entry field.

The syntax of a command is

```
[not] dates [change] [time hhmm-hhmm [change]]
```

where the value of change is on, off, or invert. Table 4.6 shows the list of valid dates, their meanings, and the syntax for time.

Table 4.6   Calendar Date Commands (Partial List)

Sunday, Monday, Tuesday, Wednesday, Thursday, Friday, Saturday	All Sundays, Mondays, and so on in the year.
WEEKDays	All Mondays through Fridays.
WEEKEnds	All Saturdays and Sundays.

continues

Table 4.6 Continued

JANuary, FEBruary, MARch, APRil, MAY, JUNe, JULy, AUGust, SEPtember, OCTober, NOVember, DECember	All days in that month.
mm	All days within the month. For example, 10 means all days in October.
mm/dd	The specific date— 10/31 is October 31.
mm-mm	A range of months.
mm/dd-mm/dd	A range of dates—for example 10/29–11/11.
*/dd	The same day, every month. For example, */01 refers to the first day of each month.
ALL	Every day in the year.
Calendar	Refers to an existing calendar by name (for example if you have defined a Holidays calendar). This includes all days on in the named calendar.

The online help in Unicenter TNG contains additional dates not found in the partial list that you can specify.

Fixed and Perpetual Calendars

TNG supports two kinds of calendars. Perpetual calendars cover every year. They handle dates that do not change from one year to another. For example, a calendar that includes only the first day in every month is a perpetual calendar. Fixed calendars are for a particular year and apply only to that year. An example of such a calendar is a holiday calendar including all days that are organizational holidays. In 1997, December 26 might be a holiday, while in 1998, December 24 might be a holiday. Check the Fixed check box to define a calendar as fixed.

General Times of Day

A calendar can also be on or off for specific times during the day. Unicenter TNG divides the day into 15-minute blocks using a 24-hour clock. The first block covers 0000–0015, and the last 2345–2400. By using the Set Time button, you can set the time blocks on or off by clicking the desired blocks to invert them. Another way to invert those 12-hour periods is to click the AM or PM button. Alternatively, you can click a block and drag the cursor over a range of blocks to invert all the selected blocks.

This *general time mask* of time blocks that you turn on will apply to each day in the calendar. Days that are outside the calendar are off throughout the day (see Figure 4.19).

FIGURE 4.19
The Calendar General Time Mask window.

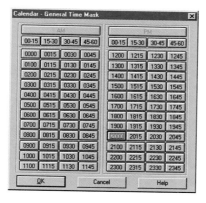

Saving a Calendar

When you have finished defining a calendar, click OK in the Calendar Detail window. The window in Figure 4.20 will appear. Enter a name and description for the calendar and then click OK.

FIGURE 4.20
Saving a Holidays calendar.

TNG's workload scheduler supports two kinds of jobs: *Scheduled jobs* run on a defined schedule, and ad hoc *dynamic jobs* run on demand.

Autoscan and Scheduled Jobs

The Workload database stores the job sets and their jobs. *Demands* allow job sets to perform the work they represent. The system can demand job sets automatically or users can do so manually. The Tracking File receives demanded job sets and their associated jobs. When a suitable time exists and resources become available, the system submits the jobs and executes the tasks.

Autoscan is a sophisticated Workload Management process. Workload Management treats a workday as a 24-hour period that begins at new-day time. By default, the new-day Autoscan happens at 1:00 a.m. Although you can configure the frequency with which Autoscan occurs, the default is every three hours.

Autoscan first selects all eligible job sets, and then eligible jobs within those job sets. It then places selected job sets and their jobs in the daily Tracking File, which comprises the current day's workload. The system automatically maintains and purges the Tracking File at midnight so that Autoscan will be able to pick up the job sets each day.

Triggers and Demand Jobs

Predictive scheduling refers to the use of calendars to schedule jobs. Jobs are scheduled and automatically placed in the Tracking File on the days you specify as workdays by using calendars. However, not all jobs need to run on a calendar basis. Occasionally situations or events may arise that require a quick, consistent, and correct response to ensure that operation continues smoothly. Recognizing this, Workload Management provides facilities you can use to identify these events and specify how Workload Management triggers handle them.

Event-based scheduling is the use of triggers and message actions to schedule jobs. The tripping of a trigger starts a message action regardless of when the event occurs. Triggers and message actions work together to execute a group of user-specified commands automatically in response to a particular event taking place on the system. There are four types of triggers:

- CA Event—Uses the CAEVENT.EXE application. This utility takes two parameters; the event name and a status code (1 to 8). Parameter entry must be in the order *name* followed by *status*. The system only invokes the trigger if both the name and the status code match the values defined in the trigger profile.

- Job Termination—The system will initiate the trigger if a named job with a specific number in a specific job set terminates with a fail code outside the range specified in the trigger profile.

- Job Initiation—The system will trip the trigger on initiation of a named job with a specific number in a specific job set.

- File Closure—The system invokes the trigger if a specified file closes after changing. Either a STAT call or an intercept method determines the closure of the file.

Triggers run jobs on a predictable schedule or in response to a particular event. In other situations, Workload Management simply runs jobs on demand. The Jobset Demand choice on the Jobset List window instructs Workload Management to "demand" (insert) a job set from the Workload database into the current workload. This allows you to place job sets into the current day's workload (into the Tracking File) that the system would not have automatically selected for processing.

When Workload Management demands a job set into the Tracking File, it also brings in the individual jobs in the job set if both of the following conditions are true:

■ The job profile specifies Autoselect = YES.

■ The calendar profile for the job indicates that today is a workday.

To bring jobs into the Tracking File automatically when you demand the job set of which they are members, both of these conditions must be satisfied. Otherwise, you must specifically demand the job into the Tracking File using the Job Demand choice on the Jobs List container window.

Defining and Running Jobs and Job Sets

To add a job set from any of the Real World Interface browsers, right-click the Unicenter Workload icon in Unispace (inside the server) and choose Jobsets from the pop-up menu. From the Enterprise Management program group, double-click Workload to open the Workload program group (see Figure 4.21) and then double-click the Jobsets icon. In either case, you will see the window in Figure 4.22.

FIGURE 4.21
The Workload program group.

FIGURE 4.22
The Jobsets List window.

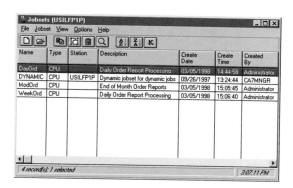

To add a new job set, choose Jobset, New from the menu. You will see the Jobset - Detail window, starting at the Main Info page shown in Figure 4.23.

First, enter a name for the job set and a description of its purpose. Next, fill in the appropriate data on each page of the notebook.

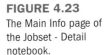

FIGURE 4.23

The Main Info page of the Jobset - Detail notebook.

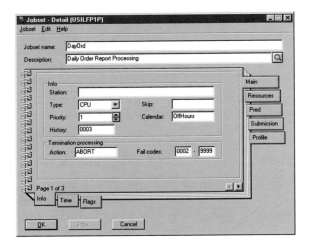

Station identifies the name of a defined station profile.

Calendar specifies those days on which the jobs can run. If no defined calendar exists, the system uses the BASE calendar.

Action identifies what should occur after the processing of a job set ends abnormally. Valid options are

  ■ ABORT—Marks the job as aborted. If this job is a predecessor to other jobs, those jobs cannot run.

  ■ CONTINUE—Marks the job as aborted. Successor jobs will still run.

Fail codes identify the limits of an exit code range. Any number within the range specified indicates a failed status. Any number outside the range indicates a good status. The default processing status is zero for good status and non-zero for failed status.

Select the Time tab on the bottom of the notebook (see Figure 4.24).

Various time values (Early Start, Must Start, Must Complete) can be defined, and the system will track the average duration. *Early Start* marks the earliest time that Workload Management can automatically mark a job set as started. You can define the date when the system can start to schedule a task and the date when the system can no longer schedule the task.

Click the Flags tab on the bottom of the notebook (see Figure 4.25).

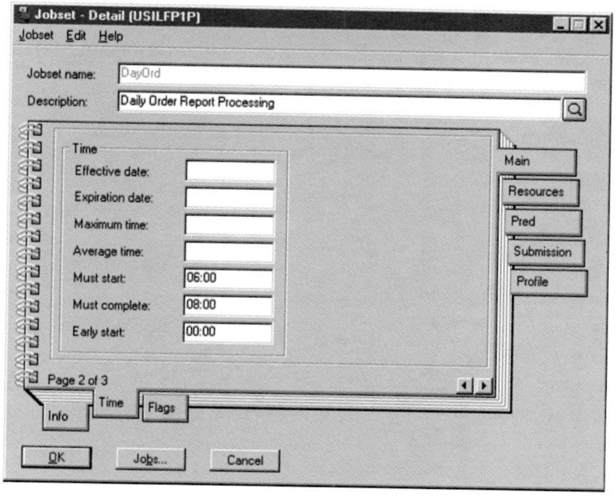

FIGURE 4.24

The Main Time page of the Jobset - Detail notebook.

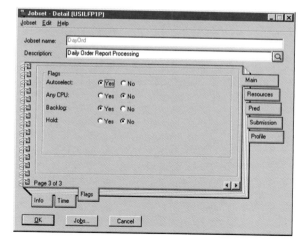

FIGURE 4.25

The Main Flags page of the Jobset - Detail notebook.

The *Autoselect* check box specifies whether the system evaluates the job set for processing "today."

- If checked, the system automatically evaluates the job set for processing as part of a Workload Management Autoscan.
- If not checked, the system ignores the job set and the jobs it contains. A job set that runs on an "as needed" basis or in response to a particular system event, such as creation of a file, is usually *not* Autoselect eligible. The system typically demands this kind of job set into the current workload as needed.

The *Any CPU* check box specifies whether any machine (CPU station) defined in the Workload client/server configuration can run the jobs in this job set or if the particular machine specified in the Station field must run them.

Ch

4

The *Backlog* check box specifies whether the system will cancel and purge the job set and all of its jobs if they have not completed by the end of the current workday.

- If checked, the system carries the unfinished job set forward as part of the new day's workload and automatically reschedules it for processing.
- If not checked, the system cancels and purges the unfinished job set (status level BLKCAN) from the Tracking File when the new workday begins.

The *Hold* option keeps jobs from running until the operator manually releases them. This is useful when you need tape mounts or paper changes.

Select the Profile tab on the right side of the notebook. Here you can specify actions to take on holidays (see Figure 4.26). Refer to the Calendar discussion earlier in this chapter for more information about holidays.

FIGURE 4.26

The Profile page of the Jobset notebook.

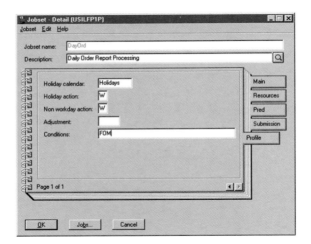

Select the Submission tab on the right side of the notebook. On this page you can enter details of the user ID profile the system will use to run the tasks (see Figure 4.27).

The following are valid options on this page:

- *Run as user*—Logon ID of the user on behalf of which the system will submit the file or program
- *Domain*—Indicates the domain under which the system will run this job
- *Password*—Password of the user for whom the system will run this job
- *Verify*—Verifies the password of the user for whom the system will run this job

If you are ready to define jobs for this job set, choose Jobset, Save and then click the Jobs button. This action takes you directly to the Jobs List container for the job set you are currently administering. This way you can immediately start to define jobs.

FIGURE 4.27
The Submission page of
the Jobset notebook.

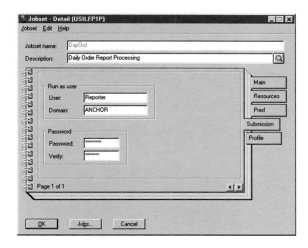

Alternatively, click OK to save the jobset profile and return to the Jobset List container. Choose File, Close to return to the Workload folder.

Open Workload from the Unicenter TNG main folder. Open Jobs from the Workload folder. Choose Jobs, New from the Jobs List container. This will open the window shown in Figure 4.28.

Ch
4

FIGURE 4.28
The Main Info page of
the Job - Detail
notebook.

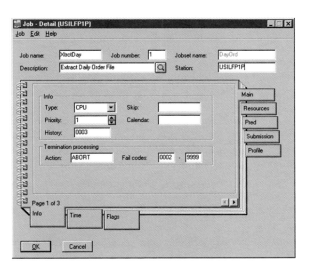

The field descriptions for Job - Detail are much the same as for Jobset - Detail, explained earlier in the chapter. Note, however, that in this window if no Calendar name is supplied, the value "Def" will appear in this field to indicate that the job inherits the calendar of the job set.

T I P The job number does *not* indicate the sequence of jobs in a job set. Often, you need to run the same job multiple times within a job set. You can use the Job Number field to uniquely identify which job is which, rather than creating new names for subsequent occurrences of the same job. For example, the first time you would use the default value 01 for the job number, the second time you would enter 02 for the job number, and so forth. We recommend that you typically use 01 for all jobs within a job set unless you have other specific requirements.

Select the Resources tab on the right side of the notebook (see Figure 4.29).

FIGURE 4.29

The Resources page of the Job - Detail notebook.

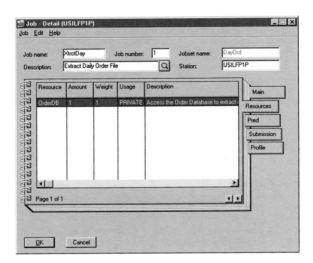

Workload balancing can be achieved by providing entries in the Resources page. Enter data in all required fields to begin defining the resources for this job. These fields are

- *Resource*—Specifies the profile that describes a resource required by this job
- *Amount*—Describes how many units of the resource are required
- *Weight*—Determines the relative priority of a resource. A higher number indicates more importance
- *Usage*—Indicates how the resource will be used by this job

  - PRIVATE—This job needs exclusive access to the resource
  - SHARED—This job can share the resource with other jobs
  - COREQ—This job may access the resource only when another job has PRIVATE access

Click the Time tab on the bottom of the notebook (see Figure 4.30).

FIGURE 4.30
The Main Time page of the Job - Detail notebook.

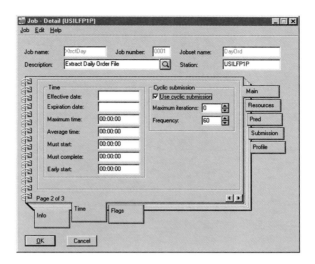

A job can be started at a particular time, run every specified number of minutes, and, optionally, run a specified number of times or until the end of the day, whichever comes first. For example, the workday ends at 20:00, and a job set to start at 16:00 has a frequency of 60 minutes and five maximum iterations. The job runs at 16:00, 17:00, 18:00, 19:00, and 20:00.

Click the Flags tab on the bottom of the notebook (see Figure 4.31).

Ch
4

FIGURE 4.31
The Main Flags page of the Job - Detail notebook.

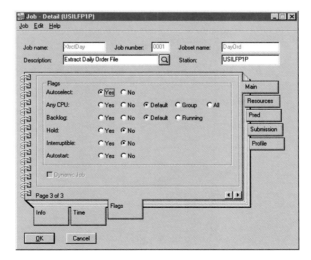

The Backlog option button appears on the Main Flags notebook page.

This button specifies whether the system should cancel and purge this job if it has not completed by the end of the current workday. The Jobset profile provides the default setting for this parameter for all jobs in the job set.

- If Yes is selected, the unfinished job is carried forward and rescheduled for processing.
- If No is selected, the unfinished job is canceled and purged from the Tracking File when the new workday begins or when the new-day Autoscan is performed.
- If Running is selected, a currently executing job is carried forward as part of the new day's workload and is automatically rescheduled for processing.

Click the Pred (for Predecessors) tab on the right side of the notebook (see Figure 4.32).

FIGURE 4.32
The Pred page of the
Job - Detail notebook.

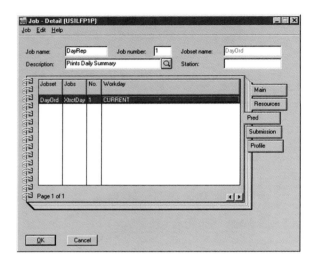

You can configure job sets and jobs to run only if one or more other jobs have successfully completed. Job predecessors identify those jobs or job sets that must complete successfully before a job can become a candidate for submission. Jobs can have both jobs and job sets as predecessors. Both job set predecessors and job predecessors must be satisfied before a job can become a candidate for submission.

Click the Submission tab on the right side of the notebook. (See Figure 4.33.)

Workload Management submits CPU jobs based on user-defined processing requirements. The task, be it an executable program, a script, and so on, must be specified. Up to 64 parameters can be specified for each task. At this point, you are ready to submit a job set, including this job.

Technically Speaking: How Scheduling Works

TNG's workload job scheduling includes a Workload Manager and Workload agents. Figure 4.34 shows the main parts of the system.

FIGURE 4.33
The Submission page of
the Job - Detail
notebook.

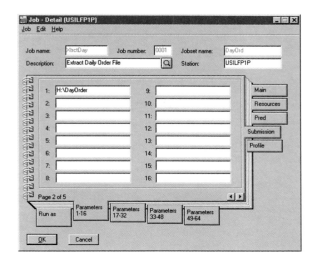

FIGURE 4.34
Workload Manager and
agent components.

Ch
4

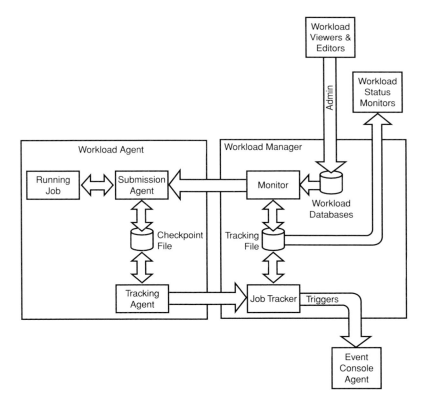

Two major subsystems comprise Workload Management—the *Workload job server* and the *Workload agent*. Typically, sites have one Workload job server running and multiple Workload agents running. The Workload agents run on all the server machines where the Workload Management job server component will submit and track work.

Workload Manager (Job Server)   The Workload job server or Manager is responsible for scheduling work, sending job submission requests to the Workload agent, processing user commands, and job tracking. It consists of two functional areas:

- The *Monitor,* which identifies jobs that should be run and determines when and where they should be submitted

- The *Job Tracker,* which collects job event data from all Workload Management agents where jobs have been submitted and uses that data to update job status and resource availability information

Workload Agent   The Workload agent is responsible for running jobs on behalf of the Workload job server and sending event data to the central Job Tracker. Workload agent processes should be running on every machine where Workload Management submits and tracks work (including the server where the Workload job server resides). The Workload agent consists of two functional areas:

- The *remote submission agent* runs the submit file specified by the Workload Management Monitor.

- The *remote tracking agent* collects job event data and sends it to the Workload Management Job Tracker.

The Scheduling Process   The basic objects of workload scheduling, as defined earlier, are jobs and job sets, resources, stations and station groups, triggers, and calendars. Operators use various workload viewers and editors to define the workload in terms of those basic objects. Those data are stored in the Workload Database in the Manager.

Within the Manager, the Workload Monitor periodically scans the database looking for work to do. This Autoscan is performed at the start of the day (at midnight) and occasionally throughout the day. The section "Autoscan and Scheduled Jobs," earlier in this chapter, describes the process that Autoscan goes through to find work to do.

When the Monitor finds a job that needs to run, it loads the job into the Tracking File. The Tracking File is where the Workload Manager keeps track of the status of each job. The Monitor watches the status of each job, job set, and so on. It evaluates dependencies, allocates resources, and balances the load to decide when and where to run a given job. When it decides a job is ready to run, it submits it to the submission agent in the station (system) that will run the job.

The submission agent actually runs the job. It sets up the environment in which the job will run and captures the status of the job in a *checkpoint file*. The tracking agent watches job status and sends updates to the Job Tracker in the Workload Manager.

The Job Tracker updates the status in the Tracking File. It also evaluates the status changes against the defined triggers. If a trigger fires, the Job Tracker sends an event message to the event log and console. There, the message/action engine described in Chapter 2, "The Unicenter TNG Framework," can be set up to kick off an action when the message is received. This is often used to start a recovery job when a job fails.

Operators view the status of jobs through various Workload Status Monitors. These all watch the Tracking File to figure out the status of jobs.

Job scheduling is tightly integrated with the Unicenter TNG event console and message/action engine. When problems occur during job execution, events are forwarded to the console, where an operator will notice and respond to them. This can also trigger an automated action such as starting a recovery job set to get the train back on the track.

One of the powerful features of Workload Management is its ability to start job sets automatically when a job in another job set fails. The recovery job set is defined like any other job set, but it is not normally defined as being Autoselectable. As shown in Figure 4.35, when a job defines a job set and a range of fail codes as a set of termination processing parameters, the defined job set will be submitted when a suitable return code is identified.

FIGURE 4.35
Defining a recovery job set.

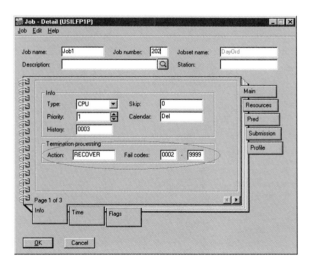

Ch
4

Jobflow

Administrators need flexible access to information in the production control environment. Sometimes they need to see the big picture; at other times, they must focus on a specific job or group of jobs.

Jobflow allows users to see a graphical representation of the workload of their enterprise. You can view relationships between jobs that are defined in the scheduling database and monitor the status of jobs in real-time. The graphical interface allows you to tailor your view of the workload. You can limit the number of jobs to view by specifying job names, time span, and number of successor levels, and display the results as either a Gantt or Pert chart. You can zoom in on the successors and triggers for a single job or zoom out for a larger perspective.

Jobflow provides two views:

- Jobflow forecast views
- Jobflow status views

Jobflow forecast views display job relationships (predecessor-successor or job-triggers) for selected jobs within a given period. You can view dependencies (requirements) for any job in the flowchart.

Jobflow status views display real-time status information for selected jobs within a given period. Color coding allows easy identification of job status and helps pinpoint trouble spots. For example, abended jobs appear red and late jobs appear yellow. Status information is updated at regular intervals, so your view of the workload remains current.

Jobflow works with, and serves as an enhancement to, the Unicenter TNG Workload Management function. Workload Management allows you to see scheduling details for a specific job (for example, detailed predecessor and dependency information). Jobflow expands your view of the workload to include multiple job relationships (see Figure 4.36). In addition, when you need to change the schedule (add a job, for example), you can access the Workload Management detail windows to update the scheduling database.

FIGURE 4.36
Unicenter's Job Flow window.

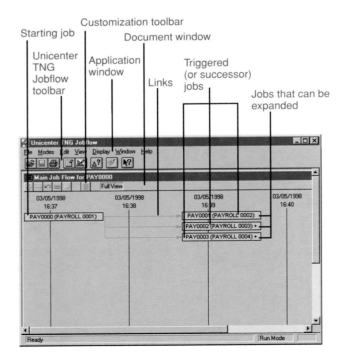

The Jobflow Forecast View

The Jobflow forecast view allows you to view relationships between jobs that are defined in the database.

In Figure 4.37, the application window (the Jobflow window) contains a document window (the Jobflow Forecast window), which presents the Jobflow forecast view of a single job. This job (the *starting job*) is the one you specify in your selection criteria.

The jobflow forecast presents each job as a bar extending across the appropriate number of time increments that represent the job's start and end times. Jobs that are related to the starting job are connected by *links* (or arrows). The jobflow consists of the starting job and either

- The jobs that are triggered by the starting job (for job trigger-based scheduling systems)
- The jobs that are successors to the starting job (for scan-based scheduling systems)

The Jobflow forecast view can be either a Gantt chart or a Pert chart. Gantt charts display the relationships between jobs across a time span. Pert charts display job relationships without regard to time. The previous illustration shows a Gantt chart.

Jobs with names followed by plus signs can be expanded to show additional trigger (or successor) levels. The following illustration presents an expanded view of PAY0002 (pictured unexpanded in the previous illustration), showing an additional level. PAY0002 is a predecessor (or trigger for) four jobs: PAY0020, PAY0021, PAY0022, and PAY0023 (see Figure 4.37).

Ch
4

FIGURE 4.37
The Main Job Flow window.

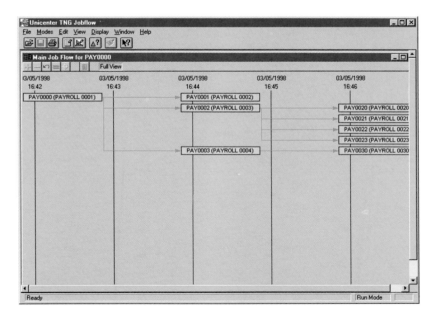

Dependency Views

Jobflow allows you to display a dependency view of any job in the job flow. A *dependency* is a condition that must be met before a job can run. The following are some examples of dependencies:

- Files (or data sets)—Files or data sets that must be created before a job can run
- Pre-CPU job—A group of non-CPU tasks that must be performed before a job can run
- Post-CPU job—A group of non-CPU tasks that must be performed after a job has run
- Jobset—A group of one or more jobs that must complete before another job or job set can execute
- Schedule—A set of instructions that tell the scheduling system when a job can run
- System conditions—operating-system–specific dependencies
- Requirements—Dependencies such as JCL overrides and hold requirements

The Dependency View window allows you to see two levels of dependency for a specific job:

- The job's predecessor (or trigger) and all of the job's dependencies (such as pre-CPU jobs, schedules, and user requirements)
- All jobs that are successors of (or that are triggered by) the specified job, as well as all the tasks (such as post-CPU jobs) that depend on the job

Figure 4.38 displays a Dependency View of PAY0002.

FIGURE 4.38
Unicenter TNG Jobflow
Dependency View.

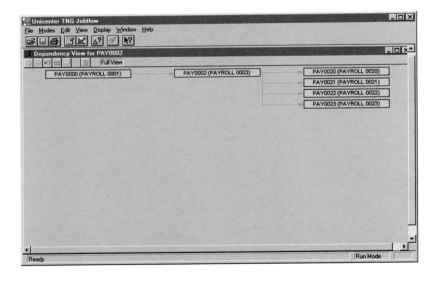

N O T E   The Jobflow application window displays two document windows: the Jobflow Forecast window and a Dependency View window. You can display multiple dependency windows in a single Jobflow window.

The Jobflow Status View

In Figure 4.39, the application window (Jobflow window) contains a document window (Jobflow Status window) that presents several jobflows (a job and its successors or a job and the jobs it triggers). Unlike the Jobflow Forecast view, the Jobflow Status view can contain multiple job flows, depending on your selection criteria.

FIGURE 4.39

The Jobflow Status view displays the real-time status of jobs within a given period.

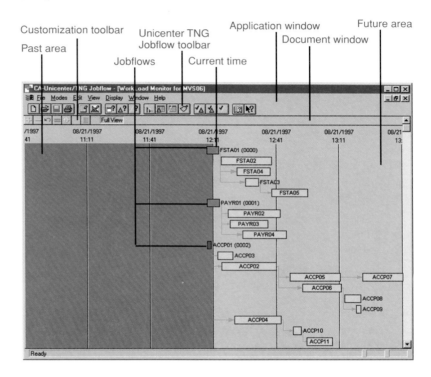

Jobs are represented by bars extending across the appropriate number of time lines that reflect the starting and ending times of the jobs. The bars are color coded to indicate their status. Jobs that are currently executing span the vertical line representing the current time. Jobs that appear in the future area have not yet executed. Jobs in the past area (ACCP01 (0002) in the previous illustration) have completed executing.

In the Jobflow Status view, as in the Jobflow Forecast view, you can display Dependency Views and expand job displays to show additional trigger (or successor) levels.

Performance Monitoring

Performance problems degrade user productivity as much or more than evident problems. Whatever the cause, working on a slow system is not only frustrating, it is the bane of creativity. Performance monitoring and management is nominally the responsibility of operations, but it often requires specialized skills to do the job.

Ch

4

Unicenter TNG's Performance Scope provides a tool for watching the performance of systems. You can use it to watch the performance of Windows NT, UNIX, and legacy servers in real-time. With it, you can drill down to gather information for diagnosing performance problems. Finally, you can use the Performance Scope to detect performance problems. Figure 4.40 shows a typical display from the Performance Scope. That scope displays CPU time used on the system as a percentage. It also shows a breakdown of the usage of that time. It shows usage both in real time in the right pane, and historically for the previous day in the left pane.

FIGURE 4.40
The Performance Scope window.

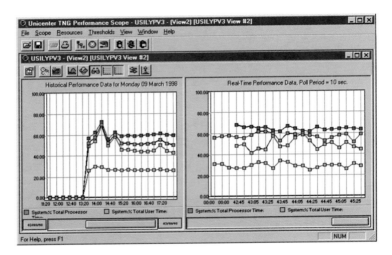

The network is also an important shared resource that can cause performance problems. Unicenter TNG's Response Manager Option (RMO) enables network performance monitoring. This chapter does not include RMO, but it was touched upon in Chapter 3, "Basic Network Management," and is covered in greater depth in Chapter 9, "Web Management."

Setting Up Real-Time Performance Agents

Real-time performance monitoring of a system depends on the Real-Time Performance Agent on the monitored system. The agent was installed on the system when you installed Unicenter Performance in Chapter 5, "Desktop Management." Once installed and running, there is nothing more to set up.

On Windows NT, the Real-Time Performance Agent hooks into all the performance metrics maintained by the operating system or by various applications in the Registry. There are hundreds of such metrics defined, and they provide information on much of what is going on inside NT and its applications.

Monitoring with Performance Scope

You can run the Unicenter TNG Performance Scope from the Unicenter TNG browsers or from the NT Start menu. To run it from a Unicenter TNG browser, like the 3D map, navigate to Unispace in the system you want to look at, right-click the Performance icon, and choose Performance Scope from the pop-up menu. To run it from the Start menu, click Start, Programs, Unicenter TNG Performance, TNG Performance Scope.

You will be asked to sign on to the Repository. The initial display will be a blank window. You must first build a *chart* or *machine view* of some data, and then let the monitor collect data for awhile.

Building a Chart

To build a new chart, first select Resources, Show Resource View from the menu. The window shows a view of all the *resources*, or metrics, that you can monitor (see Figure 4.41).

FIGURE 4.41
The Resource View window.

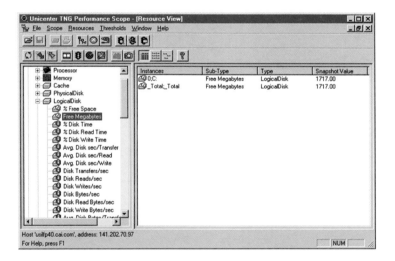

The left pane of the window displays the metrics in a typical tree view. You can expand or contract each level of the tree by clicking the plus or minus sign to the left of an object. The tree has three levels. At the top level are the systems that have the Real-Time Performance Agent installed. At the second level are major subsystems within the system: memory management, physical and logical disks, major applications such as Microsoft Exchange, and so on. At the third level are the metrics. For example, a logical disk (what NT assigns a drive letter) has metrics for Percent Free Space, Disk Queue Length, Average Disk Seconds/Transfer, and so on.

When you select a metric, a list of all the instances of that metric appears in the right pane. For example, the metric Free Megabytes occurs once for each logical disk and once as a total of all the individual disks.

You can see the current values of the metrics in the right pane by choosing Resource, Snapshot from the menu.

The metrics for Windows NT are collected by instrumentation built into the operating system or application and exposed to performance software (like Unicenter TNG's Real-Time Performance Agent) through the Registry. There are a lot of these metrics. To figure out what they mean, consult the Windows NT Performance Monitor for a short description of each metric, the Windows NT Resource Kit (about the only written documentation available), or the book *Inside Windows NT*. These resources give descriptions of how NT works in such areas as process scheduling, virtual memory management, and so on. The section "Fun Things to Watch," later in this chapter, describes some interesting metrics.

To create a new chart, choose Resources, Create New View from the menu. Then arrange the windows so you can see both the Resource View and your new Machine View (another name for a chart) at the same time. One way you can arrange the windows is to choose Window, Tile from the menu. The window will look like that shown in Figure 4.42.

FIGURE 4.42
Building a new chart.

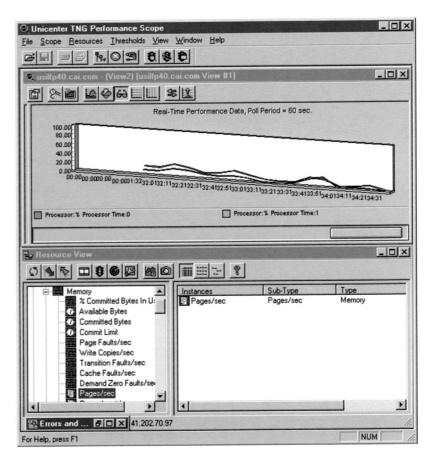

From the Resource View window, select one or more metrics from the right pane and choose Resource, Add to Chart from the menu. If multiple charts are open, you get to select to which chart the metric should be added.

Making the Chart Look Good

You can change how the chart looks in many ways. A good looking chart is easier to understand—generally, the simpler the better. Generating a multicolored 3D chart of 100 metrics plotted as a surface is probably not going to help you figure out what's wrong.

Chart Panes   A chart window (or Machine View) is divided into a left and a right pane (refer to Figure 4.40). The left pane shows historical values of the data collected by the Historical Performance Agent described in the next chapter, "Desktop Management." Since you generally collect only a small subset of the large number of metrics available for capacity planning, you will often see a message saying historical data is not available. The right pane shows the real-time data collected since you created the chart. At first it will be empty, but over time, data will fill the chart from the right. The most recent sample always appears at the right of the chart.

You can adjust the space given to the left and right panes by moving the cursor to the bar separating them, clicking, and then dragging the bar to adjust their size. If there is no historical data for a chart, you can drag the bar so that the whole window shows the real-time chart.

Each pane is divided in two. The chart itself is at the top and a legend is at the bottom. If you have a number of metrics in the chart, the legend will not have room to show them all. The line or bar separating the chart and legend can be moved by clicking the line and dragging it up and down so you can see the whole legend. You can also right-click in the legend, bringing up a pop-up menu that allows you to select the location of the legend. One of the choices is a floating legend, where the legend appears in a separate window that you can place in a convenient spot on the screen. If you close the floating legend window, you will also shut down the legend.

Changing How Data Is Collected

You can change what data is being collected in a chart and how often data is being collected.

To change the frequency of collection (how long between each sample), select a chart window and choose View, Real-time Chart Settings from the menu. You will see the pop-up window shown in Figure 4.43. Drag the slider to change the setting.

FIGURE 4.43
The Realtime Poll Period window.

Chart Properties   Selecting a chart window and choosing View, Properties from the menu opens the chart's Properties window (see Figure 4.44). This window shows each metric in the chart and its minimum, maximum, and average values.

Ch
4

FIGURE 4.44
The Properties window.

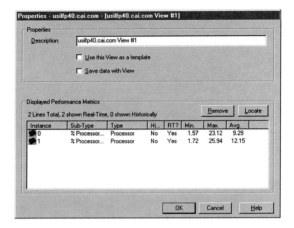

You can also change the name of the chart to something meaningful. Simply enter the chart name in the Description field of the window.

When you are done, click OK.

Chart Style and 3D charts   The Performance Scope can display many styles of charts. To choose a style for a chart, select the chart window, and choose View, Chart Style from the menu (see Figure 4.45). Pull down the Gallery Type list, and you will see a pop-up menu where you can choose a chart style (see Figure 4.46). The different charts have different strengths. Your best bet is to try out a few styles to see which seem most informative.

FIGURE 4.45
The General Options window.

FIGURE 4.46
Select the chart type from the Chart Style Selector.

To make the chart a 3D or 2D chart, click the 3D button in the toolbar (it looks like a pair of glasses). To change the 3D appearance of the chart, choose View, 3D Chart Settings. Figure 4.47 shows the resulting window.

FIGURE 4.47
Selecting 3D chart settings.

Here you can tilt and rotate the chart by dragging the small position balls. You can change the width of the chart and the size of the data-point markers. You can also choose the type of point markers used in the chart.

You can change the background color or grid color by choosing View, Chart Background Color, or View, Chart Grid Color from the menu. You can turn the horizontal or vertical grid lines on or off by toggling the respective buttons in the toolbar.

Finally, you can adjust the vertical Y axis in 3 ways. You can choose View, Fit Axis to Data so the chart will reach to the top. You can choose View, Synchronize Y Axis to make the historical and real-time charts have the same Y axis settings. You can right-click within the chart, and the pop-up window shown in Figure 4.48 will appear where you can set the exact values for the Y axis you want displayed.

Ch
4

FIGURE 4.48
The Y-Axis Properties for Real-Time Chart pop-up window.

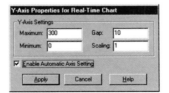

Saving and Recalling Charts

Once you have built a chart that displays the metrics you want in the way in which you want them, you can save the chart to be used again later. To save a chart, choose File, Save View As from the menu. You will be asked to name the file. The extension for saved chart files is .PSC. Give your chart a meaningful name, and then click OK.

To open a chart, choose File, Open View, and choose the appropriate file. Performance Scope lists the last few chart files you have saved in the File menu.

Printing and Mailing Charts

To print a chart, choose File, Print.

To send a chart to someone else through email, choose File, Send Machine View. The file will be attached to an email message using your normal mail program. The person you send it to must have Unicenter TNG Performance Scope installed to see the chart.

How to Monitor Thresholds with Scope

Unicenter TNG's Performance Scope can monitor the system and generate notifications and event messages when a metric exceeds some threshold. Because the Performance Scope has access to more metrics, this technique gives you the ability to watch a large number of quite detailed thresholds. When a threshold watcher fires, you can define an action that is executed. The biggest disadvantage of using Performance Scope's thresholds is that the performance scope must first be running to watch these thresholds. It's unlikely you will run the Performance Scope all the time. Instead, you will mainly use it to diagnose a performance problem on the system. Since those problems may be intermittent, the thresholds in the Performance Scope are likely to be used to notify you when you should pay attention to what's happening.

To monitor thresholds, first define the actions and threshold templates, and then apply them to particular systems (resources).

Threshold Status

The Threshold Status window, shown in Figure 4.49, shows all the thresholds that are active and their status. To open the window, choose Thresholds, Show Threshold Status… from the menu. Initially, the window will be empty. As you apply certain threshold watchers to various systems, the left pane of the window will show a tree view of the active watchers. At the top will be the systems being watched, below that will be the various threshold templates that have been applied to the system, and below that, the specific metrics being watched. The right pane will show the various instances of the metrics, their current values, the status of the threshold, and minimum, maximum, and average values.

Defining Actions

To define an action, open the Action Catalog—a list of all the available actions. To open the Action Catalog choose Thresholds, Action Catalog from the menu. You will see the Threshold Action Definitions window, shown in Figure 4.50.

Click New to add a new action, and you will see the Action Definition window shown in Figure 4.51.

Give the action a name, and then choose the things to be done. You can choose any or all of four things to happen. You can have a message box displayed. This box will pop open on your screen if the threshold fires. You can have a sound (a beep) played when the threshold fires. You can have a message logged to the Event and Notification window of the Performance Scope. Finally, you can run any command as an *external command*.

FIGURE 4.49
The Threshold Status window.

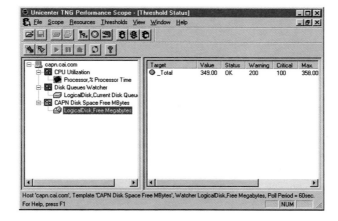

FIGURE 4.50
The Threshold Action Definitions window contains the Action Catalog.

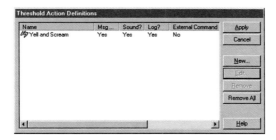

FIGURE 4.51
Defining an action.

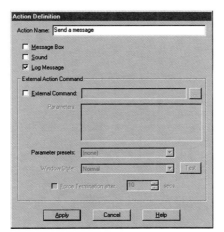

Ch
4

Using external commands, you can have just about anything happen when a threshold fires. Message boxes and sounds are useful to draw your attention to the system. The notifications appear in an Events and Notifications window. One of the options (described next) allows you to forward all of the notifications to Unicenter TNG's Event Management Console (see Chapter 2, "The Unicenter TNG Framework").

Creating a Threshold Template

To create a threshold template, choose Thresholds, Wizard from the menu. A Threshold Template Wizard will open that will guide you through the process of creating a new template. The first screen is shown in Figure 4.52.

FIGURE 4.52

The first dialog box of the Threshold Template Wizard.

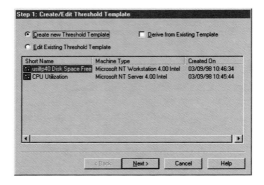

Check Create new Threshold Template to create a new threshold template. If the new template is like one you have already defined, you can start the new template from the old by checking Derive from Existing Template and then choosing the starting template from the list.

To edit an existing template, check Edit Existing Threshold Template, and then select the template you want to edit from the list.

Click Next, to advance to step 2.

The Naming and Machine Type window opens (see Figure 4.53). Enter a name for the threshold template. Select a Machine Type from the drop-down list. This will choose what metrics you can monitor and what kinds of machines to which the template can be applied.

Enter a polling period for the template, and any criteria that will describe the template's intended purpose.

Then click Next to advance to step 3—the Define Threshold Watchers window as shown in Figure 4.54.

FIGURE 4.53
Threshold Template
Wizard, step 2.

FIGURE 4.54
The screen for step 3 of
the Threshold Template
Wizard.

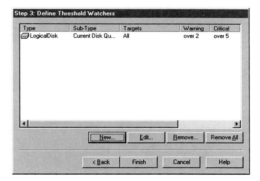

Ch
4

Now add the specific metrics you want to watch. This window lists those that have been defined so far. Click New to add a new threshold to the template. You will see the window shown in Figure 4.55. To add a threshold, you need to decide five things.

FIGURE 4.55
The Threshold Watcher
Specification window.

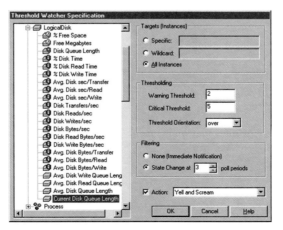

First, choose the metric you want to watch in the left pane. The metrics are organized in a tree, much as in the Resource View.

Second, choose the specific instances of the resources that are to be watched. You can watch all instances (for example all disks), a specific instance (for example, the process named SQLSERVER.EXE), or a wildcard pattern that matches specific instances (for example all processes named SQL*).

Third, choose the value of the threshold. You can set two thresholds, a Warning threshold, and a Critical threshold. Also, specify the direction of the threshold. Some thresholds, like one on the metric Pages/sec, should fire whenever they are over the threshold value. Others, like Percent Free Disk Space, should fire when they are under the threshold.

Fourth, choose if you want to apply any filtering. Sometimes a metric will occasionally cross a threshold, and you are only concerned if that happens for a longer stretch of time. You can set a filter so that the threshold only fires if three (or any number) of polls in a row are all over the threshold.

Fifth, choose an action to execute when the threshold fires. If you leave the Action check box unchecked, no action will be taken, but the Threshold Status window will show the status of the threshold.

When you are done defining a threshold watcher, click OK.

When you are finished defining thresholds for the template, click Finish.

Applying Thresholds

Once the thresholds have been defined, they can be applied to one or more systems. To apply a threshold to a system, first open the Resource View (shown back in Figure 4.41), and select the system to which you want to apply a threshold. Then choose Resource, Apply Thresholds from the menu. In the window shown in Figure 4.56, select the threshold template to apply to the system and click Apply.

FIGURE 4.56

Applying a threshold template.

Fun Things to Watch

With all the data you could watch, what is worth watching? Most performance problems are due to running out of some limited resource. Computer systems have only so much CPU availability, real memory, memory bandwidth, storage capacity, I/O, and network bandwidth. While there is not room to discuss each of these, here are a few things to watch for.

CPU Utilization

The processor (CPU) of the system is shared by all of the processes and threads running on the system. You can graph the processor's utilization (the percentage of time it is doing useful work). Operating systems like NT typically spend their CPU time in various modes, interrupt, user, and so on, and a chart can show how that is broken down.

If the CPU utilization is too high, one thing you can do is get a faster processor. While that increases capacity, it may not solve your problem. The various capacities of a system are interrelated. Without sufficient memory, the system accommodates by increased paging to virtual memory. Disk I/O, processing while making the decision to move a page out to disk, and the time spent communicating with the disk driver to send the page out to disk, all consume CPU cycles. As you can see, CPU utilization turns out to be a good overall indicator of problems, but you need to dig deeper to figure out exactly what's wrong.

Queue Lengths

Ch
4

When some component like the CPU or disk channel is fully utilized, that may not be a problem. Users are more concerned with how long it takes to get their job done than with how busy the system doing the work is. When a resource is owned by a single user, that user will get maximum responsiveness. For example, if a single user is running an hour-long, computer-intensive job, like rendering a 3D ray-traced picture, the system will take about an hour to complete the task. However, if that same job competes with many other users, it might take five or ten hours to complete. This is a common situation on a shared server, and most annoying for small tasks that otherwise might take a few seconds.

The problem is simple: When a system is doing a number of things at once, it shares resources, like the CPU, among those tasks. If a task wants to run, but the system is busy with another task, the new task waits in a queue until the processor gets around to it. A whole branch of mathematics called *queuing theory* has been developed to analyze these kinds of situations. The math shows that by assuming a large population of users and using informed estimates, rather than outright guesses about how long it takes a system to service a user and how often users ask for service, you can predict quite well the average time people will wait in the queue. Since the work determines the average utilization of the resource, this is generally drawn as a graph of waiting time against utilization. The interesting thing about this curve is that it shows a *knee* or break in the curve somewhere between 70 and 90 percent. Before the knee, queues grow slowly and gradually, but somewhere around 80 percent, the queue suddenly takes off (rises exponentially). Then, with only a small increase in the number of users entering new tasks in the system, the delays get bigger more rapidly. This does not make for happy users.

For these and other reasons, watching queue lengths can be a more sensitive gauge of user satisfaction than utilization figures. Figure 4.57 shows a graph of disk queue lengths sampled in real time. It shows numerous times when the system has queues between five and eighteen deep waiting to access a disk. What that means is that an operation that writes to a disk, such as saving a file and exiting from a word processor, will take five to eighteen times longer than "normal."

FIGURE 4.57
Busy disk queues.

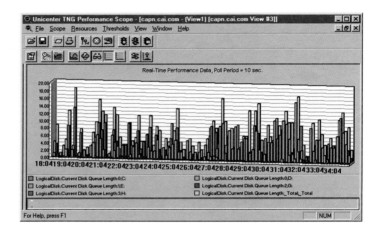

Paging

Virtual memory allows a system with limited memory to run many processes that need more memory than is physically available. Windows NT and other modern operating systems like UNIX use virtual memory. Virtual memory uses one or more disk files, known as paging files, as places to store memory *pages*. Each process actually only has a small portion of its address space (its *working set*) in physical (real) memory. When the program accesses memory in a page not actually in memory, a *page fault* occurs, and the virtual memory system finds the page and loads it from disk. Sometimes, the virtual memory system actually has the page still in memory (it is outside the working set, but not paged out to disk), so the page can be loaded into the process address space very quickly.

While virtual memory allows a system to run more programs and service more users than it otherwise could, it has a price. Page faults cost the system CPU processing time and I/O operations to input and output pages. These page faults, and paging I/O, can lead the system to a state where it is *thrashing*, spending more time moving pages around than actually doing useful work.

Just like physical memory, virtual memory is a limited resource. The size of the page files determines the total virtual memory available. When a system exhausts virtual memory, the system can't proceed unless some processes are stopped and free the virtual memory they have used.

This is a simplified description of the way virtual memory works. More detailed explanations are available in books like *Special Edition Using Windows NT* from Que.

TNG's Performance Scope can chart various metrics that show the performance of NT's virtual memory system. One important metric is the Page File Percent Usage. If this gets too high, the system will eventually fail. Another metric is various paging rates. Page Faults/sec measures the total number of page faults. Some of those page faults will be satisfied by pages still in memory. The actual I/O performed is measured by Pages Input/sec and Pages Output/sec (Pages/sec is the total of the two). While systems vary, five Pages/sec indicates that you ought to look at your memory. See Figure 4.58.

If the system is paging too much, your best bets are either to reduce the load on the system or buy more physical memory.

How to Use ObjectView for Performance Management

To use ObjectView, right-click a system or agent icon in one of the Real World Interface browsers, and choose ObjectView from the pop-up menu. You will see a window like that in Figure 4.59.

In the left pane is a tree of groups and tables (tables are represented by their entries) in the MIBs known to be supported by the agent. Clicking the plus sign expands the tree to show the variables below it. For groups, you see the group variables in the group; for tables, you see a list of the table variables in the table. Clicking a group in the tree shows all of the group variables in the right pane (displayed as a single line). Clicking a group variable shows just that variable in the right pane. Clicking a table in the tree shows the full table in the right pane. Clicking a table variable in the tree shows a single column of the table in the right pane.

You can adjust the width of columns in the right pane display by clicking the bar separating the headers of the columns, and dragging it left or right. You can adjust the order of the columns by clicking a column header and dragging it left or right to the position you want.

Viewing Another Agent   Above the two main panes of the ObjectView display is a toolbar that shows, from left to right, the IP address, DNS name, MIB, get community name, set community name, and port of the agent being viewed. In the toolbar you can select any of these fields and change them. Alternatively, you can click the small button at the left end of the toolbar, and the window shown in Figure 4.60 will appear where you can enter any of the fields. Note that once you connect to an agent, you will not see anything in the right pane until you select a group, table, or variable in the tree.

FIGURE 4.58
Watching paging I/O.

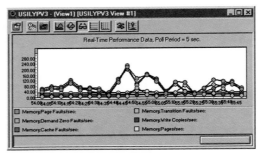

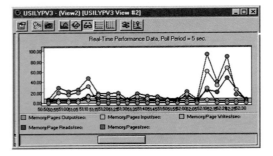

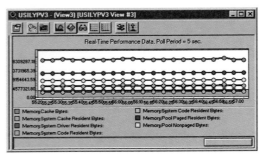

FIGURE 4.59
ObjectView looking at MIB II.

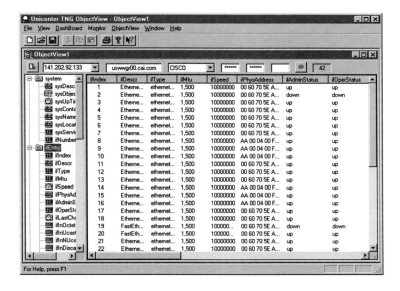

FIGURE 4.60
Connecting to an agent from ObjectView.

How to Use a Dashboard

A *dashboard* is a collection of graphs, dials, gauges, and other displays. It shows the current value of a MIB variable or the historical value of a MIB variable over the past few polls in easy-to-use graphical forms. You can also construct simple formulas that allow you to combine and manipulate the variables. You can even build a dashboard for an agent, save it, and reopen it later.

Creating a Dashboard To create a dashboard, select the MIB variables you want to display. Select the specific instances of the variables if they are in a table. To select a variable, click it. To select multiple variables, click one, hold the mouse button and drag it over the variables you want to select (you will see a small rectangle over the selection while you hold down the button). You can add to the selected variables by pressing the control key while you click.

Once you have selected the variables you want to use, choose Dashboard, New from the menu, or right click any of the selected variables and choose Add to New Dashboard Monitor from the pop-up menu. You will see a window (see Figure 4.61) that shows the current dashboard. The current dashboard shows a list of variables that can be graphed.

FIGURE 4.61
A new DashBoard.

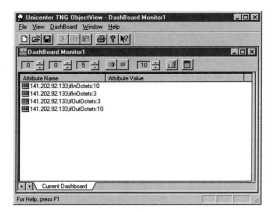

That list can include variables from multiple groups or tables, or even from multiple systems. Simply select the ÒbjectView window from the Window menu and connect to the right agent. Then show the variables, select them, and right-click the variable and select Add to DashBoard Monitor 1 from the pop-up menu.

In the left pane is the list of attributes (variables) the system can graph, as well as their most recent values. The Value column will be blank until you poll. The dashboard fills the right pane automatically.

Above the two panes is a toolbar that controls the collection of data for the dashboard. On the left are three fields where you can enter the time between polls. The three fields represent hours, minutes, and seconds. To the right are two buttons that start (the green circle) and stop (the red circle) polling. To the right of those buttons is a field where you can enter the number of polls the system will remember. If the dashboard is depicting historical data, this controls the number of visible samples. Next, there is a button to create a graph. Finally, there is a button to create a formula.

Building a Formula   If the exact value you want to graph is not in the MIB, you may be able to compute it based on available data. For example, while the Cisco MIB includes the traffic (in bits/sec) on a point-to-point line, it does not display the utilization of that line. For that, you need to divide the traffic rate by the speed and multiply by 100 to convert it into a percentage.

To build such a formula, first construct a list of attributes that includes the MIB variables needed in your calculation, in this case ifSpeed from MIB II and locIfInBitsSec from the Cisco MIB's lifEntry. Then, select Dashboard, Create Formula from the Dashboard window. You will see a formula window like that shown in Figure 4.62.

The formula will be constructed in the top window. To add an attribute to the formula, double-click its entry in the formula list. Use the calculator keyboard on the right to enter numbers, operators (like +, -, /, or *), and parentheses as needed. When you finish, click OK. The formula will be added to the list of attributes available in your dashboard.

FIGURE 4.62
Creating a Dashboard
formula.

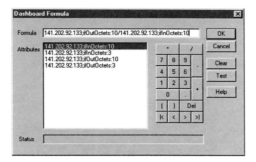

Adding a Graph to a Dashboard   To add a graph to a dashboard, select the items to graph by clicking the attribute name. Right-click one of the selected attributes and choose Add to Current Dashboard from the pop-up menu. The Graph Wizard then asks you to select the kind of graph you want to add. Most of the questions are about choosing appropriate colors. The most important step asks you to choose a style for the graph (as shown in Figure 4.63). Many styles are available. Some display the most recent value while others display the values collected over the past few polls. Simply click the style you want and continue through the wizard dialog boxes.

FIGURE 4.63
Selecting a graph style
for the dashboard in
the Dashboard Wizard.

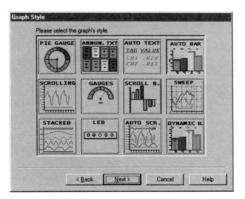

Ch
4

You can put multiple gauges, dials, or graphs in the dashboard, as shown in Figure 4.64. You can also have multiple dashboards built from the same list of attributes shown for the current dashboard. Simply choose Add to New Dashboard from the pop-up menu when you right-click the attributes you want to graph.

You can change many of the visual elements of the graph such as the title, legend, scale, and so on. To change an element, for example the axis label, right-click the graph and choose what you want modified from the pop-up menu.

FIGURE 4.64

A dashboard showing line utilization.

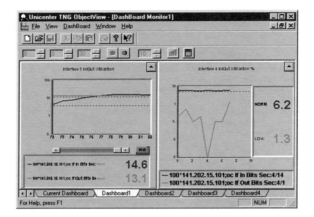

Saving a Dashboard and Loading a Saved Dashboard   Once your dashboard shows the desired information, you can save it by choosing File, Save (or Save Workplace) from the menu. The Save option saves only the dashboard, while Save Workplace saves the dashboard, ObjectViews, and Excel monitors that are open.

To open a saved dashboard or workplace, choose File, Open. The dialog box lets you choose the kinds of files you want to open.

Limitations of Dashboards   While dashboards are quick and easy to build, they have some limitations. Agent views are built for a whole class of objects, while ObjectViews, dashboards, and Excel monitors are built for specific object instances. If you want to construct a dashboard for a second Cisco router, you must start over from the beginning. There is no easy way to apply it to all Cisco routers.

Dashboard formulas are limited in their computational power. It is difficult to produce totals, compute rates, or do other sophisticated mathematical operations. For that, the Excel monitor provides a more powerful solution.

Building a Monitor (Using Excel)

An Excel monitor gives you the full computational power of Excel spreadsheets to manipulate the data you collect from an MIB.

To create an Excel monitor, select the MIB variables you want to include from the ObjectView window. Then choose Monitor, New from the menu, or right-click one of the selected variables and choose Add to New Monitor from the pop-up menu. After you collect some data, you will see a window like the one shown in Figure 4.65.

As with a dashboard, use the toolbar above the main window to set the number of polls to keep and the time interval between polls. Then click the button with the green start circle to start polling.

FIGURE 4.65

The Excel Monitor raw data sheet.

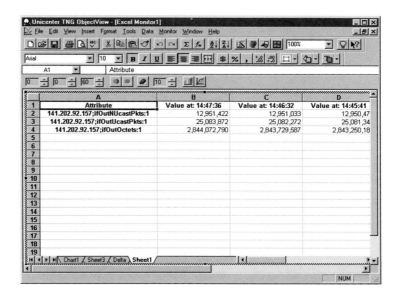

Computations in an Excel Monitor   The value of the Excel monitor comes from the power of Excel to compute values the agent and MIB don't provide. To use this, you should first become familiar with building formulas in Excel.

SNMP agents that support the standard MIBs collect performance data as counters. As their name implies, a *counter* counts the number of times something has happened since the agent started. For example, a counter is defined by the number of bytes (octets) sent over an interface since the agent started. Since that could have been weeks ago, counters often have big values that change slowly. Graphing a raw counter tells you very little. If you graphed the bytes-sent data that appears as 141.202.92.157;ifOutOctets:1 on line 4 of the spreadsheet in Figure 4.65, you would see a flat line.

To make counters useful, you usually want to convert them to a rate, for example, the number of bytes sent in the past minute. This can be computed by polling for the counter once a minute and then subtracting the values in two successive polls. Figure 4.66 shows the result of such a computation of the Delta, the value between two polls.

To compute the Deltas, first create a new worksheet for your computation. You need a new worksheet because the Excel monitor clears the raw data on Sheet1 whenever you start polling. Then set the column headings to be the same as those on Sheet1 by building a formula where, for example, cell B1 on the Delta sheet =Sheet1!B1. Then do the same for column A.

Then compute the Delta value in cell B2 by using the following formula:

```
=Sheet1!B2-Sheet1!C2
```

Ch
4

FIGURE 4.66

An Excel Monitor delta computation sheet.

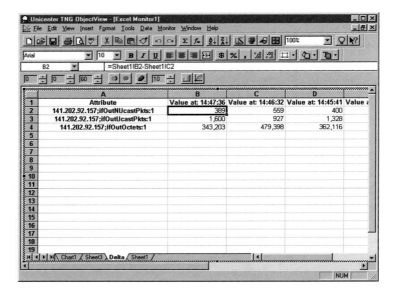

This formula can be copied to the other cells in the row—in this case columns B through K because you have polled for 10 samples—and other rows, in this case rows 2 through 4 because you have polled for 3 values. Because you have collected 10 polls, you get 9 useful Delta values (the one in column K has no data in column G to work against) so any further computations will ignore column K.

Once Excel has computed the Delta values, you can use them to compute other information. For example, you could compute the packet rate by dividing the delta of packets sent by the polling period (60 seconds). Alternatively, you could compute the outbound utilization of an interface by dividing the delta of octets sent by the speed and multiplying by 8 (bits per octet). Figure 4.67 shows a computation of the average packet size. It is computed by dividing the delta of the octets sent by the total number of packets sent on the interface. An interface can send two kinds of packets, multicast and non-multicast. Adding the two gives the total packets sent. The Excel formula is

```
=Delta!B4/(Delta!B3+Delta!B2)
```

As you can see from the data in Figure 4.67, the average packet size changes over time.

Graphing Using Excel Monitor   Once you have computed some data, you can graph it using the graphing capabilities in Excel. Simply select the data you want to graph, and choose Insert, Chart, On New Sheet from the menu. Excel's Chart Wizard will lead you through a few choices on chart style and so on. The result is shown in Figure 4.68.

FIGURE 4.67
The Excel Monitor showing average packet size.

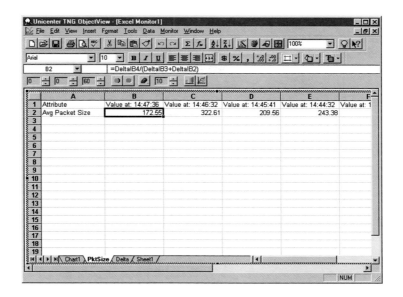

FIGURE 4.68
The Excel Monitor chart of average packet sizes.

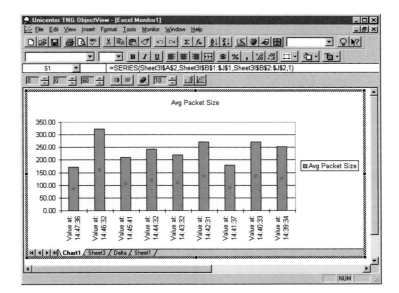

Ch
4

Capacity Planning

Long-term capacity planning for systems and networks is concerned with how workloads change over time and how systems evolve in response to those demands. By recognizing patterns, trends can be plotted that help predict when the system will run out of capacity.

Capacity planning requires knowing when major changes have occurred or are planned. This is necessary because when new applications are brought up, systems often suffer significant performance degradation. For example, when organizations first installed intranet servers and browsers became generally available, network traffic jumped, driving down overall network performance. Although such discontinuous change can't be precisely predicted, keeping an eye on what has happened and on what is coming is a key to long-term success.

Collecting long-term performance data requires planning and an initial investment in setting up the collection. To start, you should install the Unicenter TNG Historical Performance Agent (HPA) on the systems you want to monitor. The HPA runs in the background as a service on NT or a daemon on UNIX, periodically collecting system performance data and storing it locally.

As the data is collected, it is gathered into a *performance cube*. Each cell in the cube represents a particular sample of a metric, a single number to be manipulated or used. A cube organizes the collected data along three axes.

The first axis is time. The time axis determines when the data is collected. The HPA collects data at periodic intervals. You can choose the exact period—something between one and sixty minutes is typical.

The second axis represents the actual metric collected. It indicates the resource type, the specific instance of the resource, and the exact metric collected. For example, the metric `Processor->% Processor Time->0` refers to the Processor resource; the instance is `Processor 0`, and the specific metric collected is the `% Processor Time` (the time the processor is busy).

The third axis is used to gather related data from different days—in which case it is called a *period cube*—or different systems—in which case it is called an *enterprise cube*. The original data collected by the HPA for a single system on a single day is called a *full daily cube*. Full daily cubes are used to build all the other cubes.

Over time, an immense amount of data can accumulate, but things can be done to keep the volume under control. First, you can move the data from the system being monitored to a collection server (a manager system) where the data from a number of systems is gathered. The HPA and the collection manager automatically discard obsolete data.

Second, you can summarize the data by consolidating it into period cubes. Third, you can select a portion of the data for the full day as a *subset cube* that contains only the most important data.

All these controls can be set in a *policy*. Then you can apply the policy to individual systems, or whole groups of systems, from a central point.

After some performance cubes have been collected, you can begin to analyze performance trends. The Unicenter TNG Performance Trend application reads and analyzes performance cubes. Performance Trend is implemented as an add-on running within Microsoft Excel. It graphs long-term performance in numerous ways, letting you compare and contrast performance during different periods or days or on different systems. It also lets you correlate cubes to see if there are any patterns hidden in the data.

How to Set Up Historical Performance Agents

To set up the Historical Performance agents for data collection, run the Historical Performance Configuration application and use it to define a profile. Select the computers to which you want to apply the policy and then apply the policy to them. To run the Configuration application, select Unicenter TNG Performance, TNG Performance Configuration from the Start menu. You will see a splash screen and be asked to sign on to the repository. When those steps are complete, a window like that shown in Figure 4.69 will appear.

FIGURE 4.69
The Performance Configuration Application window.

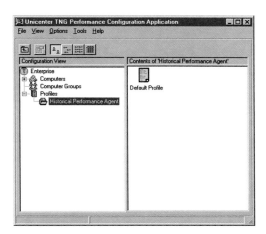

The left pane shows a tree view of various objects that can be manipulated in the configuration. At the top is the Enterprise object. Double-click it to open it. Below the Enterprise are three objects representing the three kinds of objects dealt with in the configuration, Computers, Computer Groups, and Profiles. Click the plus signs to expand the trees below the objects.

Showing Computers with HPA

Expanding Computers lists all the computer systems in the Unicenter TNG repository. Many of these will not have the HPA installed. You can discover (using Unicenter Discovery) which systems have HPA installed and filter the list of systems to include only those.

To discover the agents, choose Tools, Discover Agents, Historical Performance Agent from the menu. The Configuration application will send a message to each system to see if the agent is running there. While it is doing this, the progress window shown in Figure 4.70 will appear.

Once the agents have been discovered, you can filter the display so that only those computers appear in the tree by choosing View, Computers by Agent, Historical Performance Agent from the menu.

Ch
4

FIGURE 4.70
Performance Agent
Discovery window.

Building a Computer Group

Right-click Computer Groups. Choose Add Computer Group from the pop-up menu.

Viewing and Applying a Profile

Double-click the Profiles icon in the tree and then click the Historical Performance Agent icon. You will see icons representing the various profiles that have been defined in the right pane.

At this point, you should define a profile, either by creating a new one, as described below, or by editing an existing profile.

To apply a profile, drag it from the right pane, and drop it on a Computer, or Computer Group, icon in the tree. The configuration will then copy the profile to the agent on each system and start the agent collecting the information according to that profile.

Adding or Editing a Profile

You can either edit one of the existing profiles, like the default profile, or create a new profile to apply.

To add a new profile, right-click any of the existing profiles, and choose Add Profile from the pop-up menu. Initially, the new profile is a copy of the default profile, but you can change anything you like.

To edit an existing profile, select the profile, right-click it, and choose Properties from the pop-up menu.

Whether you are adding a new profile or editing an existing one, you will see a window like that shown in Figure 4.71. The left pane shows a tree, which you can expand or contract by clicking the plus and minus signs to the left of the icons. Each icon in the tree represents an object or page of data that makes up the profile. Clicking the icon selects that page, which appears in the right pane.

Figure 4.71 shows Agent Configuration, the top object in the tree. There, you can enter the name of the profile (if you are adding a new profile). Agent Configuration has four children. Cube Management represents how performance data is collected and processed. It is where you will configure most of the profile. Threshold groups are used to define thresholds that the HPA can monitor, much as the Performance Scope can monitor metrics against thresholds. Summarized Data and Sponsors are used in accounting and chargeback applications and will not be described in this book.

FIGURE 4.71
The HPA Configuration window.

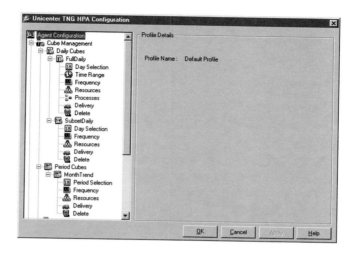

Cube Management

Selecting Cube Management on the tree displays options that allow you to set the time when the daily cube is processed (see Figure 4.72). Usually, this is immediately after the last timeband, which is when the data for the entire day is available and ready for processing. The daily cube is delivered and various Subset, Period, and Enterprise cubes are built. Here you can also set up a policy defining how long cubes are kept before deletion. Policies can be ignored for specific cube types on an exception basis.

FIGURE 4.72
Configuring the profile for Cube Management.

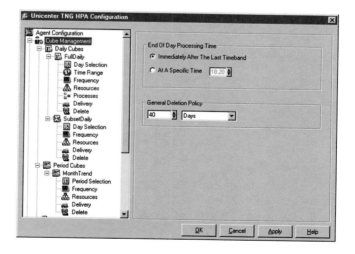

In the tree, under Cube Management, three main types of cubes appear: Daily, Period, and Enterprise. Each has multiple cubes defined with different policies, but all are based on, and derived from, the Full Daily Cube.

Ch
4

Due to the number of cubes and pages contained in a profile, this chapter will only show, in detail, how to set up the Full Daily Cube. Others are similar, and the appropriate sections of this chapter describe the differences.

Defining the Full Daily Cube

Under the Full Daily Cube object in the left pane are seven different pages. The first three control when data is collected. Resources control what data is collected. Processes control how often the data is collected.

Choosing the Days, Times, and Frequency of When to Collect   The three pages Day Selection (see Figure 4.73), Time Range (see Figure 4.74), and Frequency (see Figure 4.75) control when data is collected. The three work together, and settings on one page affect the others, so they are described together.

FIGURE 4.73
Selecting the day.

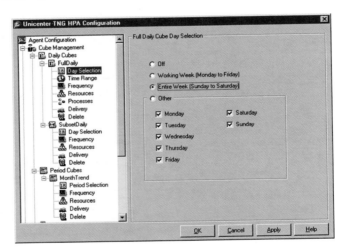

FIGURE 4.74
Selecting the time range.

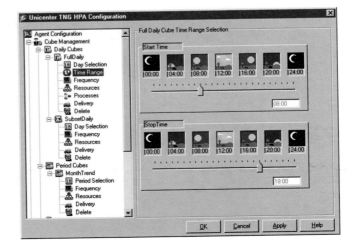

FIGURE 4.75
Selecting the frequency.

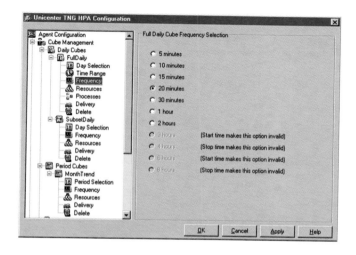

On the Day Selection page select which days of the week collection is to be done. Choose Working Week (Monday to Friday), Entire Week (Sunday to Saturday), or Other. Selecting Other lets you choose on which days data is collected. The system will only collect data on the chosen days.

On the Time Range page, choose when data collection starts and ends by clicking each slider and dragging it to the left or right to set the value. The exact time selected will appear in the field at the lower-right of the slider, as a 24-hour clock.

The Start Time and Stop Time are affected by the setting of the frequency. The values change in increments of the frequency as you move the slider. Consequently, if the frequency is ten minutes, you can change the start time to 1:00 or 1:10, but not 1:05. The Stop Time is the end of the last period for which data is collected.

On the Frequency page, choose the length of a sampling period and how often the system should collect metrics. Choose any of the values from five minutes to eight hours. The frequency is affected by the settings of the Start and Stop Times.

Choosing What Metrics to Collect   On the Resources page (see Figure 4.76), choose the policy that defines what data is collected as part of the Full Daily Cube. There are four predefined collections of metrics (Resource Sets) you can collect. They are Minimal, Standard, Extended, and Full.

The tree at the right of the page allows you to review exactly which resource types and metrics will be collected for the selected Resource Set. Because the policy you are defining can be applied to a number of different operating systems, each operating system to which this policy can be applied is listed at the first level of the tree. When you apply this policy to an HP-UX V10.00 system, only the hpx100 metrics will actually be collected.

FIGURE 4.76
Setting the policy for
selecting the data that
is collected.

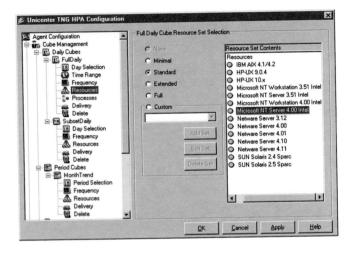

Custom Resource Sets If the predefined resource sets are not what you want to collect, you can add a custom set of your own. Check the Custom box, and you will be led through a wizard. In the first step (see Figure 4.77), just choose a name for the custom resource set and one of the existing resource sets to use as a basis (a list of metrics you can include). In the second step (see Figure 4.78), you can select which metrics will be collected. The available metrics are listed in the tree on the left. Metrics included in the custom set so far are on the right. To add a metric, select one or more metrics in the left tree and click the Add-> button. You can choose to add all the metrics for a system, all of the metrics for a resource type, or specific metrics in this way. You can also remove metrics. Once the custom set is complete, click the Finish button.

FIGURE 4.77
Custom Resources
Wizard, Step 1.

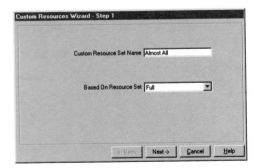

Processes

The Processes page (see Figure 4.79), lets you set thresholds against certain process metrics. Any process that exceeds (or falls below, if appropriate) these thresholds will be highlighted. By using this, you can focus on those processes using excessive resources.

FIGURE 4.78
Custom Resources Wizard, Step 2.

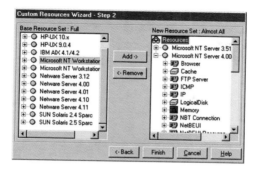

FIGURE 4.79
Set thresholds against process metrics.

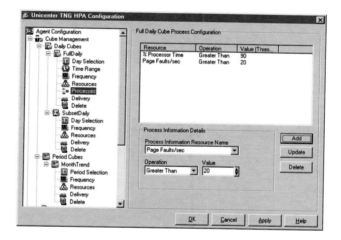

Where to Deliver the Cube   When the Full Daily Cube is collected, it can be sent to one or more other systems. Generally, a system sends its Full Daily Cubes to a collection server for processing. However, this is not always the case. Either Full Cubes can be sent, letting the collecting system subset them and build Period Cubes, or the agent system can build the various cubes and send those up to the collection machine (see Figure 4.80).

Cubes are delivered only when complete. Sending Full Daily Cubes on each update is resource intensive. Click Add Recipient Machine and enter the name. Recall that the policy can be applied to many machines, so setting the recipient here will cause all of them to send their cubes to that collection system.

How Long to Keep the Cube   The Delete page (see Figure 4.81) is where you specify when Full Daily Cubes are deleted. Enter the number of days or weeks to keep them.

Ch
4

FIGURE 4.80
The Delivery scheduler for cube delivery.

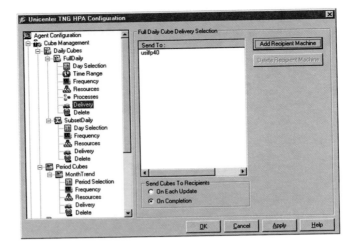

FIGURE 4.81
Setting the profile for deleting cubes.

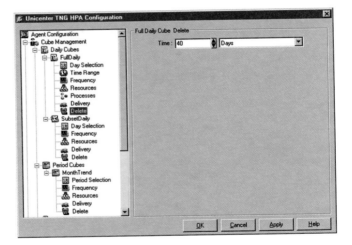

Subset Daily Cube

The HPA can build and maintain one Subset Daily Cube. To add a Subset Daily Cube if one is not in the profile, select the Daily Cubes icon in the tree, right-click it, and choose Add Subset Daily Cube from the pop-up menu. You can delete the Subset Daily Cube by double-clicking it (or the Daily Cubes) and choosing Delete Subset Daily Cube from the pop-up menu.

The Subset Daily Cube can collect data on fewer days. For example, the subset can be collected on weekdays, while the Full Daily Cube is collected every day. It uses the same Time Range as the Full Daily Cube. Its Frequency can use a longer period as long as the subset's period is a multiple of the Full Daily Period. For example, if the Full Daily Frequency were 15 minutes, the subset could be set to 30 minutes or 1 hour, but not 20 minutes. The Frequency page is also where you define when the Subset Cube is built. Unless the need is urgent, general practice is choosing Build Subset Cube At End Of Day rather than Build Subset Cube In Real Time.

The subset can also select only the most important metrics. This is done on the Resources page. By default, the Subset Cube collects the same resource set as the Full Daily Cube. The relationship between a Full Daily Cube and a Subset Cube is shown in Figure 4.82.

FIGURE 4.82

Mapping a Full Daily Cube into a Subset Daily Cube.

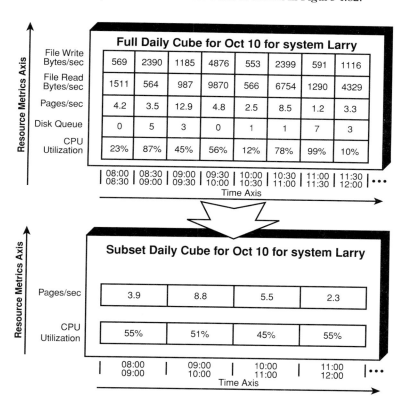

The Delivery and Delete pages are the same as those for the Full Daily Cube.

Period Cubes

Period Cubes are shown in Figure 4.83. They represent the same information as is found in a Daily Cube, but collect the data over multiple days. You can collect information for a week, a month, or a year. You can also keep a rolling cube for the last *n* days.

The Period Cube page is where you define the days covered by a Period Cube. Choose the length of the cube by choosing Week, Month, Year, or another interval.

Ch

4

FIGURE 4.83
A diagram of a Period Cube.

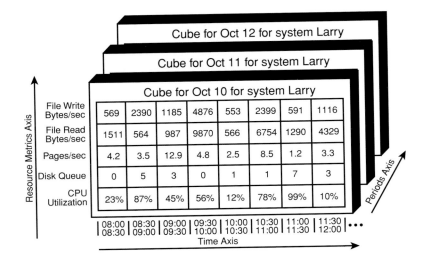

Enterprise Cube

An Enterprise Cube is much the same as a Period Cube, except it shows data for a number of systems, collected all for the same day. Enterprise Cubes, as represented in Figure 4.84, let you see how a number of systems are performing together.

FIGURE 4.84
A diagram of an Enterprise Cube.

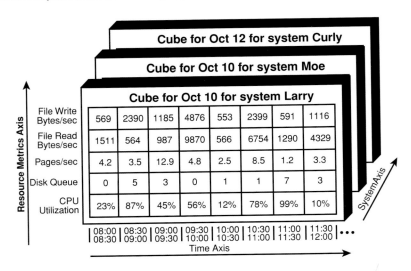

Any number of Enterprise Cubes can be defined and collected. You can build Enterprise Cubes from systems of similar types (all HP-UX systems as one example) or cubes of systems that have similar roles in your organization—for example, all servers that contain databases that are part of an SAP application. To add a new Enterprise Cube, select Enterprise Cubes from the tree, right-click it, and choose Add New Enterprise Cube from the pop-up menu. You will be asked to enter a name for the new cube.

The Enterprise Cube must be collected on a collecting system (or machine) and contains data from source systems. These are set up on the Collection page of the profile under the Enterprise Cube and shown in Figure 4.85. Add new collection systems and new systems to appear in the cube (called source machines) by clicking the Add buttons below the respective lists and entering the system names into the pop-up window.

FIGURE 4.85
Setting the profile of an Enterprise Cube collection.

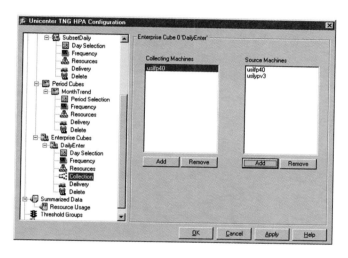

How to View Performance Trends

To view and graph a Performance Cube, choose Start, Programs, Unicenter TNG Performance, TNG Performance Trends from the Start menu.

Performance Trends is an application written to run in Microsoft Excel. The performance cube is loaded into a spreadsheet. Cube charts and graphs are displayed as Excel charts and graphs. Of course once the data has been loaded into Excel, you have all of the capabilities of a spreadsheet available to you to manipulate and analyze that data.

Selecting a Cube

To select a cube to be loaded into Performance Trends, choose Performance Trends, Generate Charts from the Excel menu. You will see the window shown in Figure 4.86. The tree on the left will display a folder for the particular collection system you are on and a folder for Enterprise Cubes. The table on the right will display each cube the system has and some information about the cube. Select the cube you want to view, and click OK. To help you find the cube you want, the tabbed pages at the bottom right allow you to filter the listed cubes in various ways. You can also display data about the selected cube by clicking the Properties button. You will see the window shown in Figure 4.87.

FIGURE 4.86
Selecting a cube for
analysis.

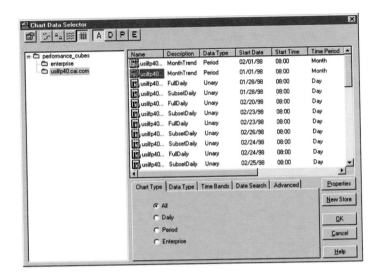

FIGURE 4.87
Properties of a cube.

Choosing Charts

Once you have selected a cube, you will be asked which charts you would like built. Check the charts you would like built in the window shown in Figure 4.88 and then click OK.

The cube will be loaded into an Excel worksheet, with sheets for the raw data, each chart, and the data used to generate each chart. Those sheets can be viewed by selecting the appropriate tab at the bottom of the window. See the Excel documentation for more information on navigating through Excel worksheets.

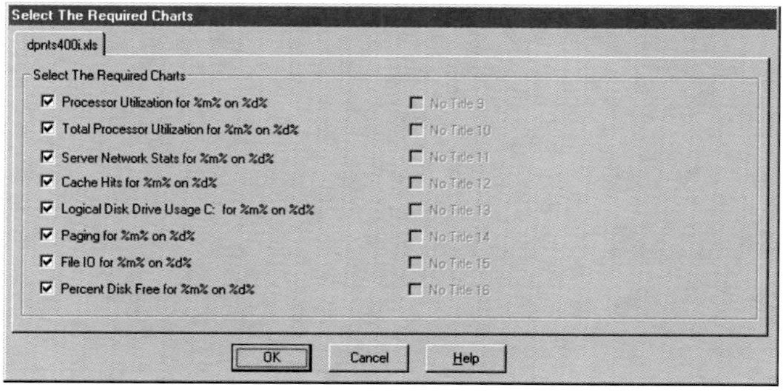

Select The Required Charts
dpnts400i.xls
Select The Required Charts
Processor Utilization for %m% on %d%
Total Processor Utilization for %m% on %d%
Server Network Stats for %m% on %d%
Cache Hits for %m% on %d%
Logical Disk Drive Usage C: for %m% on %d%
Paging for %m% on %d%
File IO for %m% on %d%
Percent Disk Free for %m% on %d%
No Title 9
No Title 10
No Title 11
No Title 12
No Title 13
No Title 14
No Title 15
No Title 16
OK
Cancel
Help

FIGURE 4.88
Selecting charts to be generated.

Final Things to Watch

There is an almost infinite list of metrics available. You should focus first on the resources that systems most often run short of, such as disk, memory, CPU, network bandwidth, and I/O. Some of these were discussed in the previous section.

Disk Space

Computers never have enough storage resources. No matter how much disk capacity is added, users and data want more. Thus, disk I/O capacity is something that we should track and analyze periodically. With Performance Trends, one can see long-term patterns of disk I/O capacity and from that decide if it is time to add more channels or perhaps rebalance the data sets.

A typical chart is displayed in Figure 4.89.

File Edit View Insert Format Tools Window Performance Trend Help
File IO for capn.cai.com on 10/22/97
25000
20000
15000
10000
5000
0
0:00
1:15
2:30
3:45
5:00
6:15
7:30
8:45
10:00
11:15
12:30
13:45
15:00
16:15
17:30
18:45
20:00
21:15
22:30
System->File Write Bytes/sec
System->File Read Bytes/sec
System->File Read Bytes/sec System->File Write Bytes/sec
File IO for capn.cai.com_1
File IO for capn.cai.com_1_data
Paging Rate_1
Paging Rate_1_data

FIGURE 4.89
Daily chart of I/O rates.

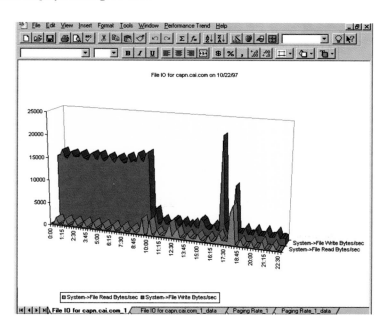

Application Workload

Applications use resources, and the capacity of the system to provide those resources can be measured. The other side of that equation is that the demands on the system depend on the workload on the system. The total load on a system is the product of the number of "transactions" the system performs and the average work done per transaction. So one of the more important metrics is the number of "application transactions" a server performs. Exactly what makes up an application transaction depends on the specific application, exactly what it does, and exactly what resources it needs.

For example, consider an NT system used primarily as a Web server. Here an application transaction delivers a Web page to a user over the network. On such a system, you should measure the average and peak number of HTML pages delivered. Each Web page delivered uses network I/O (bandwidth), CPU time, and disk I/O, so they should be measured as well. You can then get an estimate of how much workload each Web page costs by dividing the workload metric (network traffic rates) by the workload transaction rate. In this case, perhaps for an hour the number of Web pages read averaged X and the percent of Processor Usage was Y. Then an average Web page read costs Y/X or Z seconds per page. ●

Desktop Management

The advent of the desktop computer has changed the face of management forever. Instead of having a relatively small number of computers to keep track of and manage, today an organization normally has hundreds of computers and, in some cases, literally hundreds of thousands of systems. This can make the challenge of desktop management absolutely staggering.

Desktop management is an imprecise term that applies to a number of different functional areas in the overall management domain. It will be helpful for clarity in reading this chapter to establish some common terminology. First, the domain of desktop management is comprised of the end-user computers. These may be machines running Windows, Windows NT, or UNIX. However, the desktop environment also includes Macintosh computers, as well as the stripped down Network PC, and a variety of lesser known operating environments. The definition of a desktop system is not determined so much by the physical size or computing power of a machine, but rather by its intended use. A desktop system is one that is used primarily as a workstation for an individual user.

This chapter primarily concerns itself with addressing asset management and software distribution challenges. To be sure, there are many aspects of desktop management worth considering, but these are the primary focus areas for systems administrators today. The second section of the chapter covers software delivery. An automated software delivery process ensures correct and timely installation of upgrades, enhancing the dependability of distributed computing services. As much as automated software delivery provides better and more economical service to users, its prerequisite is desktop asset management.

The top management priority for the desktop environment is asset management. There is a strong need to know what assets are in place (both hardware and software) and to exercise control over those assets. There is an industry standards body (the Desktop Management Task Force) that is focused on the issues of desktop management. As they have worked through these issues, the Desktop Management Task Force (DMTF) has concluded that asset management is the most pressing issue in the desktop domain. While many people think of asset management in terms of property tags and annual physical inventories undertaken by the Accounting department, there is much more to this issue. In the desktop environment, asset management entails knowing details about

- The physical location of each computer and any attached equipment (monitors, keyboards, and so on)
- The hardware components installed in each computer, down to the board level
- The software installed on each computer, including the version of each software product

Indeed, desktop administrators worldwide are asking similar questions. Many of these questions are related to avoiding the need to constantly be "putting out fires." For example, some of the questions are

- What hardware do we have?
- Which desktop systems have what software installed?
- Do we really need all the licenses we are paying for?
- Who has unauthorized games on the hard disk?

- How can we stop users from changing their desktop configuration?
- Can we get a warning before users' disk drives get full?
- Can we be alerted if somebody steals memory out of a system?
- Can we get a warning if somebody has a virus?
- Can we detect if somebody has not logged in for a long time?
- Is there an easier way to update software and clean up local disks than walking around with a bunch of floppies?
- What would it cost to make all PCs at least Pentium 133 with 32MB RAM?
- How many workstations are running Windows 95?

Of course, management involves much more than just knowing answers. Management also entails having the ability to exercise control over things being managed. Like management in any of the other domains, desktop management involves the formulation of corporate policies and the subsequent enforcement of those policies. The top priority for desktop management is the enforcement of policies related to the software that is loaded on the desktop machines. This translates into a desire to control what software is loaded on desktop systems (enforce common configurations, for example), prevent the installation of unauthorized software, ensure compliance with software licenses, and prevent users from modifying the configurations of their desktop systems.

It is important to be able to enforce these policies from a variety of perspectives:

- Support—Improving support for desktop users, while reducing the associated costs
- Legal—Avoiding software license agreement violations
- Security—Avoiding the introduction of viruses and foiling attempts to circumvent security measures

Any one of these reasons would be sufficient to justify the enforcement of corporate desktop asset management policies. However, given the force of all three, the argument for enforcement of these policies becomes overwhelming.

The Unicenter TNG Approach

The Asset Management Option (AMO) forms the core of the desktop management solution in Unicenter TNG (see Figure 5.1).

AMO has five basic functions:

- Hardware Inventory—This is an overview of what hardware makes up each workstation and server in or outside the network (see Figure 5.2). The inventory lists the components comprising each server or workstation. A hardware scanner identifies components and their operational characteristics such as CPU, disk size, free disk space, memory, and BIOS date and version. Proprietary scanner modules can detect additional equipment that Unicenter TNG did not automatically detect, or an administrator can enter it into the inventory database manually.

Ch

5

FIGURE 5.1
A sample AMO domain map.

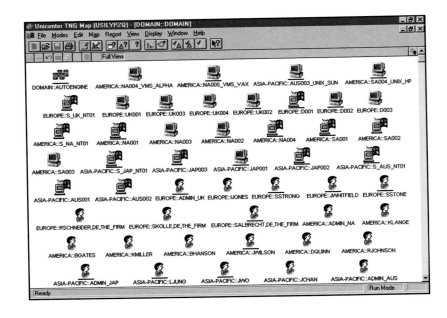

FIGURE 5.2
The AMO Domain Inventory window.

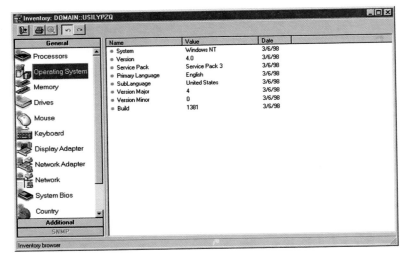

■ Software Inventory—This provides an overview of applications installed on local disks. It can also scan home directories on the network. Software is classified as known applications, main applications, or unknown applications. Administrators determine the basis of this classification. The unknown applications group, by default, contains all .exe, .bat, .com, and .dll files that are not registered as known or main applications. This allows administrators to perform a text search for application filenames. Default AMO recognizes 3500 applications out of the box and can easily recognize new applications in the network environment.

- Configuration Control—This function monitors, collects, and changes "configuration files." Typical PC configuration files are CONFIG.SYS, AUTOEXEC.BAT, WIN.INI, and SYSTEM.INI. In AMO, however, you can define any text file as a configuration file. To track changes and protect the user, the database for each workstation can store up to nine versions of the same file. Likewise, you can lock configuration files from the AMO Console. If a user unwittingly attempts to modify a locked configuration file, an AMO agent, which will restore the original file immediately and reboot the workstation, will detect the attempt.

- Software Metering—The AMO metering agent can meter any application regardless of whether it is executed from a server or local disk. AMO metering not only allows auditing of license use, but can also stop users from running unauthorized software and prevent a company from using more than the allowed number of licenses. AMO can meter suite usage so that simultaneous use of Microsoft Excel, Microsoft Word, and Microsoft PowerPoint counts (correctly) as a single suite license. Finally, you can configure metering to deny the use of SETUP.EXE and INSTALL.EXE, preventing most users from installing software on their own.

- Other Desktop Management Functions—Software maintenance is necessary for updating or otherwise adjusting installed software. This usually means adding a few files and maybe changing some settings. AMO has many features to perform these tasks locally or remotely, in real-time or as a batch function, one at a time or en masse (see Figure 5.3). Integrated job wizards and a script generator make it easy to keep software up to date. In terms of desktop security issues, both Unicenter TNG's Network Security Option (NSO) and InocuLAN have roles to play. InocuLAN is addressed in Chapter 8, "Security." The Network Security Option is covered in Chapter 9, "Web Management."

FIGURE 5.3
The AMO functions.

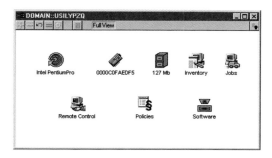

Ch

5

Getting Started

Installing the Asset Management Option is extremely simple and straightforward. Before starting the process, you need to identify which systems and directories will receive the software. There are server and desktop components to AMO. You need to identify each of these machines before beginning the installation process. There is an "express" option for the installation of AMO. This is generally the best choice for initial setup of the system. You can do any customization, utilizing the more advanced features, later.

Hardware Inventory

Hardware inventory is an essential requirement for any enterprise management solution. As a network grows beyond about 30 PCs, network managers begin losing track of the location of components and configuration of the PCs. A hardware inventory system helps them regain control without inhibiting growth and change.

AMO deploys agent software installed in a central directory on a server. All the agents and modules are available in specific versions for each operating system.

When the agent runs, it activates a number of scanners that scan for hardware, software, and configuration files.

In AMO there are different ways of scanning hardware according to operating system:

- In DOS, Windows, OS/2, and Windows NT 3.51, the AMO agent scans for data itself.
- In Windows 95 and Windows NT 4.0, the AMO scans the Registry for hardware information.

Note that there are also special scanning modules for niche environments like native OS/2, Macintosh, Banyan VINES, and DECnet.

Although AMO uses different methods for scanning, it rationalizes the data. This means that regardless of the source, AMO displays information in a consistent and coherent format.

Hardware Inventory Organization

AMO divides the hardware inventory into five sets of information, as described in the following sections.

General Inventory   The general inventory is a concentrated subset of the full spectrum of frequently requested information. In general inventory you find the most frequently requested information. This includes things like CPU type, operating system details, memory, local drives, network drives, mouse, keyboard, display adapter, network adapter with associated information, network overview, BIOS date and BIOS ID string, I/O ports, and country information. The system keeps this information consistent between operating environments.

Additional Inventory   Additional inventory contains more granular information such as the following:

- Serial numbers for hard drives
- Screen resolution
- Template information, if the workstation template is enabled
- Devices with problems (according to the operating system)
- NT services including status information

DMI Inventory   DMI Inventory contains the results of a scan if the workstation is DMI enabled.

Generic Operating System Inventory The Generic Operating System Inventory presents operating system resources and other operating system–dependent information, such as known problems (see Figure 5.4).

FIGURE 5.4
AMO UNIX inventory.

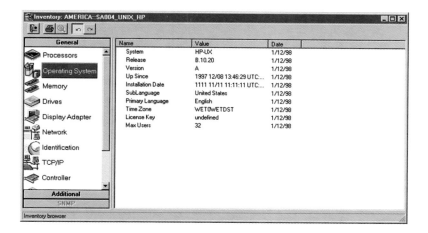

Network Inventory AMO treats network inventory as an extension of hardware inventory, since the primary components are network cards. In network inventory (see Figure 5.5), you find network adapters, loaded protocols (including extended information), TCP/IP information (including DHCP, WINS, DHCP server), and NetBIOS (protocol settings, MAC address) data.

FIGURE 5.5
AMO network inventory.

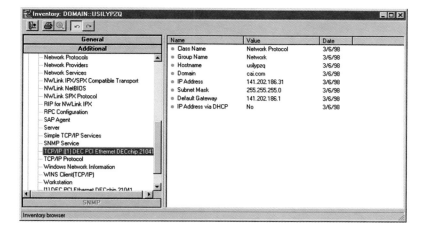

Ch
5

Software Inventory

Managing the software assets located on desktop systems can be an overwhelming task. With the proliferation of desktop systems, and with users downloading shareware and demonstration copies of application software from the Internet and loading games or other software on their desktop systems, keeping an accurate and up-to-date software inventory seems like an impossible task. However, the Asset Management Option simplifies the difficult task of keeping track of software inventories. The Asset Management Option automatically detects and inventories applications and system software on both desktop and server systems. The Software Inventory facility of the Asset Management Option scans the clients for information about the software on each desktop. Once you create the software inventory, you can view it from the console (see Figure 5.6). You can examine the inventory relative to individual workstations, individual users, and groups.

FIGURE 5.6

AMO Software Inventory.

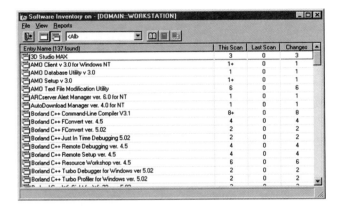

It is important for managers to keep track of where applications are installed for two main reasons:

- To ensure that the company's application license usage is within the number of purchased licenses
- To ensure enforcement of company policy concerning unauthorized applications (such as games)

The basis for software inventory is a complete file list delivered by the agent and stored in the database by the engine. Additionally, the engine scans the file lists and compares each file list with a list of defined applications stored in the database.

In AMO, the predefined list of applications contains about 3500 titles. Normally AMO is set up so that the engines only scan for a subset of these applications. There are several reasons for configuring AMO in this way. Most organizations find that they do not care about more than a few hundred applications. Moreover, because you can easily prevent execution of any application you choose, it may not make business sense to track every application on a large network.

Configuring Software Inventory

Before you use the Software Inventory facility, you should configure it to ensure that the settings are tailored for your environment. Configuration is a simple process. On a series of screens, you select options that affect how the Software Inventory scans run. You can configure the Software Inventory for a unit (workstations or users) or a group of units.

 TIP When a configuration is done for a group, it will set the configurations for all of the workstations or users that are defined in that group. Doing the software configurations in this way will result in a quicker setup. Still, it is important that you do not define multiple conflicting policies.

You can view Software Inventory on several levels:

- All files listed in directory order (File Manager)
- All files defined as main files listed separately
- All files defined as known applications listed separately
- All other executables listed separately
- Query any classification of files

You can classify any application as a member of any number of user-defined software classes such as office applications, databases, games, sniffers, and so on.

Configuration Control

Configuration control is comprised of three tasks: collecting, locking, and monitoring changes in configuration files. Why bother? Many times users independently install software on their desktops. Frequently an employee needs to install a licensed copy of a software product. Often a manager decides to make her employees more productive by purchasing a package for the server her people use, despite the fact that the company has not yet approved it. So what? To begin with, unauthorized software might conflict with other products running on the desktop. Additionally, new applications often make changes to the system configuration (CONFIG.SYS, AUTOEXEC.BAT, and so on). Those configuration changes can cause problems or conflicts that cost time and money to resolve.

If that were the only exposure, perhaps configuration control would not be such a pressing issue. The reality is, however, that inevitably some employees try to install "bootleg" copies of the latest game a friend gave them, or install an illicit copy of an application they have used elsewhere. If an employee installs such illegal programs on a company desktop, the corporation is quite likely violating copyright laws and software license agreements, and ignorance is no excuse in the eyes of the law.

Collecting and Monitoring Configuration Files

It is important to be able to monitor and control workstation configurations to prevent renegade users from tampering with the setup. The system can collect and monitor configuration files on a business unit or group level, even in a heterogeneous environment. This is important, because every operating system has its own set of key files, and configuration control must be set up accordingly. You can define any ASCII file as a configuration file. The database can store up to nine different versions of the same file. After the system has reached that threshold, it discards the oldest version of a file whenever it collects a new version of that file. The Configuration Control utility can also retrieve text files (log files and so on) that custom applications and utilities may produce.

Locking Configuration Files

Asset Management contains a Secure System Files function that enables the system administrator to ensure that the configuration file is controlled from the console and cannot be changed locally. The system compares the configuration file (usually CONFIG.SYS) on the local client to the configuration file set up on the asset management console. That comparison is done every time the workstation connects to the network. If the Secure System Files function detects any difference between the two files, it copies the configuration file on the console to the workstation and overwrites the existing one. You can lock any configuration file. The "lock job" can also reboot the workstation automatically after a restore. You can use this feature to enforce configurations across groups as well (see Figure 5.7).

FIGURE 5.7
The Select Revision window.

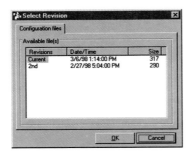

Configuration Control

Under DOS and 16-bit Windows (version 3.x), control of AUTOEXEC.BAT, CONFIG.SYS, WIN.INI, and SYSTEM.INI is the most important. The system can also monitor and control these files under 32-bit Windows (Windows 95 or Windows NT). On these systems, however, it is more important that you control the Registry.

The AMO script language can read, edit, and change any Registry setting. If Registry backup were requested, the method would be to export the critical part of the Registry to an ASCII file and then define that file for configuration control. If special monitoring needs to exist, you can use the scripting language for monitoring any file, including the Windows 95 or Windows NT Registry.

Software Metering

A typical enterprise has a multitude of desktops scattered throughout the organization. Each desktop probably has several, if not many, applications running on it. Without automation, the administrative nightmare of keeping track of the number of licenses running at any point in time is horrendous. The Asset Management Option can automatically monitor desktops for license compliance.

Overview

The Software Metering module in AMO gives desktop administrators the following capabilities:

- Monitor how many employees use specific applications.
- Restrict access by additional employees to applications when the organization has reached its license limits.
- Prevent use of certain classes of applications (no games allowed, for example).
- Audit what software is in use, regardless of the original scan configuration.
- Forbid software installations by preventing execution of INSTALL.EXE or SETUP.EXE. This prevents users from running the installation programs for any application, whether that program is located on a CD-ROM, floppy disk, or the system's hard drive. Note, however, that this solution cannot prevent loading software that does not require "install" or "setup" for installation. For example, some applications require only copying them from a disk to the hard drive of a target machine. A more absolute method is to use Directory Synchronization, which is discussed next.

Directory Synchronization

The Directory Synchronization function is another AMO tool that can control the unauthorized installation of applications on a remote workstation. This option locks the contents of the workstation's directory to the directory of the console. In other words, Directory Synchronization keeps the contents of a directory on a workstation identical to the contents of that directory on the console. If a file is on the target directory (the user's system) but not on the source directory (the system where the console is located) and the user attempts to delete it, the system will delete the file. If a file or directory is on the source directory but not in the target directory, the system will copy that file or directory to the target directory. Strictly speaking, this method does not prevent users from installing their own software. However, if the user logs on to the network, directory synchronization can automatically delete any unauthorized software. You can also use this utility to automate backup of critical files from a notebook to a network server for later archive to tape.

Ch
5

Software Metering Configuration

By definition, the system conducts software metering on a group (or unit). Therefore, the first step in Software Metering setup is defining the members of a group. In addition, you must identify the applications the system will meter for each group.

A group (or unit) is a collection of individuals and/or workstations. AMO has considerable flexibility regarding the definition of groups. First, a workstation or user can be a member of several groups. Moreover, individual users and workstations that are both geographically and organizationally dispersed can form the membership of a group. For example, members from several different servers can make up a group.

User and workstation groups provide important assistance to management in specific situations. Software inventories provide useful information about what software is on the network, but most administrators need to know its location as well. Software metering based on groups might deliver information that is more useful because it can report exactly who is playing a game at 9:00 a.m. on Tuesday morning.

How Software Metering Works

The basis of software metering is an agent that runs on each client system. The agent logs all necessary activities and communicates with a central server managing the queuing system. The Software Metering module, unlike other AMO agents, stays resident and reports software usage at all times. The module locally logs information about what the workstation is using, and when, and then transfers it to the console the next time the system runs the AMO agent.

Active and Passive Metering

AMO performs metering in two ways:

- Passive metering logs all information locally and uses no network connection. Passive metering provides the necessary information and, except at startup, generates no network traffic. Passive metering prevents access to specified applications entirely by setting the allowed limit to zero, but it does not provide a way to limit access to a specified number of users. Figure 5.8 shows a graph of metered software usage.

FIGURE 5.8

The OffLine Utilization window.

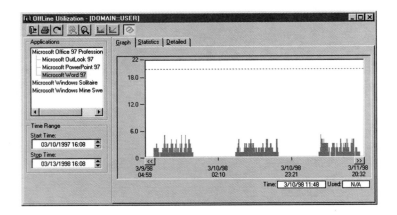

■ Active metering requires a network connection to a shared drive. There are three ways to do Active software metering:

- Monitor only—If the system surpasses the allowed limit, the module does nothing.
- Monitor with message—When the system surpasses the limit, it sends a customizable message to users, but still allows them to use the application.
- Monitor with enforcement—When the system surpasses the limit, the system prevents users from working with the application. (See "Queuing," later in this chapter.)

Software Audit

Software audit registers everything that is started on the workstation. You do not need to specify which applications you want to monitor. It audits executables, DLLs, and Windows NT services.

Positive and Negative Lists

Instead of defining the applications users cannot run, which is the way normal software metering works, you can do the exact opposite. A system administrator can define which applications users can run, and they can execute no other application on the desktop.

Suite Metering

AMO can monitor application suites. Suite metering simplifies license control. Without this feature, you must set up metering for each individual application. However, if you configure metering to monitor the group of files that makes up a suite, such as Microsoft Office (Word, Excel, PowerPoint, and Access), the system gives a more accurate picture of application usage. When a user is accessing one suite application, the system counts one suite license. When a user launches three suite applications at the same time, the system still reports only one license. You can view the metering information on the suite level or broken down to show each member application.

Queuing

When using the Active Software Metering mode, the system gives users the option to enter a queue when it reaches the approved license limit. The queue works on the FIFO principle. This means that the system gives the next available license to the first user in the queue.

AMO sends a notification to the first queued user when a license for his or her application becomes available. The system then launches the application if the user responds affirmatively to the notification.

If users do not respond within a customizable interval, the system releases the license and gives it to the next in line. Special users, deemed "VIPs," can bypass licensing restrictions. If a VIP user attempts to use an application that has reached the license limit, they will always be successful.

Ch
5

Offline Metering

You may want to meter two types of offline devices:

- Mobile computers or those that intermittently connect to the network
- Isolated computers that never connect to the network

To perform software metering on computers that sometimes connect to the network, use the normal Passive Metering mode. You will not be able to get live data from these computers, but you will receive the data when they connect to the network.

To perform software metering on computers that never connect to the network, set the computer up as an offline client. You will need to collect the metering information (along with other inventoried information) by using a portable media such as a floppy disk, Zip drive, and so on.

Displaying Data

Because AMO distinguishes between users and computers, you can configure the metering module accordingly. This way you can have separate metering configurations for different personnel groups, for example, one metering configuration for people in the Finance department who are allowed to use two licenses of PowerPoint, and another metering configuration for the Marketing department, which has 12 licenses for PowerPoint. Whichever way you configure the metering module, the system will log both user and desktop as using the application. This way you are not limited when you perform queries.

Queries   One of the main reasons for doing software metering is that system administrators want to use the data collected to make better decisions. Administrators need to decide when to buy new software or upgrades, and they need to plan its delivery. There is no need to buy or distribute upgrades to users who never use the products. Because a standard database (SQL) stores the software metering data, you can perform very complex queries. You can also combine different data, such as hardware inventory, user information, or software inventory, with the software metering queries (see Figure 5.9). Some possible examples include:

- How many of my desktops with less than 16MB of RAM have been using PowerPoint, and for how long?
- Who has tried to use WordPerfect in the last month and been denied?

Viewing Historical Data

Asset Management provides several useful tools to allow the system administrator to view software metering information. There is a Graph view, a Statistics view, and a List view. Each of these views displays the software metering information in different formats.

As suggested by the name, Graph view provides a graphical representation of the metered information. This view shows the actual usage of the software compared to the authorized number of licenses, over time. Graph view makes it relatively easy for the administrator to assess whether a license violation for this software is a common occurrence necessitating some kind of action or if it is rare. When the administrator notices messages that the license limit has been exceeded for a particular piece of software, the View Historical Information Graph view graphically illustrates the actual usage compared to the authorized licenses threshold, over a period of time. Using this tool, the administrator can see if license violations for this software are a commonplace occurrence or just an anomaly. The administrator may decide to purchase additional licenses if the trend of violations seems to be commonplace. If the violation is an anomaly, the administrator may just continue to monitor this particular software until usage becomes a problem.

FIGURE 5.9
Using Query Designer to create complex database queries.

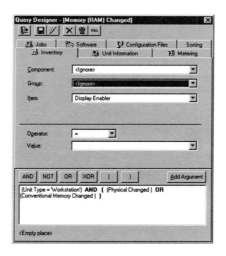

Statistics View   The Statistics view presents detailed information on the units (workstations or users) that were using the application during the selected time interval. The application being metered is identified, and the time interval appears at the top of the folder. The time interval can be changed in the Filter/Setup folder of the Software Metering On window.

Ch
5

The Usage section of the folder displays the following information:

- Maximum number of concurrent users of this application
- Minimum number of concurrent users of this application
- Average number of concurrent users of this application

The Action Distribution section of the folder displays the following information:

- Execution Was Prevented
- Started Normal Stopped Normal
- Started with Warning Stopped Normal
- Started Normal Stopped Strange
- Started with Warning Stopped Strange

The Miscellaneous section of the folder contains the following information:

- Number of Times Application Was Started
- Total Number of Different Users Running Application

This view can be very useful when gathering information about the use of the application. For example, if the average number of concurrent users for this application is above the number of authorized licenses, the administrator should consider purchasing more licenses. The Total Number of Different Users Running Application can show that this application is either widely used or used by a small number of users in the enterprise. The other statistics can be helpful in many other ways.

List View   The List View folder displays a report on the application usage during the time interval that was used for the graphical display. It contains a list of units that used the application, along with the start and stop times. The report is divided into three columns:

- Unit—The name of the unit (workstation or user)
- Date/Time—A time stamp
- Additional—Action that was taken at the unit, if the license policy was exceeded

There are also two sections of the report. The information about when the application was started is listed first. The information about when the application was stopped is listed at the end of the report.

The following is an example of how this report can be used. A user may be abusing the availability of games on the workstation. The administrator could use this report to see when the user started the game application and when the user stopped the game application. If the user started and stopped the game application several times during the day, this would all be recorded in List view. Another way that this report could be used is to see whether users are logging on to a particular business application for long or short periods of time. If users are logging on to a graphics application for long periods of time, and if many users throughout the enterprise use this software, perhaps more licenses are needed. The system administrator may use the information from each of these views to determine licensing requirements and current usage.

Remote Management

Desktops may be deployed throughout the enterprise, some within the same building as the administrators, some across the country, and some across the world. In this environment, it is critical to have remote management capabilities to economize on the time and money it could cost to manage these remote desktops. If personnel must be flown to the remote sites to handle problems, the costs for supporting desktops will rise astronomically. However, if they could handle the problems remotely, it would save money and time.

Remotely Possible, a Unicenter TNG option, allows the console to "take over" remote workstations. The console can have direct online control of the keyboard and mouse of multiple remote workstations. The console displays the screen of each remote workstation. It can also reboot the remote workstation. This capability allows administrators to work on the remote workstation without having to be at the remote site. This is the basic function, but remote management also includes the following:

- *Education and Training*. Organizations can set up virtual classrooms. Students can view an instructor's PC, no matter where they are, with Remotely Possible. Control can also be passed from the teacher to any student to promote hands-on learning.
- *Telecommuting Remote Access*. Mobile users can connect to an office PC to execute desktop applications, check email, and transfer files. Remotely Possible delivers fast remote control, making telecommuters and mobile users feel they are sitting in front of the remote PC.
- *Help Desk Support*. Help Desk support personnel can understand and resolve issues faster by directly manipulating remote users' machines. Remotely Possible allows support staff to do such things as remotely use applications, set up printers, or adjust network settings. Sessions can be recorded for training other support personnel.
- *Call Center Quality Control*. Call center managers can view and record the activities of staff to monitor service quality, audit usage, and identify problems and trends.
- *Server Administration*. Single-point administration of multiple servers eliminates unnecessary travel for problem resolution. Administrators can manage remote NT servers by creating and editing user profiles, modifying Registry information, troubleshooting and rebooting servers, and viewing performance monitors from any location.
- *Multitasking Capability*. Control one or more systems simultaneously to help a user, monitor another, chat with a third, and transfer files among them.

How It Works

Connectivity: Users connect to any host PC via network access, dial-up, or the Internet. Whether the PC can be accessed on a LAN, WAN, or remote node network, such as RAS or PPP, it can be controlled by Remotely Possible. This works seamlessly through bridges, routers, and switches, and supports multiple network protocols. Its multitasking capabilities can be used to view one or more Windows PCs, exchange files, and have interactive chat sessions—all simultaneously. Furthermore, multiple viewers can connect to a single host.

Security: Multilevel security allows administrators to restrict access to remote systems. Data encryption is used for secure data transmission and access and can restrict bidirectional file transfer between a viewer and host.

Record and Replay Sessions: Remotely Possible enables users to record and playback sessions. Designed to emulate a VCR, it is easy to use and provides optimum video replication of host graphics and color. User sessions can be recorded, archived, and then replayed in real-time or in fast forward. This capability is ideal for help desks, call centers, and support centers in monitoring service quality and facilitating group training and distance learning.

Interactive Training Tool: A "baton passing" feature allows for transfer of control between a student's host machine and the instructor's viewer. Training personnel can hold interactive training sessions and have trainees demonstrate to the trainers the concepts they have learned.

Technically Speaking: How AMO Works

The AMO architecture is somewhat different from what many would expect from a PC management tool. Usually PC management tools install an agent that resides in memory on each workstation and connects directly to a database.

With AMO, the agent software is not installed on the workstations, but in a central directory on a server. Upon execution of the agent, it terminates.

The advantage is that the AMO client is non-invasive and therefore does not conflict with other programs or consume memory or CPU cycles while users are working. The agent can be scheduled to run periodically or as a service on Windows NT.

Agents

The AMO agents are directories with several executables—each being an agent main program or an agent module. An agent can scan, meter, or perform administrative chores. Both agents and modules are available in versions for their specific operating system.

When the agent runs, it activates a number of scanners, searching for hardware, software, and configuration files. A scan usually takes up to 30 seconds, depending on how many modules are enabled, disk size, and the number of files on disk(s) scanned. If a large job is scheduled, it can take a longer time before the agent terminates.

Detected information and status messages are stored in proprietary files, usually in the directories C:\CLIENTWS for workstation data and C:\CLIENTUS for user data. When the scan is over, a delta scanner compares the information from last scan with the present scan and the differences are stored in the directory called SECTOR on a server.

Sectors

Within AMO the sector functions as a communication area where components (agents, consoles, and engines) exchange data and messages with other components. A sector is implemented as a directory with a structure of subdirectories. It is located on any file share. It is recommended to create at least one sector per 500 workstations and to let each sector reside on its respective file server. Except during logon peaks, it is not particularly demanding for the file server to have a sector installed.

There are four kinds of sectors: online preconnected, online autoconnected, offline network, and offline portable media sector.

- The console and the engine update an online preconnected sector. They both read and write information directly into the sector. Console and engine both have a drive mapped to the online preconnected sector. This limits the number of sectors to the number of available drive letters.

- The console and the engine update an online autoconnected sector. They both read and write information directly into the sector. Console and engine do not have a permanent drive mapped to the online autoconnected sector, but they do connect a predefined drive letter when needed. This limits the number of sectors to the number of available drive letters.

- An engine updates an offline sector. The engine always maps a drive to connect as needed. Using offline sectors makes it possible to utilize any number of sectors.

- An offline portable media sector resides on a portable media for devices such as a floppy disk or a Zip drive. This sector is collected and updated by a special engine process started from within the console.

Engine(s)

Engines are the most active part of AMO. At least one engine should always be running in each AMO installation. An engine can service several sectors. It is recommended to set up one engine for each 1000–1500 workstations. This can vary from 500–2000 workstations per engine, depending on setup, network, and equipment.

The engine takes care of the following:

- Distribution of unit jobs to sector(s).
- Collecting data from the sector(s) and storing it in the domain database.
- Internal communication between AMO components via database or sector(s).
- Communication between AMO and Unicenter TNG.
- Performing queries, updating dynamic groups, and executing alarms.
- The engines can be set up to perform a number of automation tasks for the whole network, such as Directory Synchronization, virus scanning of servers, SQL scripts, deleting temp files on servers, and so on.

An engine can run as a service under Windows NT. If an engine has to collect from more than 500 workstations, it is recommended to have it run on a dedicated machine. There is heavy traffic between engines and the database, especially if the database is an Access database.

Ch
5

Domain

In AMO, the term *domain* covers two items:

- The installation itself, meaning all the units to be found in the console/database. The AMO domain is defined independently of network domains unless intentionally coordinated. This means an AMO domain can contain several network domains, or the reverse can be true.

- A directory called Domain, containing the most important system settings and, if Access is chosen as the database, the domain database itself. Consoles and engines must have a drive mapped to the Domain directory. In AMO version 2.0, the NCDB directory holds the database.

The internal AMO license control takes place in the Domain directory. In addition, the Domain directory has a settings file for each AMO administrator.

Enterprise Repository

The Enterprise Repository is a repository and console that can simultaneously work with units and data from a number of AMO domains. AMO alone might not be adequate for working with more than 14,000 units, depending on database and server setup.

The Enterprise Repository adds genuine enterprise functionality to AMO. This allows a world-wide company to install one or more AMO domains in each country and concentrate the information in an Enterprise Repository (see Figure 5.10), allowing company management to see an enterprise-wide overview and plan accordingly.

FIGURE 5.10
List of AMO Network domains around the world.

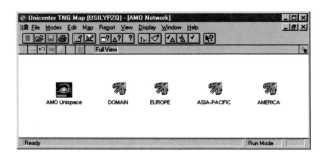

The Enterprise Repository resides on any of the available database types. It is recommended that only ODBC databases be used, to keep network traffic down in an enterprise installation. Special engines replicate data to and from the enterprise database.

Software Delivery

Local area networks (LANs) and wide area networks (WANs) represent two of the most powerful means available for fulfilling your corporate data processing needs. With a LAN/WAN structure, the information systems (IS) administrator can ensure that hundreds—or even thousands—of users' needs for data and software can be met.

With this great ability, however, comes a corresponding responsibility to manage the vast amounts of software and data so that all users have access to the latest and most productive tools. As the number of network users grows, the traditional methods of individually distributing, upgrading, and monitoring software on individual users' PCs becomes an increasingly difficult task.

Problems with Manual Distribution

The task of manually installing and updating new software packages can pose problems for system administrators, especially when the software has to be distributed along a heterogeneous network. The more people and locations that are involved, the greater the chances are that errors will be made and the harder it is to guarantee deadlines are met.

The problems with manual distribution can be divided into several categories. These issues, which grow in proportion to the number of computers involved, include

- Organization—In larger organizations, the use of remote sites requires that you maintain a balancing act between standardized upgrade procedures and the effective use of key personnel. Software installations and upgrades performed by on-site personnel may or may not adhere to company standards. On the other hand, sending a technician from the central site to respond to all remote-site software needs could mean your key technicians will be spending a lot of time on the road.

- Personnel—Even if all of your systems are located close together, each one will still need to have the changes applied. This could mean that your key technical staff members are too busy to perform the other improvements to your system that your business depends on to remain competitive.

- Cost—Valuable processing and worker time can be lost while software is manually distributed. The cost incurred increases when errors are made.

- Errors—Ensuring that all changes have been correctly applied to each system is another concern. It is easy for manually applied changes to be inconsistent. This could have disastrous consequences when the new system goes live.

- Inconvenience—When all systems have been changed, there is still the problem of switching the whole network over to the new version at the same time.

- Timing—Finally, if there is a problem with a new software version, you need to be able to revert back to the previous version as quickly as possible.

Software Delivery—The Automated Solution

Software Delivery is the automated solution that enables you to do the following:

- Work with existing Windows NT or UNIX servers to access and administer programs installed on remote Windows NT, Windows 95, Windows 3.x, NetWare, OS/2, and UNIX workstations.

- Track all software installed at a particular location and identify when, where, how, and by whom the programs were installed.

- Distribute new software packages and upgrades to existing packages to all or to a selected group of computers from a central location or through local administrative workstations.

- Maintain a centralized record of all software installed in the Software Delivery network regardless of whether or not it was installed through Software Delivery.

- Alert the administrator when a computer's available disk space drops below a certain percentage.

- Monitor logged events that track the installation and activation of item procedures associated with programs registered in the Software Delivery library.

■ Identify installed software that has not been distributed or registered through Software Delivery.

■ Create customized installation diskettes, or a directory for automatic registration, for site-written applications that can utilize the CA-Installer program.

Software Delivery Architecture

The Software Delivery structure consists of the following (see Figure 5.11):

■ An optional Central Site, from which the Enterprise Administrator can send programs, documents, and orders to Local Sites. The Central Site database, which includes the Enterprise library and Local Site distribution and installation data registers, is maintained on the Enterprise Server at the Central Site.

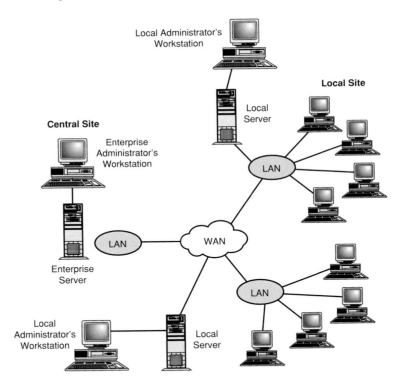

FIGURE 5.11
Software Delivery architecture.

■ One or more Local Sites, each of which may be managed by its own Local Administrator. A Local Site consists of a local server and all computers networked to that server on which the Software Delivery Agent has been installed. The agent is the program that maintains communication between a local server and its networked computers.

- A local server is the server from which software distribution orders are sent to the target computers. A local server maintains registers with information on all machines in the Local Software Delivery network and the software installed on them.

- Optional Fanout Servers, which function as "traffic concentrators," to reduce network load on the Enterprise Server for distributions to the Local Sites.

- Optional Staging Servers, each of which is a connection between a local server and agent computers. The agent computers communicate with a Staging Server, and the Staging Server communicates with the local server on behalf of its agents. This can reduce traffic between the local server and the target computers.

- Several target computers, on which software packages will be installed and monitored. For a computer to receive software distributions and communicate with the local server, the Software Delivery Agent must be installed.

Fanout Servers

Fanout Servers provide an optional level of traffic control between the Central and Local Sites (see Figure 5.12). For example, the DALLAS, HOUSTON, and IRVING Local Sites may be registered with the TEXAS Fanout Server. When a distribution is targeted for any or all of those sites, the distribution is first sent to the TEXAS Fanout Server. From there it is sent to the individual Local Sites. By operating as a network traffic concentrator, the Fanout Server reduces the network load that would ordinarily be on the Enterprise Server.

FIGURE 5.12
Fanout Servers relay distributions from the Enterprise to selected Local Sites.

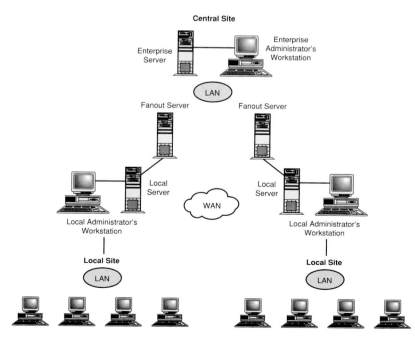

Staging Servers

Staging Servers also provide an optional level of traffic control. However, unlike Fanout Servers that reduce traffic between the Central Site and Local Sites, Staging Servers can reduce traffic between a local server and its target computers (see Figure 5.13). That is, if a job is targeted for an agent downstream of a Staging Server, the job is first sent to the Staging Server. From there it is distributed to the agent computers. This option is particularly useful if the local server is managing a large number of agents. This is because the workload can be distributed to a number of Staging Servers, with each managing some of the agents. It can also be useful if there is a slow link between the local server and its agents, since large amounts of data are only sent once from the local server to a Staging Server.

FIGURE 5.13

Staging Servers receive data from the local server and distribute it to the agent computers.

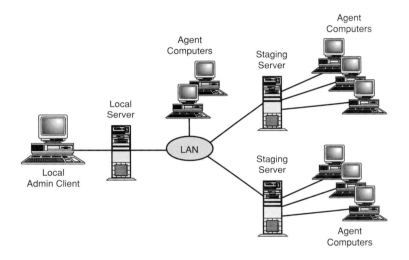

You can simultaneously have agents connected to the local server directly, or via an intervening Staging Server. There can be many Staging Servers for a local server. However, there can be only one Staging Server (registered at the local server) between an agent and the local server. At agent installation time, you determine the type of server to which to connect the agent when configuring Server net address and Library access.

Software Delivery Attributes   Software Delivery attributes are computer attributes that are displayed for Windows, NetWare, OS/2, and UNIX agents (see Figure 5.14). They can only be accessed from a Local Admin Client machine. A sample Computer Attributes dialog box is shown in the following figure.

Information listed in the computer register includes the following:

- Current operating system type and version
- Available memory and disk space
- System model

- Floppy disk drive, capacity, and format
- Fixed disk drive, capacity, and file system
- Keyboard and serial ports
- Processor type and disk drive capacity (both available and used)

FIGURE 5.14
The Computer Attributes
dialog box.

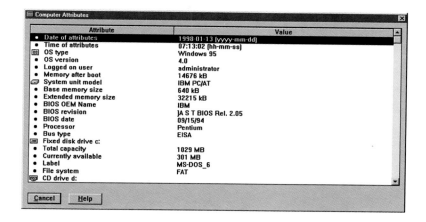

Software Delivery GUI   The Software Delivery graphical user interface (GUI) is available from any Windows computer on which the Admin Client component has been installed.

On a Windows NT Admin Client, the folder selections for Windows NT servers are shown in Figure 5.15 for the Enterprise Server and Figure 5.16 for the local server.

FIGURE 5.15
The Software Delivery
folder on an Enterprise
Server.

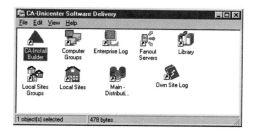

FIGURE 5.16
The Software Delivery
folder on a local server.

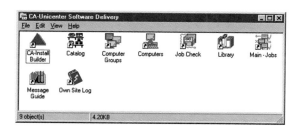

Ch

5

Each folder contains a main access icon (Main Jobs for the local server; Main Distribution Jobs for the Enterprise Server) from which all Software Delivery administrative tasks can be performed. It also contains several specialized icons that perform specific tasks, such as defining a computer group or reviewing the Enterprise Log.

These icon selections and the subsequent differences in dialog boxes reflect the different responsibilities and authority levels allotted to the Enterprise and Local Administrators.

Distributing Software   The distribution of software through Software Delivery is a three-step process. First, the software must be defined to Software Delivery through the *registration* process. This can be done in either the Enterprise or the Local library, depending on the intended target computers and on the distribution structure and policies employed. Second, the software must be sent from the library to the target computers through the creation of *orders*. If the orders are *distributed* from the Enterprise Server, they are bundled into a *container*. If they are sent from the local server, they are issued as individual jobs. Third, the orders are *monitored* to ensure that no errors occur.

Registration

Library item *registration* actually requires two actions. First, the item is identified (by name, version, and so on) to Software Delivery. Then the requisite files are copied into the appropriate library.

The amount and type of information that must be supplied when the item is identified depends on the type of library item being registered.

Registering Documents   Documents do not have embedded item procedures; therefore, you only need to provide a name and version when registering documents.

Registering Programs   Registering programs with embedded item procedures requires further steps to identify additional parameters, such as startup procedures.

When registering programs, you can take on the files that make up the package from a variety of sources, including diskette, CD-ROM, directory, or tape.

Once the library item and its associated item procedures have been registered in the library, they can be distributed throughout the Software Delivery network.

Automatic Registration   If you have a large site with multiple Enterprise Servers, an existing program registration in one Enterprise library can be copied to its original source medium (directory, diskettes, tapes, writeable CD-ROMs) and used to perform an automatic registration in subsequent Enterprise libraries. All details provided during the initial registration of the program (name, version, parameters, location, and so on) will be copied along with the actual program files and will not have to be re-entered.

Automatic Registration can also be used to register the software programs supplied with Software Delivery (the Admin Client, agents). Completed registration information files are already included with each component.

Distribution

Once a software package has been registered in either the Enterprise or Local library, you can distribute it to other networked computers by creating and sending an *order*.

Orders   Software Delivery uses several types of orders, each designed to perform a specific task:

- Registration Orders—Distribute registered items and item procedures from the Enterprise library to a Local library.
- Installation and Uninstallation Orders—Install or uninstall a program on a computer or computer group.
- Fetch Item Orders—Retrieve or "fetch" a specific file or files from the Local Sites to a designated place on the Enterprise Server.
- Deregistration Orders—Deregister and delete items from the Local library.
- Activation Orders—Start a program. For example, an activation order can be used to trigger the start of an archive program on a remote machine.
- Configuration Orders—Initiate changes in the configuration files on a remote machine. When orders are sent from the Enterprise to a Local Site(s), they are bundled into *containers*. When an order is sent from the local server to individual computers at that site, each order is distributed as a single *job*.

When an order is received and activated on a targeted computer, it proceeds as if the item procedure was initiated directly on that computer (see Figure 5.17).

FIGURE 5.17
Flow of orders from the Enterprise Server to the local server to target computers.

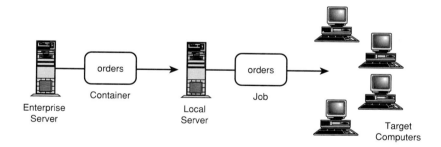

Distributing Orders from the Enterprise   Orders are distributed from the Enterprise Server to the local sites through the use of a *container*. A container is basically a "to-do list," or list of orders, sent from the Central Site to Local Sites. Containers can include any of the orders listed previously (see Figure 5.18).

The container may include one or more orders selected from the Order menu of the Container dialog box. A sample container with one order is shown. Although the example contains a single order, there is no limit to the number of orders that can be included in a single container.

FIGURE 5.18
The Container Contents
window.

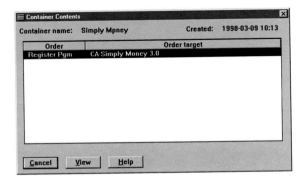

Containers can be distributed to a Local Site(s), Local Site group(s), or computer group(s); they cannot be distributed to individual computers.

When orders from the Enterprise are received at the Local Site(s), the appropriate jobs (installation, uninstallation, activation, and so on) are automatically created and sent to the target computers at that site.

Orders are executed in the same sequence that they are listed in the container. Therefore, if you place a software installation order and its corresponding registration order in the same container, you must place the registration order in the container first, because a library item must be registered in a Local library before it can be installed on a computer or computer group at a Local Site.

Distributing Orders from the Local Server   When orders are received from the Enterprise by a local server, they are processed automatically without intervention by the Local Administrator, if one exists.

A Local Administrator can also originate orders. When an order originates from a local server

- The item must be registered in the Local library before it can be distributed to the attached computers.
- Both computer groups and individual computers can be targeted.

Fetch, registration, and deregistration orders cannot originate from a local server. There are three options for distributing orders from a local server:

- Select an item from the library, and then select the target computer(s) or computer group.
- Select a target computer, and then select the library items to be sent.
- Enable an item procedure for the Software Catalog, so a target computer user can select and install a program or document.

Although the example contains a single order, there is no limit to the number of orders that can be included in a single container.

Containers can be distributed to a Local Site(s), Local Site Group(s), or computer group(s); they cannot be distributed to individual computers.

When orders from the Enterprise are received at the Local Site(s), the appropriate jobs (installation, uninstallation, activation, and so on) are automatically created and sent to the target computers at that site.

Orders are executed in the same sequence that they are listed in the container. Therefore, if you place a software installation order and its corresponding registration order in the same container, you must place the registration order in the container first, because a library item must be registered in a Local library before it can be installed on a computer or computer group at a Local Site.

Distributing from the Local Library   The local server Library dialog box (see Figure 5.19) lists all the items in the library, along with their version number, type, time, and date of registration.

FIGURE 5.19
The local Library dialog box.

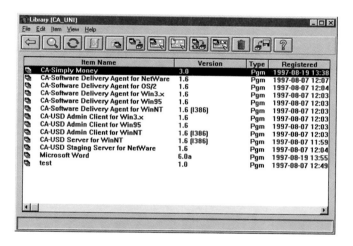

To begin distribution from the Local library, you would first select the appropriate software package and item procedure. Second, you would select the computers that will be targeted to receive this package. This approach is helpful when you know which computers to target, but you still need to review the list of available software packages.

Distributing from the Computer List   The Computers dialog box (see Figure 5.20) displays the list of all computers attached to the local server that have the Software Delivery Agent installed.

This dialog box lists the name, owner, operating system, and (communication) state of each computer. Since Windows, NetWare, OS/2, and UNIX computers are in constant communication with their local server, the value listed in the State column for Windows NT and UNIX computers indicates whether that computer is on or off.

Ch

5

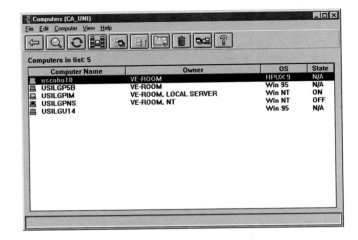

Communication between Windows 3.x and Windows 95 computers and the local server is intermittent; therefore, the State column for those types of computers will always display N/A (for Not Applicable). The attributes information listed for these computers is only as current as the last communication.

To distribute an order from the Computers dialog box, select the target computer from the list of candidates and proceed to the library to determine which software package and item procedure will be sent. This approach is helpful when you need to review the list of suitable targets before distributing software.

Enabling an Item Procedure for the Software Catalog   The Software Catalog is a feature of Software Delivery that enables agent users to request software from their Local Site library by means of a graphical user interface. Agent users can only request items that have been enabled for Catalog selection. For an item to be enabled, the local administrator must check Include in Catalog when registering the item procedure. A sample Register Item Procedure dialog box can be seen in Figure 5.21.

An agent user accesses the dialog boxes needed to install, activate, configure, or uninstall available library programs and documents by opening the Catalog icon, provided on the target machine. A sample Software Delivery Catalog dialog box is shown in Figure 5.22.

FIGURE 5.22

The Software Delivery Catalog window.

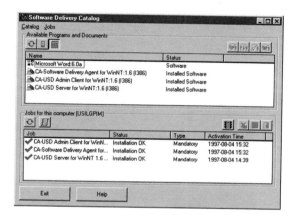

For more information regarding the Software Catalog, refer to the *Agent User Guide*.

Activating Orders on Target Computers   When the Software Delivery Agent on the target computer detects an order, the startup procedure identified by the item procedure initiates. If the administrator had selected the Prompt User option on the installation order, the user is prompted to choose whether to start the installation immediately, at a later time, or not at all. A sample screen is shown in Figure 5.23.

FIGURE 5.23

The Computers – Installation window.

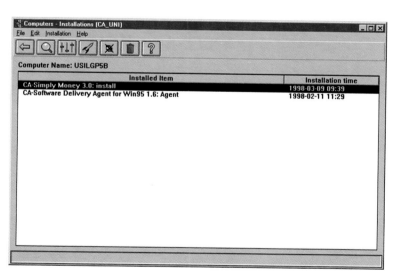

Ch

5

If the order has been received and accepted, the degree of user interaction required is determined by the item procedure. You can create customized item procedures for installing or activating software. These procedures are written as batch, command, or executable files and must be registered along with the software program itself.

At the conclusion of an item procedure activation, users will be prompted to indicate if the item procedure completed successfully. If it did not complete successfully, the user can specify the reason for the interruption. Then the installation register will list this installation as an error. The user's response helps maintain the local server's installation register.

Monitoring Status   After you send a container (from the Enterprise server) or a job (from the local server), it is often useful to monitor the status of the distribution. You can view whether the distribution is waiting to start, is partially completed, has been halted, or has completed successfully from the appropriate Admin Client workstation.

Viewing Installed Computers and Items

Software Delivery maintains a record of all current product installations. You can view this record in terms of the number of products installed on a particular computer or in terms of the number of computers on which a particular program has been installed.

Viewing Installations by Computer   Starting from the Computer Register, you can see what software packages are already installed on a particular computer (see Figure 5.24).

FIGURE 5.24
The Computers - Installations dialog box.

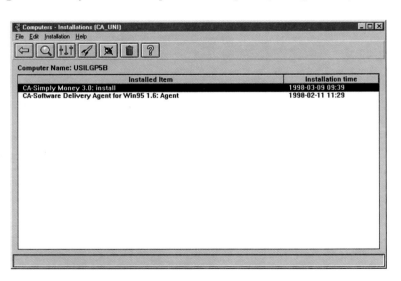

This screen displays the name of the computer, all installed items, and the date and time these items were installed. This option is very useful if you are a local administrator who wants to check whether a particular item was installed on a specific machine.

Viewing Installations by Item   Starting from the Local Server Library, you can see on which computers a designated library item has already been installed (see Figure 5.25).

FIGURE 5.25

The Library - Installations window.

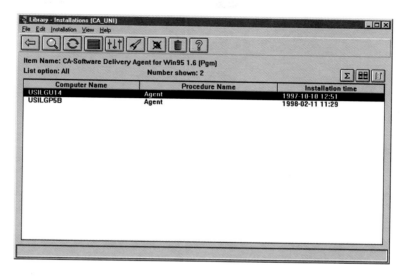

This screen displays the name of the item and all computers on which it was installed. Also, this screen displays the name of the item procedure and the date and time the item was installed. This option is very useful if you are a local administrator who wants to check the number of machines—and their names—on which a particular item was installed.

Unicenter TNG Integration

Software Delivery is a Unicenter TNG option. As such it works in conjunction with Unicenter TNG on the Enterprise and local servers. Software Delivery directly interacts with the following Unicenter functions:

- Event Management to track and manage events distributed from the Software Delivery event logs
- Security Management to control access to Software Delivery assets, such as the Libraries and Logs

In addition to these two functions, once a Software Delivery message has been sent to the Unicenter Event Management console, the Machine-Generated Problem Tracking (MGPT) function of Problem Management can be used to automate how that message is received and what type of response is issued.

Event Management   All Software Delivery Log entries are automatically sent to the Unicenter console and are indicated by the prefix CASWD. Events, commands, and messages monitored by Event Management can be associated with the following:

Ch

5

- *Message Records* that identify the message to be trapped.

- *Message Actions* that indicate what will happen to those messages. Message actions range from simply highlighting a message in the console to triggering a command to sending that message up to Problem Management for further processing.

The processing flow of an event from Software Delivery to Unicenter is illustrated in Figure 5.26.

FIGURE 5.26
The processing flow of an event.

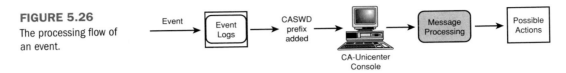

Depending on your configuration of Event Management, messages can be handled on individual nodes or redirected to a central or other Unicenter console. You can collect related messages network-wide for display on a single console or send them to multiple locations as needed.

Because the Unicenter TNG Event console processes all standard Windows NT and UNIX message traffic, messages from non-Unicenter TNG controlled nodes can also be redirected to the console. Additionally, Unicenter TNG Console events can be freely forwarded between Windows NT and UNIX consoles.

Using Machine-Generated Problem Tracking with Event Management   Messages forwarded to MGPT are given a status code, priority code, responsibility area, and escalation table assignment. The escalation table determines how Problem Management will respond if the message is not responded to in a designated period of time. For example, if the primary technician (named in the responsibility area) does not respond in one hour, the message may become the responsibility of his manager.

Using Event Management in conjunction with Problem Management's Machine Generated Problem Tracking component, you can improve overall operating efficiency and reduce the potential for error by automating the process of interpreting and responding to events.

Security Management   Software Delivery resources on the Enterprise or local servers can all be secured through the Security Management functions of Unicenter TNG.   ●

Help Desk and Problem Management

Murphy's Law definitely applies to the environments managed by IT organizations! The IT infrastructure is composed of thousands of individual elements from the major domains of networks, systems, applications, and databases. In a large organization, the number of potential points of failure may easily exceed 100,000! The networks may be brilliantly engineered. The applications may have been exhaustively tested. The systems may have been configured with extreme care. The databases may have been designed flawlessly. No matter how nearly perfect the IT infrastructure may be, it is inevitable that problems will occur. Even if nothing in the infrastructure ever failed, there is the human element (the end user), which can be relied upon as a source of problems. When a problem does occur, it must be resolved. In addition to resolving the problem, information about the problem must be captured for both real-time tracking and historical analysis.

Real-Time Tracking

There is normally an interval between the occurrence of a problem and its resolution. That interval may be only a few seconds, as when a user has forgotten his or her password. Alternatively, the interval from occurrence to the resolution of a problem may be several days. Whenever work on a problem is interrupted, there is the potential that responsibility for the problem will fall through the cracks. The interruption in the problem resolution process may come when a problem is transferred from one person (or group) to another person (at the end of a shift, when a specialist is asked to look into a problem, for example). An interruption could also occur when a person is asked to look at another problem that is more critical; it could be caused by the need to talk with a friend about plans for the weekend. Regardless of the reason, there is the potential for the problem to be forgotten and its resolution delayed unnecessarily whenever work on a problem is interrupted. This is one of the reasons IT organizations have found it so valuable to have a system in place to track problems from inception to resolution.

In its real-time use, a problem-tracking system needs to be able to capture essential information about the problem (when it occurred, nature of the problem, person working to resolve it). In addition, the system should allow managers and operators (system users) to query the system in order to review outstanding problems for anomalies. Also, the system should be able to automatically send warnings when certain types of problems have been unresolved for too long.

Historical Analysis

Tracking problems to ensure that they are not lost is an important capability required by every IT organization. However, this is not the only value that can be derived from some type of process for capturing data about problems and the processes followed to resolve them. Historical analysis of data encompassing numerous problems can reveal trends or even root causes that may not be apparent in the rush to fix a problem. Unicenter TNG does not only provide the capability to monitor the problems while they are outstanding; it also allows the data to be archived for subsequent analysis.

The problem-tracking system should archive all of the available data about each problem. This data should be available for report generation. It should also be possible to extract the data for input into a statistical analysis tool—Unicenter TNG is able to meet these requirements. The Advanced Help Desk option is also available for more advanced users. This provides even greater capabilities for problem management.

The Unicenter TNG Approach

There are two subsystems in Unicenter TNG that facilitate the process of problem identification and tracking. The first, Unicenter TNG Problem Management, is a part of Unicenter TNG's Enterprise Management component. The second component is the Unicenter TNG Advanced Help Desk (AHD), which significantly expands Unicenter TNG Problem Management's capabilities and adds a Call Management module—a front-line Help Desk support tool. This chapter covers the basics of Unicenter TNG Problem Management as well as the Unicenter TNG Advanced Help Desk.

Problem Management

Unicenter TNG Problem Management defines and tracks items and events. *Items* and *events* are the components and activities typically found in a data center or processing environment—items such as PCs, printers, and file servers, and events such as program and network activity. The Problem Management system creates problem records, tracks the progress of problems toward resolution, and eventually closes and archives the problem records. A problem record can either be opened by Help Desk personnel or created by the system through Machine-Generated Problem Tracking (MGPT), in which selected events from the Event Management subsystem automatically open a problem record. Asset Management Option (AMO) 2.0 or later can use policies to open a trouble ticket automatically based on changes in PC inventory information.

Getting Started with Problem Management

As noted in Chapter 2, "The Unicenter TNG Framework," one of Unicenter TNG's main components is Enterprise Management; Problem Management is one of the components of Enterprise Management. Therefore, Problem Management is installed automatically, as part of the initial Unicenter TNG installation. Consequently, Problem Management is ready to use once Unicenter has been installed.

However, it is possible to gain additional functionality and value from Problem Management through some additional setup and configuration steps. Those steps can be grouped into three phases:

1. *Establish the equipment configuration.* Identify those system components that are candidates for problem tracking. AMO inventory discovery can generate the information required for this step so that Advanced Help Desk can access it.

2. *Establish the Problem Management policies.* Identify how problems are to be classified and assigned (problem categories, status codes, and responsibility areas, for example).

3. *Establish Problem Escalation policies.* Define how priorities and responsibilities are to be changed based upon how long a problem has been unresolved.

While none of these phases is required, this information enables you to manage your Help Desk more effectively. It gives detailed information on system components, identifies problem status, assigns responsibilities, and automatically escalates problems before they become critical.

Define the Equipment Configuration   The first optional phase in maximizing Problem Management's functionality is to populate the database. The database should be populated with information about those components (managed objects) that are candidates for problem tracking. Some of the components you may want to monitor include the following:

Displays/monitors	Routers
Keyboards	Printers
Telecommunications equipment	Office automation equipment
PC equipment	Workstations
PC software	

The equipment configuration database can be populated with a variety of information that may be useful to have readily available when a problem occurs. For example, it is useful to record information for a router, such as the location of the device, warranty or maintenance contracts, maintenance history, user and departmental information, and relationships to other components (the network in which it is located, for example). Recording this information in the database speeds the problem resolution process; Help Desk personnel will not need to spend time searching for this data.

N O T E   All of the instructions in this chapter begin from the Problem Management folder.

Populating the database with equipment configurations is quite simple. Go to the Component - Detail window; it can be reached by selecting Component, New from the Component list container. You can then enter the information about a component. See Figure 6.1.

You can also use information from the Unicenter TNG Asset Management option to populate AHD's Network Resource Detail fields with information such as IP address, host name, or MAC address of workstations managed by Unicenter TNG.

It is also possible to enter supplementary information about a component. There are three optional categories (marked with tabs) available: user information, warranty information, and maintenance information. To enter information related to one of these categories, select a tab and then enter the information. Once finished, save the component definition (by clicking OK) and return to the Problem Management folder.

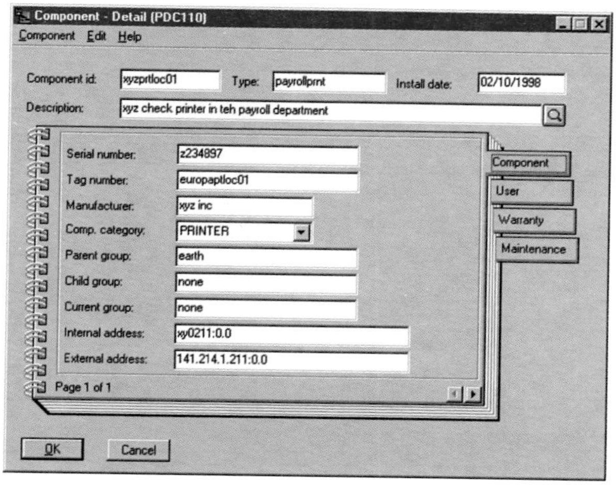

FIGURE 6.1

The Component - Detail window.

Specify Problem Management Policies   Problem Management policies tell the system how to handle certain types of problems. Specifically, these policies define the seriousness of the problem (Severity level), the person or group to whom the problem should be assigned, and so on for each type of problem. These definitions, while useful in themselves, are even more important because they make possible further automation of the Problem Management process. These codes are used to establish automatic escalation policies. It is this feature that makes Problem Management so powerful—the capability to ensure that problems do not get lost and that the appropriate people are notified about the progress of a problem.

In order to populate the database with management policy information, open the Category Code - Detail window (see Figure 6.2) and select Table, New (see Figure 6.3) from the list container. Enter the requested information, save the information, and exit.

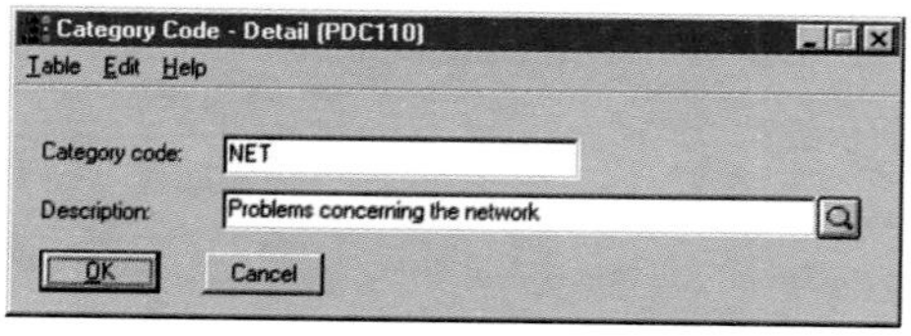

FIGURE 6.2

The Category Code - Detail window.

Ch
6

Establish Problem Escalation Policies   While it is true that a problem is a problem until it is fixed, the significance of that problem can change over time. The change may be due to the length of time that the problem has been outstanding. Alternatively, the significance of the problem may change as the result of new information.

FIGURE 6.3

The Table menu.

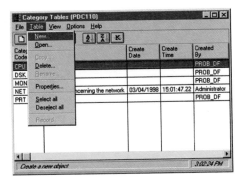

This is easily illustrated with a non-technical example. Consider a problem with your car. You notice a very annoying squealing whenever you accelerate. From this sound, you make a preliminary diagnosis that the problem is due to the fan belt slipping—a very minor problem. You make an appointment to take your car to the dealer to have the fan belt tightened. They are busy, so you leave the car and their courtesy shuttle takes you to your office. You plan to pick up the car at lunchtime. Shortly before lunch, you call to see if your car is ready. You are told that it is not ready, but are assured that it will be ready by the end of the day. At this point, the problem is still minor. Late in the day, the service manager calls to tell you that they have started working on your car and that the problem is more serious than you thought. The fan belt is slipping because the bracket that holds the alternator has cracked and sagged—the bracket will need to be replaced. Fortunately, the bracket is inexpensive and can be replaced in with just a few minutes of work. Unfortunately, this is an unusual problem and the dealer does not stock the part. This means that your car will not be ready today, but you are assured that they should have no problem getting it ready tomorrow. In addition, you are told that in the interim, your car should not be driven because there is the possibility of either creating an electrical short and destroying the car's electrical system or causing a fire. At this point, the problem has become slightly more serious because you were scheduled to drive for your son's school field trip. The following day you are told that there has been a rash of this type of problem and that the part will have to be ordered from the factory in Japan (approximately 2 weeks wait). Now this problem has become a crisis because you were planning to use your car when you went on vacation this Friday.

In this example, the severity of the problem changed over time due to the inability to rapidly resolve the issue when it was first reported. With these changes in severity, it became necessary that various people be notified. You might even have considered contacting the car's manufacturer to complain. Similar things occur in the IT environment. A cable may be cut at 10:00 p.m., isolating a router. This, in turn, may cause congestion on the remaining portions of the network. Because of the congestion, the overall response time for all transactions is degraded. This may initially be considered a serious, but not critical, problem. However, if the cable cut has not been repaired by 8:00 a.m., when the volume of transactions being processed increases significantly, the problem will have a greater impact and becomes more serious. Moreover, if this happens to occur at a critical time (pre-Christmas for a mail order merchandiser, for example), the problem may actually be considered critical. Most businesses want to escalate awareness of problems as the seriousness increases. Table 6.1 illustrates an extremely simple example of an escalation policy.

Table 6.1 Simplified Escalation Policy Example

	Low	Moderate	High	Critical
0–15 minutes	None	None	Group Manager	Group and Department Managers, CIO
16–60 minutes	None	Group Manager	Department Manager	CEO
1–8 hours	Group Manager	Department Manager	CIO	
>8 hours	Department Manager	CEO		

A more robust policy might include specific actions such as contacts with the impacted user organizations, raising of the severity level assigned to the problem, and the like.

Unicenter TNG allows administrators to define policies that will ensure the automatic notification escalation. The use of this feature provides the assurance that no one will "forget" to escalate a problem or to take the associated actions. In order to take advantage of this capability, the administrator needs to define the various policies that will take place and the criteria that will trigger those actions.

Once the escalation policies have been established, Unicenter TNG can automatically associate the appropriate policy with each problem when a problem record is opened. The escalation policy is associated with a problem based upon the criteria previously defined. The priority of a problem can be escalated or responsibility for it transferred according to those criteria. These actions are intended to ensure that the problem receives attention and action at the appropriate points in the organization. All escalation actions (changing of priority or responsibility) resulting from escalation policies are triggered by the amount of time that has elapsed since the problem originally occurred. This, in turn, results in a new policy being associated with the problem and the appropriate notifications being made.

To define the escalation policies to Unicenter TNG, open Open Priority Escalation and select Table, New from the Priority Escalation Tables list container. Enter the data in the Priority Escalation table (see Figure 6.4) relevant to the policy being defined.

Ch

6

FIGURE 6.4

The Priority Escalation
Table - Detail window.

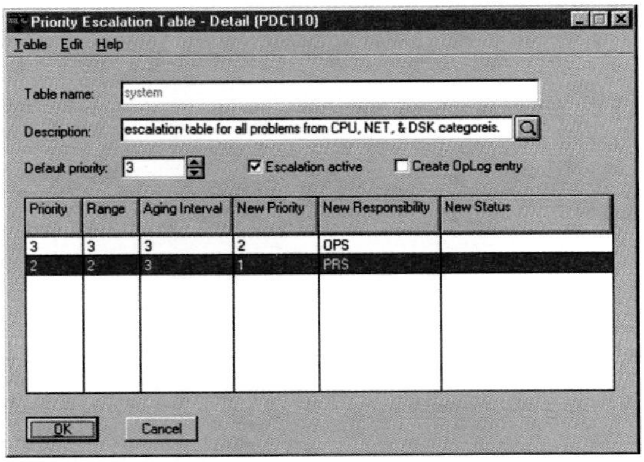

There are some important criteria that can be specified:

- Table Name—A policy name for the table
- Description—The purpose of this table
- Default Priority—The initial priority level
- Priority—The lower boundary of priority
- Range—The upper boundary of priority
- Aging Interval—Number of minutes before escalating
- New Priority—The new priority level
- New Responsibility—The new responsible individual
- New Status—The new status code
- Escalation Active (NT and UNIX only)—Is this policy active?
- Create OpLog Entry (NT and UNIX only)—Create a log entry

Once the appropriate data has been entered, save the data and then either enter another policy or exit.

Manually Managing Problems

Regardless of whether a problem is managed with an automated Help Desk tool, there are four basic tasks involved in manually managing problems: recording the occurrence of a problem (creating a trouble ticket), recording changes in the status of the problem (updating trouble tickets), modifying the problem's status, and recording the problem's resolution (closing trouble tickets). With Unicenter TNG, all of these activities can be performed manually, and certain ones can be set up to occur automatically (creation and escalation).

Creating a new trouble ticket (problem report) is quite simple. The user selects the problem icon in the Problem Management folder and then selects Problem, New.

Go to the Problem - Detail window (this can be reached by selecting the Problem icon in the Problem Management folder and then selecting Problem, New. Enter the requested information about the problem on the screen that's shown in Figure 6.5.

FIGURE 6.5

The Problem status page of the Problem - Detail notebook.

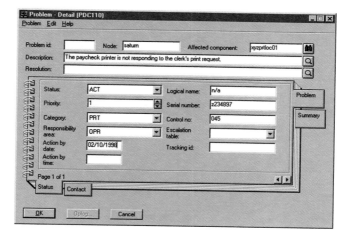

The following lists some of the data that can be entered about a problem:

- Affected component—The particular component affected
- Node (NT version only)—The Windows NT machine on which the problem occurred
- Description—Symptoms or description of the problem
- Status—Status of the problem (active, resolved, closed)
- Priority—The priority level
- Category—Problem category (printer, CPU, software?)
- Responsible area—Individual or group responsible for solving

N O T E The problem Description is the only mandatory field. The others are optional.

Once the information about the problem has been entered, save the information and exit, or enter another problem.

Update, Change Status (Escalate), and Close a Problem Record   The Help Desk personnel, as a part of solving the problem, must keep track of its actions and activities, escalate problems where additional resources may be required, and eventually close problems that have been solved. All of these activities are recorded by updating problem records. The process for manually modifying a trouble ticket is similar to the one used for opening a trouble ticket. Select a problem to update from the Problems screen and then select Problem, Open. This takes you to the Problem - Detail window, where there are four places information can be updated: the Main notebook page, the Status page, the Contact page (as shown in Figure 6.5), and the Summary page (see Figure 6.6).

Ch

6

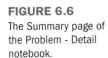

FIGURE 6.6

The Summary page of the Problem - Detail notebook.

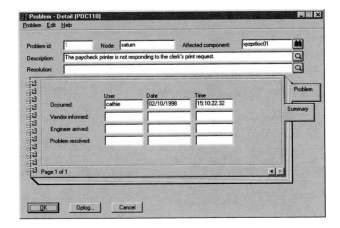

The screen(s) you need to access in order to update the record depends on which information is being updated. Figures 6.7 through 6.10 show the fields for each of these screens.

Modifying the priority assigned to a problem and closing the problem report are the Status notebook's key functions.

These four notebook pages allow the user to enter most relevant information about a problem. However, it is impossible for a system to anticipate every piece of data that might need to be captured. Unicenter TNG has provided a screen (Operations Log) where supplementary information can be entered in anticipation that a user might want to enter additional status information (beyond what is captured on the Main, Status, Contact, and Summary notebooks). This can be thought of as a "notes" page on which the user can type in any information. For example, a person working on the problem might want to enter a note with details of a conversation with the failed device's manufacturer. This Operations Log window can be accessed from any of the Problem Detail windows by clicking the OpLog button at the bottom of the screen.

FIGURE 6.7

The Operation Log - Detail window.

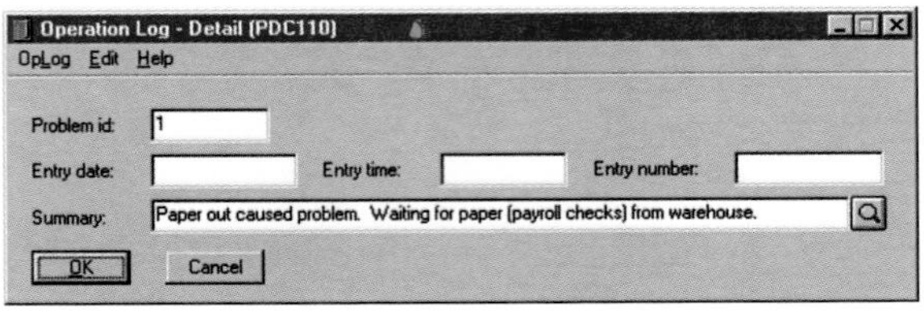

Automating Problem Management Processes

An important Help Desk system requirement is that it can automate two of the essential problem management processes. Those two processes are the creation of problem reports (trouble tickets) and the escalation of those problems in accordance with administrator-defined policies.

Automating these processes offers certain benefits. First, having the software create the problem report ensures consistency. The operations personnel monitoring Unicenter TNG for the occurrence of problems are faced with an enormous amount of data in the typical IT environment. It is possible for them to fail to notice a problem when it occurs, or to forget to document the occurrence by creating a problem report. It is indeed more important to fix the problem than to take to time to create an accurate problem report, particularly when serious problems occur. Unfortunately, memories about details may be imprecise after the problem is fixed. Automating the process guarantees that all problems (that have been defined as requiring a problem report) will be documented in a problem report and that the information will be accurate. The accuracy of problem reports is important. They are often used as part of the basis for service-level agreements. They also may be used for performance and capacity analysis, helping form part of the basis for major capital investment decisions.

Manual problem escalation has some of the same pitfalls associated with the creation of problem reports. Many people are afraid to escalate a problem. That fear may be based upon any of several possible reasons. There is the possibility that doing so may cause them to be viewed in an unfavorable light. For example, escalating the problem may cause them to be perceived as being unable to resolve the problem and therefore not suited for the position they hold. There is also the problem, irrational though it may be, of "killing the messenger." Some executives and managers become frustrated and angry over a serious problem and vent their emotions on the person informing them of the problem. Another cause of problems not being escalated is the thought (or hope) that the problem can be fixed in a few more minutes. In addition, during the heat of the moment, people may simply forget a part of an escalation policy (contacting the head of the impacted department, for example). Regardless of the reason, there may be times when problem escalation policies and procedures are not adhered to completely. The result can be delays in resolving a problem and the subsequent business impacts.

Obviously, it is desirable to automate the creation and escalation of problem reports whenever possible. As described earlier in this chapter, Unicenter TNG will automatically handle the escalation of any problem for which a policy has been defined. It also has the capability to automatically create problem reports for any problem if it is aware of the problem. The Unicenter component for automatically generating problem reports is Machine-Generated Problem Tracking (MGPT). To automatically create problem reports, the Event console (or the Windows NT Event log) is monitored for events that require the creation of a problem report, based upon the criteria specified by the system administrator. Here are some examples of problems that might be set up for automatic problem reports:

- Hardware failures
- Failures of scheduled batch processes
- Excessive CPU usage
- High paging rates
- Unusual file activity
- Security violations
- Changes to the configuration of a PC: hardware, software, or a configuration file

Setting up Unicenter TNG to automatically create problem reports involves two basic steps: defining the criteria for use in deciding to create a problem report and the action to take when those criteria have been satisfied. The criteria are defined in two places: MGPT tables and the Message Record. Tables can be set up by selecting the Table, New option in the MGPT Tables list container. This brings up the MGPT Table - Detail window (see Figure 6.8), where the administrator fills in the fields specifying the values that must appear in order to require action to be taken.

FIGURE 6.8
The MGPT Table - Detail window.

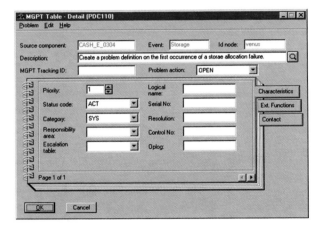

Once the appropriate data has been entered, save the data and then either build another table or exit.

Since every message will not have exactly the same format, the next step is to define for Unicenter TNG how to interpret the messages that are received and relate them to the fields in the MGPT table. This straightforward process is begun by selecting Open Messages from the Event Management folder. In that folder, select Message, New in the Message Records container; this takes the administrator to the Message Record - Detail window (see Figure 6.9). Enter the data requested. Additional information can be supplied by selecting the More notebook tab and going to that screen. There also is a Config notebook tab and a Scan notebook tab. Once all of the necessary information has been provided, save the data and then either build another Message Record definition or exit.

FIGURE 6.9
The Message Record -
Detail window.

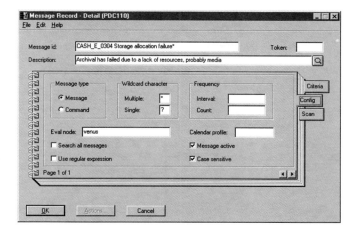

Once the criteria have been defined by building a Message Table and a Message Record, the next step is to define what Unicenter TNG should do when this condition occurs. This is done by defining the Message Action (see Figure 6.10). To begin, select the message for which an action will be defined. The message is then opened by selecting Message, Open from the Message Records container. This causes the Message Record - Detail window (see Figure 6.9) to be displayed. From there, selecting Actions and Selected, New causes the Message Record Action - Detail window (see Figure 6.10) to appear. This is the window in which the system administrator will provide the information that will define the action to be taken. Some additional, optional data can be entered by selecting the Overrides notebook tab. Once all of the necessary information has been provided, save the data and then either specify the actions for another message or exit.

FIGURE 6.10
Message Record Action
- Detail window.

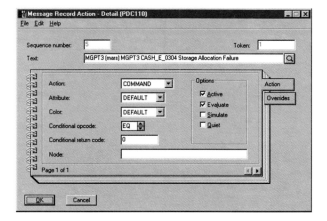

Ch
6

Advanced Help Desk

Unicenter TNG Advanced Help Desk (AHD) option is the second component of problem identification and tracking. This module adds a number of data input forms for better identification and tracking of user-initiated Help Desk requests. AHD also adds more complete incident reports in Problem Management. Finally, AHD adds trouble tickets, which allow the combining of multiple incidents into a single problem and facilitate problem tracking with additional reporting options. Advanced Help Desk can either be integrated with Unicenter TNG or run as a standalone module.

Advanced Help Desk is a high-end Help Desk management system that streamlines the definition, tracking, and resolution of caller issues and problems. It is composed of two separate but tightly integrated functions—Call Management and Problem Management. Call Management provides a central point for all caller interactions with the Help Desk and is used to collect, record, disseminate, and track caller issues. Problem Management extends the Unicenter TNG Problem Management process by providing automated incident recording, tracking, identification, and escalation of corrective actions and automatic notification of key personnel. It also includes extensive MGPT capabilities, so that significant events occurring on the network are automatically brought to the attention of Help Desk personnel and other interested parties, as well as automatically inserted into the problem queue.

Advanced Help Desk provides one of the features most commonly requested by Help Desk personnel—external notification. This is the capability to contact personnel by means outside of the system. In other words, Advanced Help Desk can contact people via email, fax, pager, or voice message. This is particularly important during those times when the Help Desk or management center is unattended.

In order to make AHD easier for individual operators to use, its interface can be customized to meet their needs and preferences. AHD's capability to filter trivial and redundant messages is another feature designed to make the Help Desk personnel more productive. In addition, AHD has APIs that allow it to extract event information from Unicenter TNG, as well as from other products such as Hewlett-Packard's OpenView and SunSoft's SunNet Manager.

AHD supports extensive reporting and analysis of historical data. This is facilitated through its capability to store data in its own proprietary format database, CA-OpenIngres, Sybase, Oracle, or Informix. This flexibility allows the system administrator to set up this system with the database preferred by his or her company.

Getting Started with Advanced Help Desk

The basic features and flow of information in Advanced Help Desk are shown in Figure 6.11. There are two sources of external input: user requests, which can come in via telephone, hard copy messages, electronic media, or walk-in, and the computer network through event notification from network management platforms, and messages from Unicenter TNG.

FIGURE 6.11

The basic features and information flow in Advanced Help Desk.

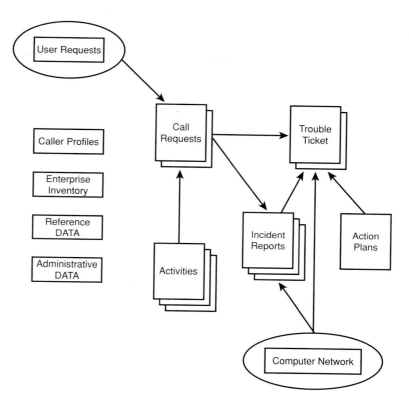

The Help Desk is the first line of support for system users. When a request arrives, the information is entered in the Help Desk system, associated with the user, and associated with any equipment that might be involved. Actions taken by Help Desk personnel are recorded in the activity log. While Help Desk personnel will often be able to solve the problem very quickly and close the incident, this is not always possible. Perhaps equipment needs to be repaired, so a work order needs to be prepared. Perhaps there are symptoms of something going wrong on the network but it's unclear exactly what the problem is, so additional personnel must become involved in the problem-solving process. A problem may take time to solve and fix for a variety of reasons, and it needs to be monitored. At this point, Help Desk personnel would transfer the incident to Problem Management.

The Problem Management side of Unicenter TNG Advanced Help Desk uses incident reports generated by Help Desk personnel or the computer network, and it creates trouble tickets, which are used to track a problem from start to finish. The incident reports focus on problem reporting, and several incident reports can be consolidated into a single trouble ticket. Trouble tickets focus on solving the problem and identifying the actions taken and people involved in the solution. These two documents are used to track the problem and to ensure that all personnel involved are properly notified of the problem status and progress made in solving the problem.

Ch
6

Action plans can be associated with trouble tickets. These can be prepared as soon as the problem and solution are identified. However, these can also be prepared well in advance so that classes of problems have action plans associated with them, and the time between problem recognition and problem solution can be shortened. For example, an action plan could specify which vendor or maintenance contractor should be contacted, what internal individuals need to be notified, the timeline of events and the expected downtime, what backup procedures are available, or what alternative services can be provided to users. In short, an action plan can specify all information necessary to facilitate the repair process, keep people notified, and provide alternative end-user services. The action plan states who is to do what, at what time, and to what equipment.

Much of the Advanced Help Desk's power comes from thoroughly documenting the organization's networking environment, setting up basic equipment information, developing codes for various activities, and developing administrative policies. Much of the information in the following table can come from the Asset Management option, reducing the amount of manual entry required. This information includes:

- *Inventory Tables.* These identify the resources, people, and locations associated with the network:
  - *Resources and resource classes.* The devices, software, and services that make up your network. A record uniquely identifies each resource and its location.
  - *Models.* Information about the types of devices.
  - *Sites.* Groupings of equipment, typically geographical.
  - *Locations.* Physical places where inventory, contacts, and network resources may reside.
  - *Organizations.* Internal departments, divisions, or workgroups.
  - *Contacts.* Any person associated with the network, including analysts, technicians, administrators, vendor representatives, customers, and network users.

- *Reference Data.* The tables and codes that control how and when to apply management policies. These are used by Call Management and Problem Management:
  - *Contact types.* Classifications of people, such as vendor, user, or analyst.
  - *Coordinate types.* Coding for geographic locations, such as city, telephone exchange, or longitude and latitude.
  - *Location types.* Customer or vendor.
  - *Manufacturer codes.* Identification of hardware and software manufacturers.
  - *Vendor types.* Vendor classification codes.
  - *Resource families.* Network resources such as hardware, software, and services.
  - *Call areas.* The generic category into which a call request can be organized, such as application or hardware.

- *Trouble codes.* Identify the type of problem, such as device failure, failed connection, or intermittent malfunction.
- *Impact codes.* How the issue or problem impacts work being performed.
- *Severity codes.* Extent of equipment affected by the issue or problem.
- *Urgency codes.* Importance of the user tasks supported by the affected network resources.
- *Priority codes.* Specifying level of attention on caller issues or problems.
- *Service types.* Category or level of service provided to a caller, such as standard or premium.
- *Escalation levels.* Intensity of concern about the trouble ticket.
- *Ticket status codes.* Possible states of a trouble ticket (open, fixed, or closed).
- *Action status codes.* The status of work on a trouble ticket (started, delayed, or completed).
- *Call status codes.* Status associated with a call request (open, closed, or in progress).
- *Service status codes.* Readiness condition codes for network devices (in repair or in service).
- *Reason codes.* Explanations for a trouble ticket status being changed.
- *Action delay codes.* Reasons for delays in completing action assignments.

■ *Administrative Data.* These are the definitions of valid users, notification rules, escalation rules, and sequencing of call requests.

- *Automatic notification policies.* Identification of significant events (network events and call request activities) and notification rules (who to notify and how). Call Management activities can include any change in the status of the system, such as creating new requests, transferring requests to Problem Management, and problem escalation.
- *Escalation policies and rules.* Trouble tickets are escalated based on priority and length of time since the last change in status. Escalation can result in automatic notification of responsible individuals.
- *Service level agreements.* SLAs are associated with network resources. Elapsed time is measured, responsible individuals automatically notified, and vendor performance evaluated.
- *Event monitoring.* Specification of conditions and actions that state where, when, what, and how call requests should be tracked, and actions to take if a condition still exists.
- *Event handling.* Event messages generated by network devices can automatically prepare incident reports and trouble tickets.

- *Incident filtering.* Network devices may generate hundreds of event messages, and incident filtering can be used to screen for specific needs. You can specify event counts within time intervals so that random errors are filtered out but repeated errors create trouble tickets.
- *Security.* Users of Help Desk and Problem Management can be assigned to security levels to control access to various activities and options within Advanced Help Desk.

Unicenter TNG Advanced Help Desk comes with some data already defined and loaded:

- Resource classes corresponding to valid enterprise types, including OSI equipment types
- Model data corresponding to valid manufacturers
- Reference table data, including call request codes and trouble codes
- Administrative data, including notification rules

This basic information is more than sufficient to begin using Unicenter TNG Advanced Help Desk. The data can be refined over time to more accurately reflect the organization's resources and operational procedures. The key information needs include the following:

- *Equipment configuration.* Particularly those system components that are candidates for problem tracking.
- *Problem Management policies.* How problems are to be classified and assigned (problem categories, status codes, and responsibility areas, for example).
- *Problem Escalation policies.* How priorities and responsibilities are to be changed, based on how long a problem has been unresolved.

In order to automate problem tracking and make it a particularly effective tool, notification policies should be the first category of additional information. *Notification policies* identify who needs to be notified as problem status changes and how are they to be notified.

Using Call Management in Advanced Help Desk

Advanced Help Desk includes features for recording more complete call request information, for assembly of incident reports that can be attached to trouble tickets, and for recording action plans that can be attached to trouble tickets. A high degree of flexibility and control is added to the basic Unicenter TNG system when you completely integrate Call Management (the frontline Help Desk support tool for assisting analysts in tracking caller issues) and Problem Management (the core support tool for tracking network problems and more complex user issues).

The Call Management main window (see Figure 6.12) is the starting point for Call Management users. It displays any Help Desk announcements posted by the manager or system administrator, summarizes outstanding call requests, displays information about call requests (this section is customized by the system administrator to show system-specific information), and active call requests by priority status.

FIGURE 6.12
The Call Management window.

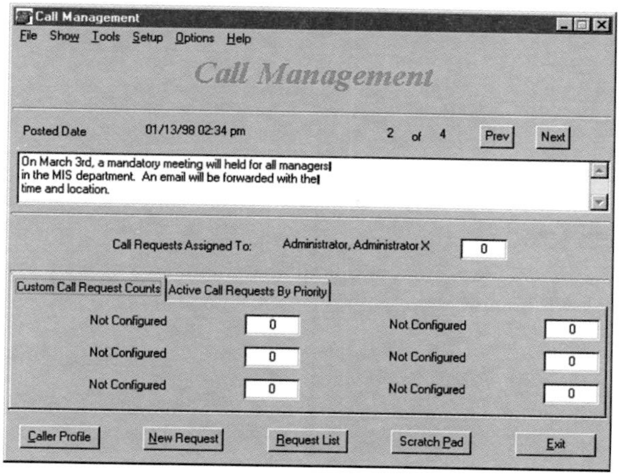

When a user calls in with a problem, Help Desk personnel can click Caller Profile to identify the individual making the call or can click Scratch Pad to begin entering information concerning the problem. Help Desk staff can also use the Remote Control option, Asset Management option, and Software Delivery as tools when solving user problems.

The Caller Profile window is used to identify the individual requesting help. It provides information about the caller, provides a history of calls from this individual, identifies the organization, provides information about the configuration of equipment, and shows a history of calls from the caller's organization. The individual and organizational history is particularly useful because it can indicate a pattern of problems that point to a general system failure rather than just an isolated incident. Each section contains administrative and technical information to help the analyst log, classify, and resolve call requests.

The Caller tab provides information about the individual. The caller information can be collected and entered during the telephone call if this is a first-time contact.

The Caller History tab displays historical information related to previous call requests. You can check for previous reports on similar problems or select open reports to update the current information.

The Organization tab is used to check and enter information about the caller's organizational unit, the organization's equipment configuration, department location, and other administrative information.

The Organization History tab displays information about previous call requests from this organizational unit. This listing's main purpose is to determine whether call patterns exist, which may indicate a systemwide rather than an individual problem.

The Scratch Pad is used to enter information about a call request. Information entered on this form will automatically be transferred to a new or existing call request. It is frequently the first

Ch
6

place information is entered because the customer may begin describing the problem before indicating who he or she is. This gives the Help Desk analyst a way to start taking notes online, and that information will never have to be entered more than once.

The Call Request Detail window is opened to enter information necessary to resolving the problem or reporting the issue. It is opened by clicking New Request either in the Caller Profile window or in the Call Management window. If the caller has been identified, information from the Caller Profile is transferred to the Call Request Detail window. If information has been entered on the Scratch Pad, it is automatically transferred to the Request Description block in the Call Request Detail window (see Figure 6.13).

FIGURE 6.13

The Call Request Detail window.

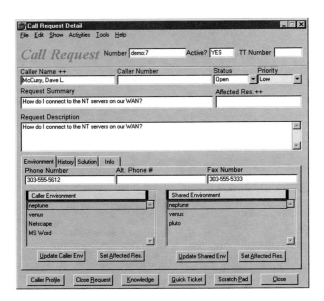

The Environment tab contains information about the Caller Environment and the Shared Environment. The History tab is used to enter activities, and the Solution tab to enter the problem resolution. Note that all relevant information is consolidated on the Call Request Detail window so that it is unnecessary to pull information from a variety of sources. The Call Request Detail window is the Help Desk's central information source regarding the problem, its status, and the solution.

Help Desk personnel need to record information about their activities as they work on the problem. The Activities pull-down menu is used for changing problem status, closing the problem, recording manual notification of personnel involved, manually escalating the problem, logging and recording, transferring the issue to Problem Management, and a variety of other activities. Transfer to Problem Management can be accomplished by clicking Quick Ticket, which will create an incident report and trouble ticket.

The Call Request list is what the Help Desk analyst uses to view open calls and find status information. This window is used to select the specific call requests to work on or to review.

Using Problem Management in Advanced Help Desk

The Problem Management function of Unicenter TNG Advanced Help Desk is designed to simplify problem solving and management of distributed computer networks. There are three key Problem Management components:

- Incident reports—Created by Call Management or network-management platforms when events pass through filtering criteria. Incident reports contain symptoms of problems.

- Trouble tickets—Created by and attached to one or more incident reports. Trouble tickets describe the problem, assign responsible personnel, and monitor corrective actions.

- Action plans—Attached to trouble tickets. Action plans describe specific steps that must be taken to solve the problem, including personnel assignments and scheduling.

The Problem Management main window is the starting point for Problem Management function users. It provides Help Desk personnel real-time status information by providing current counts and priorities of all open trouble tickets; it also provides counts and impacts of all unattached incident reports. It is possible to review outstanding items, print reports, create new trouble tickets, and create new incident reports from this window.

The Incident Report window is used to record events that indicate potential problems on the network. While they can be created manually, they are usually created one of three ways:

- By dispatching a problem from Call Management to Problem Management
- By the network-management platform reporting events that have passed the filter
- By message records and actions in Unicenter matching an input event message

The Incident Report list is used for selecting unattached incident reports. The fields on the bottom third of the window are used to enter search and selection criteria, and the resulting incident reports are displayed in the top part of the window. You can select outstanding incident reports via a variety of criteria such as date, network resource, location, and contact.

To solve and track an incident after it has been reported, you must attach it to a trouble ticket. This can be done by creating a new trouble ticket, which is done by clicking the Quick Ticket button on the Incident Report window. It can also be done by selecting one or more incidents from the Incident Report List window and adding these to a new or existing trouble ticket.

When incident reports are automatically generated, trouble tickets will also be created and the incident report will be attached. The Trouble Ticket window (see Figure 6.14) contains summary information about the attached incident or incidents. In addition to details about the problem, it will contain details about the individual and organization involved, as well as logging data.

Ch
6

FIGURE 6.14
The Trouble Ticket window.

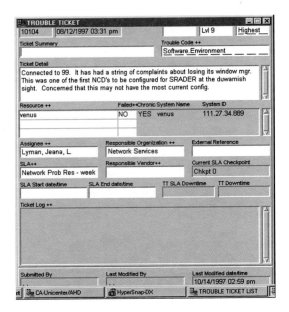

Templates can be created for common problems, and these can have fields with automatic information, such as priority, urgency, assigned responsibility, and applicable service level agreements. This can speed the process of entering data and save a significant amount of Help Desk time.

The Trouble Ticket List window is used to track open trouble tickets. You can enter selection criteria such as date, trouble codes, or resources in the bottom part of this window. Only trouble tickets meeting the criteria are displayed in the top part of the window. Trouble tickets can be updated, have their status changed, have new incidents attached, and be closed.

Action plans can be attached to trouble tickets. Simple actions can be entered directly into an Action list. The steps can be listed directly on the Action list, or you can select the Detail button to create a more detailed description of each step. ●

Storage Management

In this chapter

It is widely accepted that information is a valuable corporate asset. Indeed, corporate data often defines the very nature of an organization. In terms of contemporary technology, electronic information (whether stored on disk drives or not) more or less corresponds to an organization's memory. It needs to be preserved, while remaining easily accessible. Managing the quantity, diversity, and widespread distribution of data across today's typical enterprise is a daunting task. Terabyte databases in the glass house, hundreds of gigabytes on departmental servers, and thousands of PCs with a few gigabytes each add up to a complex problem.

The owners and users of corporate data understand and value it, but they alone cannot be counted on to safeguard it. Due to the complexity and scope of storage management, not to mention the very high cost of failure, it is inevitable that IT will be called upon to ensure that these corporate assets are reliably secured; so while storage management is not sexy or glamorous, it is an absolutely essential to IT's role in the enterprise.

In part because it receives scant attention, there is some confusion regarding the term *storage management*. Storage management focuses on efficiently and dependably protecting and retrieving files leveraged by applications and employees. It is not concerned with such things as file structures, database design and organization, and the like, except as those issues impact the space requirements, backup times, and so on. Storage management is basically the function of ensuring that data is available as needed, at a reasonable expense.

- Integration—A key to efficient storage management is providing a comprehensive solution. This means that storage management should be integrated with other disciplines such as security, job scheduling (workload management), antivirus, Help Desk (problem management), and even network management. This is important for two reasons: First, nobody wants to back up data with a virus infection or to an insecure destination, so higher quality storage management is a direct benefit of integration with other management components. Second, business applications can leverage the storage capabilities to make processes more reliable and secure. For example, whether backups are triggered in response to an anticipated problem (via pattern recognition) or through a regularly scheduled program (via workload management), business information ought to be protected on multiple levels, in many ways. Unicenter TNG provides the needed integration across multiple environments including Windows NT, UNIX, and legacy platforms.

- Backup and recovery—Doubts concerning the importance of protecting data can be quickly dispelled by a short conversation with anybody who has suffered through the painful process of desperately trying to re-create lost information. Making sure that data is available when and where required is a multifaceted problem, however. The most fundamental part of this challenge is the file backup and recovery process. In order to ensure the availability of files, it is first necessary to make copies of them. However, regular backups on anything other than casual use systems (such as home PCs) require more than copying files onto removable media (disc or tape, for example) and hiding it. A definable, repeatable process supported by reliable software mechanisms is necessary.

  Data is dynamic—accordingly, it should be backed up periodically, generally speaking at least once a day. Constantly making a full backup of everything, while comprehensive, takes a lot of unnecessary time, space, and machine resource. Making an *incremental backup* that copies only those files that have changed since the last backup is usually sufficient. Each time a back up is performed, it creates a *saveset*, a file that contains copies of the backed up files. As files change and savesets accumulate, multiple versions of individual files are created. This presents the challenge of identifying which saveset contains the particular version of a file required for retrieval.

■ Archiving—Another aspect of making sure that files are available when needed is the problem of selecting the appropriate storage media. This is relatively simple if cost is not a consideration. Everything is kept on blazingly fast hard discs attached directly to servers. Unfortunately, although disk drive pricing is constantly decreasing, costs remain a very significant consideration. Archiving selected data to lower cost (and so usually slower) media is a common means of containing overall data storage costs. The challenge is determining which files should be migrated and which media is appropriate. In addition, another challenge exists once files have been migrated—keeping track of and retrieving the files. If this aspect of storage management is not performed effectively, it can end up creating serious bottlenecks and offsetting any of the benefits that it offers.

■ Media management—The need for an effective media management capability is implicit in the archiving function as well as in the backup and recovery function. Effective media management capability entails knowing the contents and location of all removable media (magnetic tape, for example). In fact, this functionality is an important requirement of any IT organization's everyday production operations. It is through this that such things as tracking files to specific storage volumes are accomplished. Media management consists of software and processes for the use of the software. Companies have lost billions of dollars because of inadequate media management. Consider the case of a careless tape librarian. Several tapes had arrived in the library during a previous shift. On those tapes were the billing records for services the company had provided. The tapes had been sent to this facility to have the bills printed. A check of the Media Management system (which was linked to the system used by the company to schedule computer jobs) would have shown that these tapes had not been processed and needed to be sent to the computer room. Instead, the librarian decided to clean and certify the tapes—a process that included overwriting each tape, thereby destroying all of the original billing data. The value of the services that could not be billed was nearly $1 million! This was not a failure of the Media Management system, but a failure of processes around that system. Both parts are essential to success.

■ Other functions—There are a number of other miscellaneous, but still important, functions that relate to storage management. Things such as file compression (to reduce the space required), disk compression (to reduce fragmentation and wasted space), and media inspection (tape certification, surface scan of disks) fall in this area; they are used to ensure the reliability of the media and avoid the loss of data. There are functions related to the use of specialized hardware (RAID devices, for example) and strategies coupled with hardware (Hierarchical Storage Management—HSM). While each of these is important, they do not make up the fundamental basis of storage management and will not be dealt with in depth in this chapter.

Ch

7

The Unicenter TNG Approach

Unicenter TNG's focus on basic storage management is in the file management part of the product. This component addresses the key functions of media management, archiving, and backup/recovery. There are additional components—Unicenter TNG Automated Storage Management and Unicenter TNG Advanced Storage Option—that can address some of the more advanced storage management functions, such as hierarchical storage management and online backup. Like file management, these solutions are integrated with Unicenter TNG and available across heterogeneous, distributed environments.

In addition to these items, Computer Associates also offers an extensive set of products targeted at specific environments, such as standalone LANs as well as special-purpose storage management products. These offerings are not part of the Unicenter TNG suite, however, and are not addressed in this chapter.

Getting Started with File Management

File Management is a part of Unicenter TNG's Enterprise Management component. Enterprise Management is one of Unicenter TNG's main parts, and as such is included in Unicenter TNG's installation; Enterprise Management's installation includes File Management.

Unicenter TNG installs and configures File Management so that it can be used immediately. However, some optional tasks are suggested before beginning use of File Management in a production environment. Those phases are as follows:

- Verifying that all of the storage devices have been discovered by Unicenter TNG
- Tailoring Unicenter TNG's default policies for File Management to match those of your organization
- Using File Management to back up all of the Enterprise Management files

Phase 1: Verification

The first task is defining for Unicenter TNG the devices that will contain the files to be managed. This is done by building a Device Table. The ASM Device Table (`dev.tab`) is a configuration file that Enterprise Management uses to cross-reference the media class and type to a physical device. It defines the devices that File Management can use for backups and restores.

File Management will automatically discover eligible storage devices and build the Device Table as part of the installation process; this saves time and effort (see Figures 7.1 and 7.2). It is important to note that this process can only detect those devices that were attached and online during the system boot process. If the program finds tape devices during this discovery process, it will ask the system administrator to tell it whether the tape drives are 4mm, 8mm, or DLT. Other than this limited interaction, the process will be able to discover the storage devices and create entries for them in the ASM Device Table.

FIGURE 7.1

Files program group.

FIGURE 7.2

Backup Devices window.

You have to review the ASM Device Table after it has been created; do so to verify that all of the storage devices were detected (see Figure 7.3). It is also a good idea to verify that the information supplied about tape drives is correct. If any devices were not turned on while Discovery was running, they would not have been detected (see Figure 7.4). It is possible to manually create entries for those devices at this point in time. Alternatively, another Discovery process can be run with the missing devices turned on.

FIGURE 7.3

Editing the backup Device Table.

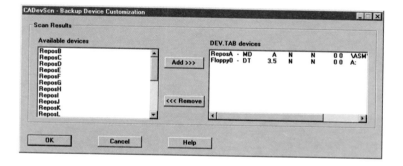

FIGURE 7.4

Adding a new backup device.

Phase 2: Customization

Another file is created for use by File Management during the initial Unicenter TNG installation—the defaults file. This is sometimes referred to as the defaults table. This file contains the default parameters shipped with Unicenter TNG. These parameters define and run the policies for the backups, restores, and archives. Although this file is loaded with the default parameters when installed, the system administrator should review this file and change any of the settings necessary so that the file reflects the policies for that company. Therefore, the next phase is to review the defaults file and make any changes that might be appropriate. (Any text editor can be used for this review.) Some of the variables in this file follow:

- Number of times to retry a database operation that was rolled back due to a deadlock
- Number of seconds to wait before retrying a deadlocked operation
- Default number of days to keep an archived file
- Default number of days to retain a file backup
- Maximum number of days to retain a file
- Minimum number of days to retain a file
- Default number of versions to keep for any file
- Maximum number of versions to keep for any file
- Minimum number of versions to keep for any file
- Buffer size, in kilobytes, used for data transfer
- Number of buffers to use for data transfer operations
- Boolean for tracking empty directories (for backup/archive)
- Boolean for defining the tape media as appendable
- Perform incremental backup on file size change (Yes/No)
- Perform incremental backup on update date change (Yes/No)
- Perform incremental backup on file system update date change (Yes/No)
- Perform incremental backup on file system access date change (Yes/No)

It is important to remember that the defaults file is installed with default values to each of the entries in the table. While it is advisable to review these values, it can be run initially without modifying them.

TIP It is a good idea to make a copy of the defaults file before making changes to it. If necessary, the original configuration settings may be referred to in the future or restored.

There is one change that the user is likely to make in the defaults file: activating IXR. Intelligent Transparent Restore (IXR) is a feature in which files that have been archived are automatically restored to disk for access by the requesting user. This is totally transparent to the user.

Phase 3: Backing Up

The last phase of getting ready to use File Management is strictly precautionary. It is recommended that all of the Enterprise Management databases be backed up. This can be done using the File Management program `CADBBKP.EXE`. (A description on running this program is listed in the next section.) It is recommended that all Unicenter TNG database activity be stopped before you do a hot backup of the Unicenter TNG databases. When the database activity has stopped, `CADBBKP` can be run against the Unicenter TNG database.

Once these initial installation steps have been completed, File Management is ready to use each of its functions: backups, restores, and archiving.

Performing Enterprise Backups

One important part of backing up files is to define the policies that are to be followed in the backup process. These policies need to be defined and then implemented in Unicenter TNG's File Management. An example of a backup policy is defining which files are backed up and the criteria to use for determining when to take a backup (for example, elapsed time since last backed up, back up only if modified, and the like).

The user has a variety of ways to define the backup policies when following the initial File Management configuration. Perhaps the simplest way to do this is with the graphical user interface (GUI). With this interface, the user simply selects the files to be backed up by graphically dragging and dropping the files onto the desired backup device. This method is preferred for requesting the backup of individual files or a small number of files.

N O T E   Unicenter TNG supports the use of most types of storage device for backups, including fixed or removable disks, magnetic tape, and writeable optical disks. However, as a practical matter, most organizations prefer to use tape as the storage media for backups.

Another choice is to run a backup automatically, in Batch mode, at a scheduled off-peak time. In this scenario, File Management integrates with Unicenter TNG's Workload Management component (discussed in Chapter 4, "Server Management") to schedule and track the backing up and archiving of files. More details on backing up individual files are provided later in this chapter.

File Management provides the option (on an individual file basis) of either backing up or archiving files. The distinction between these two options lies in what is done with the original copy of the file. If a file is backed up, the original, online copy is left in place and a duplicate copy is written to the backup media. If a file is archived, the original, online copy of the file is deleted after a copy of it is written to the backup media. The advantage of archiving files is that it frees valuable disk space. However, access to files that have been archived can be delayed.

When a file is backed up or archived, File Management stores summarized information about that version of the file in the File Management database. This information can be displayed at any time, and it provides a productivity tool for the operators responsible for storage

Ch

7

management. Summary information enables administrators to quickly locate a file when needed for a restore operation.

Unicenter TNG supports four broad categories of backups:

- User requested—Specific files are backed up at the explicit request of a user.

- Incremental—Only those files that have been modified since the last time they were backed up are copied in this type of backup.

- Differential—Backs up to a single saveset those files created or updated since the last full system backup (a cumulative incremental backup). This is not available through the GUI's drag-and-drop method.

- Full system—Backs up all files on an entire file system, including directories and subdirectories.

Backing Up Databases

Relational databases have become the heart of most organizations' critical business-data processing. These databases are usually very large, complex, and "fragile" and are often in continuous use by online applications. Therefore, relational databases require special precautions. It is for this reason that File Management provides a special program for backing up SQL Server databases. The program (CADBBKP.EXE) can be used interactively through a GUI or on a scheduled basis in Automated Batch mode. Because of the pervasive nature of SQL databases, this program is the one that will be used to back up the majority of the enterprise's files.

As noted, the relational databases are both critical and sensitive. That is, it is vital that the backups are successful and that they not do interfere with use of the database. Therefore, the Unicenter TNG program (CADBBKP.EXE) backs up the database in two phases. In the first phase it dumps the active database (using an SQL DUMP DATABASE) to a temporary database. This is done to keep the time required to capture an image of that database to an absolute minimum. Once this has been completed, the second phase moves (archives) the dump datasets to the media of your choice. You need to use CADBBKP in order to take a backup of an active database. This program requires several variables to be specified (name and location of the dump directory, for example). Details about specifying these variables and running CADBBKP are provided in the *Unicenter TNG Administrator's Guide*.

When CADBBKP has finished execution, the File Management list container will list the backed up databases as part of the dump directory. Their names will be identical to the name of the database, with a .dmp extension.

Backing Up Individual Files

It is very simple to request that File Management back up a single file, or a small number of files, by using the graphical user interface (GUI). This consists of selecting the desired files and then dragging and dropping the files onto the appropriate backup device. (This is described in detail later.)

Begin by opening the Devices window to view the available backup devices. To do this, select Files from the Unicenter TNG main folder. The `Files` folder appears.

Select Devices from the Files Program Group window. The Devices window displays the icons of the devices defined to the system and Unicenter TNG. Place the cursor on an icon that represents the type of device to be used for the backups and click the right mouse button. A pop-up menu appears.

If you're backing up a number of files and folders, you may want to gather the files in a *batch saveset*, rather than create an *immediate saveset* for each set of files you drag and drop onto the backup device. Click Process Mode to choose whether the saveset is a batch or immediate. Select Batch to run the backup later; select Immediate to back up now. Using the Immediate option is recommended if you're backing up a small number of files. However, using the Batch option is best if a larger number of files or folders will be backed up.

At this point, move the Devices window to an area of the desktop where it will remain visible. Windows that must be viewed simultaneously with the Devices window are now opened. The Windows NT File Explorer is opened first. Open the Windows NT File Explorer and select the files to be backed up. Using the left mouse button, drag and drop the selected files onto the icon for the backup device that was selected (see Figure 7.5). This causes the Backup Object(s) window to open (see Figure 7.6); it lists the files that are selected for backup. Backup is automatically selected.

FIGURE 7.5
Drag and drop the files to be backed up.

FIGURE 7.6
Backup Object(s) window.

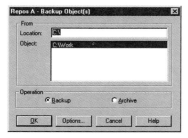

Ch
7

Ensure that Backup is selected, and then click the Options button. The Backup Options window, as shown in Figure 7.7, is displayed.

FIGURE 7.7
Backup Options.

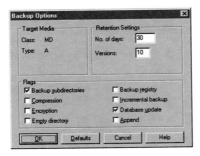

This window allows the selection of various options that determine how the backup will be executed. Table 7.1 describes the fields and what the settings do.

Table 7.1   Backup Options

Option	Description
Number of Days	The number of days the backup is to be retained.
Versions	The number of versions that should be retained.
Backup Subdirectories	If selected, any subdirectories of the disks or directories selected will also be backed up.
Encryption	If selected, the saveset will be saved in encrypted form. A window opens, asking for a password to be entered. To restore the encrypted files, the same password that was entered here must be used.
Backup Registry (NT)	If selected, the Windows NT Registry will be backed up. This option is recommended when doing a full system backup.
Incremental Backup	If selected, only those files that have changed since the last backup are backed up.
Append (NT)	If selected, this backup saveset may be appended to a tape or other media that already has files backed up on it. If not selected, the backup will be written to an empty tape.
Database Update	If selected, File Management will record information about the backed up files in the database. If not selected, no record of the backup will be kept.

Click OK twice after all of the selections have been made. If Immediate was selected, the backup is performed now.

If Batch was selected, the job must be released for processing (described later). If files from other directories and drives must be backed up in the batch saveset, drag and drop additional files onto the backup device, selecting the appropriate backup options for each set of files. To release the batch job for processing after all of the files have been selected, click the right mouse button to open the pop-up menu. Select Process Mode and Immediate.

Multiple drives can be backed up using the `cautil` command. For more information on this command, refer to the *Procedures Guide*.

If backup is being performed on a tape and a valid scratch tape is not already mounted, Unicenter TNG automatically prompts an operator at the Event Log console to mount one. Messages will be sent to the Event console when the backup is completed, notifying the operator that it is done.

Archiving Files

Archiving is used to store older files or files that are not expected to be used in the near future. This saves valuable disk space. Instead of simply deleting the files from the disk, the files are saved to the archive in case they are needed again.

The same commands and procedures used to back up files and databases are also used for archiving. The only difference is that Archive, instead of Backup, is selected as an option. Using the same drag-and-drop technique as described for backing up, select Archive (from the Backup Objects window). Click Options. The Archive Options window appears.

FIGURE 7.8
Archive Options.

The options are the same as those described earlier. Table 7.2 describes the options that are unique to archiving.

Table 7.2   Archive Options

Option	Description
Archive Subdirectories	Any subdirectories of the disks or directories selected will also be backed up.
Mandatory Data Move	The file will always be copied to the archive media, even if a current backup exists on some other tape. If not selected, the existing backup file version will be changed to an archive. Generally, this should be selected; that way, the backup file versions can expire at their natural times and the tapes can be reused. This also concentrates the archived file versions on a single medium, whereas leaving it unchecked can spread the archive copies over many tapes.
Confirm on Release	You will be asked to confirm the Archive operation when the Archive operation is released for immediate processing.

Performing Incremental Backups

Performing full backups on all servers and systems is a time-consuming process. Doing a full backup of every database every day may not be practical in some cases; the combination of full backups and incremental backups is generally used. An incremental backup only backs up those files that have been modified since the last time they were backed up. This saves time for the operations staff, while at the same time providing the enterprise with the security of a reliable backup.

File Management allows the system administrator to select from one of three options for determining whether a file has changed and needs to be backed up. The first method (the default) bases the determination on the file size. If the file's size has changed, Unicenter selects the file to be backed up in the incremental backup. The second method is the update date (the date and time the file was last modified). If that has changed since the last backup, Unicenter assumes that the file has been changed and selects the file for the incremental backup. This option may be useful because there are applications that can change a file without changing its size. The third method involves examining the date and time the file was last accessed. Under this schema, Unicenter looks at the last time the file was read or used by some application. This changes whenever the file is read or accessed by an application. This last option is not recommended because many files that were not changed would be selected for backup, thus defeating the time-saving benefits of incremental backups.

You follow the same steps outlined for backups in order to perform an incremental backup, but instead you select the options for Incremental Backup. Select the Incremental Backup option on the Backup Options window via the GUI method.

Performing a Restore

The ultimate test of the completeness and efficiency of an enterprise's backups occurs when restoring files is required. If user or system files are deleted, destroyed, or overwritten, the files should be recoverable by restoring them from the backups. Restoring the files is an easy task if the backups were done properly. Unicenter TNG tracks all versions of the files that have been backed up, which makes it easy to recover from disasters such as these.

To restore a file, the file must first be located in the file table. You can locate the file from the Unicenter TNG `File` folder.

1. Click Main.
2. Select Files.
3. If applicable, select a server.

In this window, select the files on the system to display by specifying the criteria for including files. If the initial values are selected, all of the files that are recorded in the database will be displayed (see Figure 7.9). Once all of the selection criteria have been entered, click Include. The Files container, shown in Figure 7.10, will appear.

FIGURE 7.9
Selecting files to include.

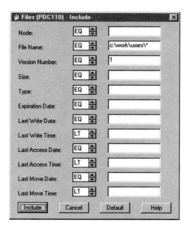

FIGURE 7.10
Files list.

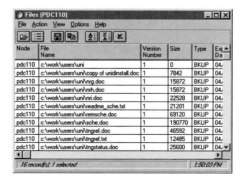

To restore all of the files shown, first click Action, and then click Select All. Alternatively, you can select only the directories and files that should be restored by clicking them individually. This list may be long, so scroll through the display to view all available files (see Figure 7.11). Once all of the files have been selected, click Action and then click Restore. The Files-Restore window appears.

FIGURE 7.11

List of a user's files.

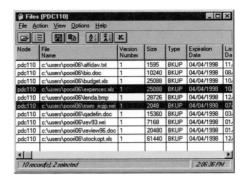

Unicenter provides the option of restoring from a version that is older than the most current one. This is quite easily done. In order to use an older version for a restore, begin by selecting the file and click Action; then click Open (as version list). A file version table appears (see Figure 7.12).

FIGURE 7.12

File Versions List.

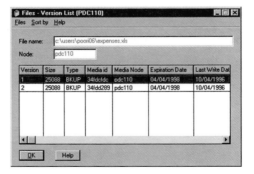

Select the appropriate version to restore. To restore the file from this window, click Files and then select Restore. The Files-Restore window is displayed.

If multiple file versions are to be restored, the window in Figure 7.13 appears, asking for confirmation. If desired, click to deselect any items that were previously selected, and then click Restore. The File Restore Options window opens.

FIGURE 7.13
Restore confirmation.

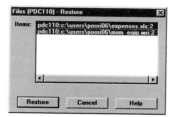

Selecting Restore Options

Now that the file versions to restore have been selected and confirmed, the user must select the options, shown in Figure 7.14. The location to which the file should be restored should be entered in the Restore To field. The Overwrite Options tell File Management what to do if it encounters files in the directory that have the same names as the restore files. The choices are as follows:

- Never—Never overwrite duplicate files.
- Always—Always overwrite duplicate files.
- Older—Only overwrite files that are older than the version being used for the restore.

FIGURE 7.14
Restore Options.

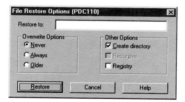

You can select other options:

- Create Directory—Allows directories to be created if they do not exist in the directory.
- Recursive—Performs a recursive restore for files and subdirectories of a restored directory.
- Registry—Restores the Windows NT Registry.

When all options have been selected, click the Restore button to begin the restore process. The restore executes immediately, and the display returns to the Files container. To exit from restore, select File and click Exit. Close the `Files` folder to return to Unicenter TNG's main folder.

When a restore is initiated, Unicenter TNG prompts the operator at the Event console to mount the tape (or other backup media) where the backup copy of the file is located. A message will be sent to the Event console when the restore has been completed.

Ch

7

Managing the Backup Media

The operators who run the backups and restores must deal with hundreds of tapes. When working with so many tapes, the chances for misplacing, mislabeling, or mixing up tapes or copying over current backup files increase. That, in turn, increases the risk that the current backups may not be in proper order when they are required. Unicenter TNG assists the operators' managing tapes by tracking each tape (or other media) it uses in storage management. It tracks whether the tape is *active*, meaning that it is in use, or is a *scratch* tape, meaning that it is available for use. It also tracks which savesets are stored on the tape and which files are stored on those tapes.

All of this information can be viewed from the Backup Media table. To open the table from the 2D or 3D map, right-click on the system's Unicenter File object in Unispace and select Media.

Alternatively, you can do this from the system's Enterprise Management program group: Double-click the Files icon to see the Files program group, and then double-click the Media icon. In either case, the Backup Media window, as shown in Figure 7.15, displays a media list.

FIGURE 7.15
Media list.

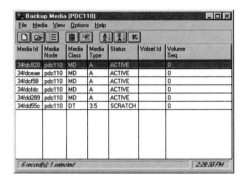

Media and Tape Labels

Storage media, tapes in particular, have *labels*. Labels are text strings that identify or name the media. That label appears in two places. An *external label* is the sticker a person can read on the outside of the media . An *internal label* is the data written on the media in a special place. American National Standards Institute (ANSI) describes how to write an internal label on a tape. Internal labels are what the computer reads and uses to identify the media. Obviously, it will be easier for everyone concerned if a tape's internal and external labels are the same. Tape labels can be up to six characters long and can contain letters or digits. Unicenter TNG expects the letters at the beginning or end of the tape label rather than interpersed throughout it. The label ABC123 is fine, as is 123ABC; 1A2B3C is not allowed.

Adding New Media

Adding new tape media simply adds a record of the media to the database so that Unicenter TNG can track it. To add new tape media, choose Media, New from the menu. You see a window like that shown in Figure 7.16. Choose the media type; see Table 7.2 for an explanation.

FIGURE 7.16
Adding new media.

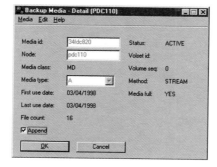

To add a tape, enter its label in the Media id field.

If this tape should only store a single backup or portion of a backup, do not check the Append box. However, check Append if you want to allow multiple savesets to be stored on the tape.

Other Functions

What has been discussed in this chapter presents a few highlights about the more commonly used File Management functions. There are many other important functions that are not addressed here. For example, when backing up a file, it is possible to specify that it be encrypted for security purposes. Another example is the capability to link File Management with Workload in order to automate the scheduling and running of backup jobs. Yet another is the capability to centrally administer the backups for all of a company's geographically dispersed servers. These are just three examples of additional functionality. Readers interested in learning more about Unicenter TNG's storage management capabilities are encouraged to refer to the *Unicenter TNG Administrator's Guide*. ●

Ch

7

Security

Security Management

It is an inescapable fact that enterprises have a significant investment in their IT infrastructures. The hardware, software, and other resources (networks, personnel, and so on) IT organizations require to serve their clients represent a huge investment on the part of an enterprise. The magnitude of that investment alone is justification sufficient to require the implementation of a comprehensive security solution.

However, even more important and more valuable than those resources is the data IT stores and the services necessary for the business to function. The IT services are essential to the functioning and survival of most businesses today. Just as every organization is heavily dependent on its IT function, those same organizations are targets for attack through those same IT functions. IT represents the Achilles' heel of most companies. It is through the IT function and its resources that organizations are most vulnerable to attacks, and through which the greatest amount of damage can be done with the lowest probability that the perpetrator will ever be caught. Attacks may come from outside the company in the form of viruses and hacker attacks. There are, however, also internal threats. Employees actually represent a far greater threat to an organization than do all of the external threats. It is well recognized that a disgruntled employee may pose a threat. However, an even greater risk can be posed by the curious or the well-intentioned but inept employee.

Access Control

Two broad areas comprise the security function. The first is ensuring that access to information resources conforms to the organization's policies. This area can be thought of as being much like the newspaper axiom of "who, what, when, where, why, and how." To begin, access needs to be limited to those who have been authorized to access the data (who). Control over this aspect has traditionally been implemented through the use of user IDs and passwords. Unfortunately, these have proven to be moderately effective; more and more organizations are turning to more sophisticated techniques (smart cards, biometrics, and the like).

However, access is usually limited. Many users are restricted in terms of the functions that they can perform (what). Some are permitted only to read the information in a file. Others may be authorized to update the file as well as read it. A smaller, trusted group may be permitted unrestricted access to the information, having the authority to delete information or even the entire file containing the information. This aspect of security is focused on controlling a user's access to information resources and controlling the authority the user can exercise over any of those resources.

It is sometimes determined to be appropriate to restrict access to certain files to certain times of the day, days of the month, or year (when). It is the role of the security system (both human and electronic components) to enforce the policy that determines when information can be accessed.

The "where" question can better be characterized as "from where." That is, a company may want to restrict the retrieval of some information to certain physical locations. For example, it might be considered desirable to limit the retrieval of employee's medical histories to workstations located in the medical department. Salary information might be limited to retrieval from locations within human resources, or payroll. "From where" also raises the question of connecting to the Internet and what types of information will be allowed to pass back and forth between the company and the outside world.

In general, "why" can be thought of as being beyond the purview of security administration. Security administrators who question the level of access being granted to someone do not normally find a ready audience for their question.

The final aspect of access control is "how." The common security access is centered around individuals who will be attempting to access the data via internal network connections. However, the security policy must also include a provision addressing the question of access to the corporate information assets by unsecure methods (remote [dial] access, Internet access, and so on). These types of access can be points of much higher risk. Therefore, the policy must address whether access by these unsecure methods will be permitted, and how they will be made more secure if they are permitted.

Without the use of security tools, it is all but impossible to implement an effective security policy to control access to information resources. Fortunately, there is a wide variety of tools available. Unicenter TNG, along with some of its options, is able to address many of the requirements for effective security administration.

Viruses

Computer viruses represent the second major area of concern for security administration. For some reason, there has arisen in the high-tech world a group of people who derive pleasure from devising computer viruses. These people are unlikely to ever realize any personal gain from their efforts, yet they willingly spend hundreds and even thousands of hours to create a piece of software in the hopes that it will be able to wreak havoc on some unsuspecting individual or organization. A large percentage of today's computer users have had one or more encounters with this scourge of the modern age.

The threat of computer viruses is very real. The potential sources of infection seem to be endless. They can come in electronic copies of internal documents. Files copied from the Internet are also a potential source. Employees who bring files into work from home (sometimes after having worked on a company project at home) are often a source of infection.

Just as it is impossible for an individual to keep from being exposed to biological viruses every day of his or her life, it appears to be impossible to prevent the introduction of viruses into an organization's computing infrastructure. However, just as exposure to a biological virus does not mean that a person has to get sick, it is possible to limit, or even eliminate, the adverse effects from the introduction of a virus. The key to minimizing or avoiding damage caused by viruses is to detect and isolate them as soon as they are introduced and then eradicate them. Even more than the control of access to information resources, and probably more than any other management function, the detection and eradication of viruses can only be done with some type of software solution.

The Unicenter TNG Approach

IT organizations are now faced with the challenge of securing the IT resources without making it prohibitively difficult for users to access those resources. Unicenter TNG's Security Management component is a policy-based security system that works in conjunction with the native operating system's security. It is an extra level of security, rather than a replacement for the native operating system's security. Access to assets (applications, files, system functions, log-on, and so on) is controlled with security policies that define what actions a user is permitted to perform. Access can also be permitted or denied based on date and time, as well as by asset or group of assets. After Unicenter TNG approves an action, the operating system's security features are invoked to provide an additional review.

Unicenter TNG Security Management is a part of the Enterprise Management component. Security Management's integrated functions allow it to work with Enterprise Management functions to trigger events that are sent to the event console log, notifying the administrator when a security violation is attempted. Real-time security monitoring can help blunt attempted attacks and avoid the damage they might cause.

Unicenter TNG Security Management includes a feature that detects viruses. This feature also notifies the administrator when a virus is detected. *InocuLAN* is an add-on component that works with Unicenter TNG to provide even greater virus protection for the server as well as for the clients. InocuLAN scans files, including zipped files, that are to be loaded on a system. When InocuLAN detects viruses, they can be *cured* (removed). This is a higher level of virus protection.

The Single Sign-On option works with Unicenter TNG Security Management to provide a productivity tool for users who must sign on to multiple systems. Instead of having to remember different passwords and different sign-on procedures, Single Sign-On allows a user to sign on once and have access to multiple systems that the user has authorized access to, by pointing and clicking. The sign-on procedures for each system are transparent to the user.

Getting Started

Like so much of Unicenter TNG, Security Management is a component of Enterprise Management. As an Enterprise Management component, it is installed during Unicenter TNG's initial installation. This will provide some basic Security Management functionality. While the basic Security Management is available as a result of installing Unicenter TNG, there are some extra steps that expand and enhance its capabilities. That work falls into four phases:

1. Review the Security Management options and client/server preferences. Select the options that are relevant to your needs and set them to values that are appropriate for your environment. (These are described in detail in *Unicenter TNG Administrator's Guide.*)

2. The Security Management database needs to be populated with information from the user IDs that are on the native operating systems.

3. Validate the security policies.

4. Activate enforcement of the security policies.

Select Options and Preferences

When installed, Unicenter TNG Security Management has default values for the options and preferences. These parameters help define the security policies that Security Management enforces. It is important to review and modify the settings for these parameters in light of the specific policies of the company implementing Security Management. See *Unicenter TNG Administrator's Guide* for a listing of all the parameters you should review or possibly modify.

Populate the Database

Security Management needs to know the IDs for every user who will be attempting to access any of the resources controlled by it. This means that Security Management needs to know the user ID for every person on every system that it will manage. This could be an extremely tedious and error-prone process if done manually. Fortunately, Security Management has the capability to discover all of the user IDs on a system. This is done by running a program: `secadmin`. This defines a user profile in the Security Management database for each of the user entries found on a Windows NT system (in the SAM database) or on a UNIX system (in the `/etc/passwd` file).

N O T E   When `secadmin` is run, it overwrites the existing Security Management database. Therefore, it should be run only when Security Management is being first set up. After that, the use of `secadmin` will cause the loss of other data stored in the database.

Validate Security Policies

Once defined, security policies can be rigidly enforced. This is vital to having effective security. However, if those policies are incorrect, there is the potential of either denying users legitimate access to data or permitting access by unauthorized users. Therefore, it is important you are certain that security policies are correct before beginning to enforce them. Security Management provides vehicles for testing the policies against the needs of the business. It is possible to set Security Management to run in a mode that will detect but permit deviations from the defined policy. This permits the security/system administrator to analyze the results of the policies defined to Security Management and to verify that the desired results are being obtained. The following settings should be used in order to run Security Management in test mode:

- User default violation mode—SYSTEM
- System violation mode—QUIET
- User default violation action—CANUSER
- Default permission—ALLOW

Activate Enforcement of the Security Policies

Once it has been confirmed that the settings in Security Management are producing the intended results, it is time to activate security policy enforcement. This is done by changing the options selected in Phase 3 (validate security policies). There are a number of ways the policies can be enforced. These are discussed in detail later in this chapter.

Adding a User

The addition of users is a regular activity in most companies. As explained, the initial addition of users to the Security Management database is an automated process. Subsequently, new users can be added with a minimum amount of effort. It is done by defining a User Profile. Select Users from the Unicenter Main folder, and then select the Security User Profiles list container. From this, select User, New. This last step will cause the User Profile - Detail main window to appear (see Figure 8.1). Enter the requested information on that screen. The only mandatory field on this screen is User ID. Next, you will probably want to go to the Security Login notebook (to reach it, click the Security tab on the User Profile - Detail window); see Figure 8.2. As you did on the User Profile - Detail main window, enter the requested information. At a minimum, it is necessary to provide the status for the user ID (*Active*, for example) and the effective date (when the system should activate this user ID).

FIGURE 8.1
The User Profile - Detail window.

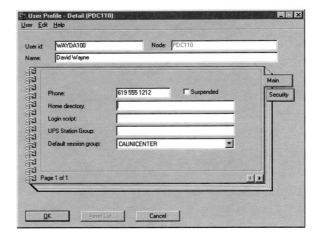

After providing the information requested on the Security Login, go to the Security Enforcement notebook page (see Figure 8.3). (This is reached by selecting the Enforcement tab at the bottom of the screen.) Mode and Action are the key pieces of information you need to supply on this screen. These tell Security Management what to do when violations occur.

FIGURE 8.2
The Security Login notebook window.

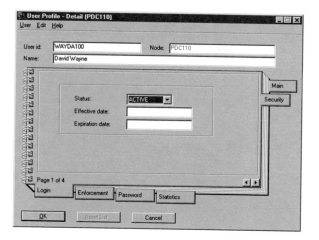

FIGURE 8.3
The Security Enforcement notebook page.

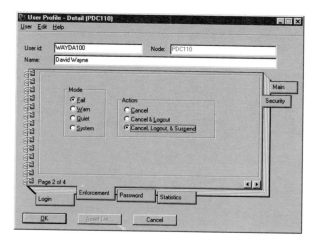

Security Management has three basic options for Mode:

- It can permit access to all resources regardless of permission and take no other action.
- It can permit the access and send a warning to the event console.
- It can deny access and log the event.

The other half of the enforcement equation is Action. This defines how to handle the user. There are three alternatives:

- Cancel the process from which the access was attempted.
- Cancel the process and log the user off the machine.
- Cancel the process, log the user off, and suspend the user's ID.

The last alternative means that, having attempted a violation, the user will not be able to log onto the system again until the system administrator reinstates the user ID.

Figure 8.4 shows the Security Password notebook page. This is the next piece to be filled in. It is reached by selecting the Password tab at the bottom of the screen. Enter the information requested into the fields. Options that allow the administrator to set password policy for a user are on this page. The password may be assigned by the system. The user can be allowed or restricted from changing the password, setting minimum and maximum days between password changes, and setting an expiration date for the password. For help on the fields, highlight the field and then press the F1 key. The required and other important fields are: Password, Verify, Change Control, Minimum, Maximum, and Expiration Date.

FIGURE 8.4

Security Password notebook page.

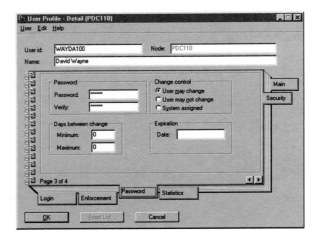

Next, click the Statistics tab at the bottom of the notebook page. The Security Statistics notebook page is an informational screen only. This page displays how many times the user has violated the policy, when the user was suspended, or when the suspension was revoked. Display the Statistics Page Help for an explanation of the information contained in this window. More advanced users are able to use this information to help them create even better enforcement of security policies.

Once the necessary information has been entered, click OK to save the user profile. This returns you to the Security User Profiles list container. From here, either enter another user profile or exit. Finally, after all of the user additions, deletions, and changes have been completed, the commit process must be run in order for this change to be reflected in Security Management. This is done by entering `run secadmin /c` at the command line.

Controlling Access to Resources

The basic objective of access management is to control which information technology resources a particular user may utilize. Asset Permissions is one of the components of exercising effective control in Security Management. Asset Permissions controls users' access to resources, as well as how the resources can be used once they are accessed. Permissions are granted through the Security Management GUI. If a user attempts to access a resource without authority (Access Permission), a violation results. The violation does not necessarily mean that the user will be stopped from accessing the asset. That is a decision that must be made by the system administrator at the time the permissions are defined. This is done through the Enforcement Mode in the user profile. This option determines whether the user will be able to use the asset in the event of a violation.

It is recommended that the System Violation Mode be set to WARN when setting up rules for production. If any user is in violation of rules that have been set to WARN mode, the Security Management system will execute the following tasks:

- The user will be allowed access to the asset even though he or she has not been authorized to do so.
- The event is logged to the event console log.
- A warning message is sent to the user who caused the violation.

This approach allows for testing and fine-tuning of the rules without affecting any users' ability to work during the rule setup phase. In order to set the System Violation Mode to WARN, click Configuration from the Unicenter TNG Main folder. Next, click Settings; this causes the Settings window to be displayed. From there, click the Options tab. Set the System Violation Mode's option value to WARN. Save the change by pressing Enter and then Exit. Security Management must be stopped and restarted in order for this change to take effect.

The next step is to create an Asset Permission, which grants users permission to access assets. This is accomplished by first selecting Assets from the Unicenter TNG Main folder. Next, click Access Permissions, which causes the Access Permissions list to appear. Select Access, New in that container. The Access Permissions - Detail window (see Figure 8.5) appears.

FIGURE 8.5

The Access Permissions - Detail window.

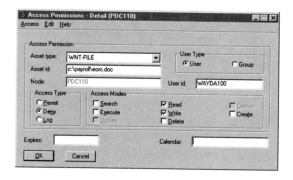

Enter the requested information in the Access Permissions - Detail window. Fields with multiple options are as follows:

- User Type—User, Group, User ID
- Access Type—Permit, Deny, Log
- Access Modes—Search, Execute, Update, Read, Write, Delete, Control, Create

Save the new access permission by clicking OK and Exit. The commit process must be run in order for the changes to take effect.

The system can administer both users and assets on a group basis. Information about both of these options is contained in the following sections.

User Group Administration

It will always be necessary to address individual users on a singular basis when creating new user IDs. Beyond that, it is often possible to manage users as part of a group and thereby save both time and effort. Much of the administrative work done for security actually applies to entire groups of users. For example, a work group of 20 people is transferred from the Accounting Department to the Human Resources (HR) Department. The corporate security policy specifies that all of the users in the HR Department have access to the same set of files. That is, they are able to access all of the information in an employee's personnel record. Previously, as members of the Payroll Group in the Accounting Department, this group of 20 people only had access to information that was directly related to payroll issues. Now all 20 of these employees need to be authorized to access the same information the other HR Department employees access. At this point, the system administrator responsible for making the necessary changes has two options. The first option is to change the access permissions for each person individually, as described in the previous section. The other option is to define (if it has not been done previously) these 20 people as members of a common user group and then to change the access permissions for the group.

A user group logically connects users and asset permissions together. Defining user groups is not required, but it is a convenient administration tool. An administrator can assign users to a specific user group. That user group can be granted access to a set of files, which results in all members of the user group automatically having access to the set of files. This is much quicker and more efficient than individually defining the permissions for each user. In order to define a user group, the system administrator needs to select Users from the Unicenter TNG Main folder, and then select User Groups. Following that, the Security User Groups list container appears. In that container, select Group New, which causes the User Group - Detail window to appear.

In the User Group - Detail window, enter the requested information and then click the New button. The Users Group Management window (see Figure 8.6) appears. A new user group can be created from this window; you can also add users to or delete users from an existing group. To add a user group, select a user type of GROUP and enter the group's name in the Userid field.

To add a user, select a user type of USER and enter the user's name in the Userid field. In either case, enter the requested information into the fields, click Add to save the definition, and then exit. Finally, as with the addition of an individual user, the commit process must be run in order for this change to be reflected in Security Management.

FIGURE 8.6
The User Group Management window.

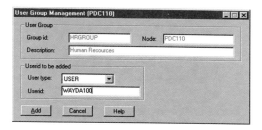

Creating an Asset Group

An *asset* is any resource (files, applications, Unicenter resources, user IDs, and so on) defined to Unicenter TNG. Just as users can be assigned to an asset group and administered collectively, assets can be assigned to an asset group, which logically links related assets together. The asset group allows administrators to grant user authority to groups of files at a time. Continuing with the example of 20 employees transferred from the Accounting Department to the Human Resources Department, the administrator could define all of the files accessed by the HR Department employees as a single group. Therefore, with the new employees defined as a user group and the files accessed by the Human Resources Department employees defined as an asset group, granting the new group access to the additional files becomes a very simple task.

The process of defining an asset group is similar to those followed for creating a user group. Begin by selecting Assets from the Unicenter TNG menu. Follow that by selecting Asset Groups. This causes the Asset Groups list container to appear. From the Asset Groups container, select Asset, New, which will cause the Asset Group - Detail window (see Figure 8.7) to appear.

FIGURE 8.7
The Asset Group - Detail window.

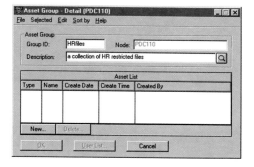

Enter the requested information in the Asset Group - Detail window. (Group ID is the only required field.) Next, click the New button. This causes the Asset Group Management window, shown in Figure 8.8, to appear. Enter the requested information. Once finished, save the information by clicking Add. Continue adding assets to the group. When finished, select Cancel. The Asset Group - Detail window appears, showing the asset groups that were just added in the Asset list area of the window. The commit process must be run in order for this change to be reflected in Security Management.

FIGURE 8.8
Asset Group
Management window.

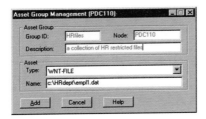

Single Sign-On

Users often need to log on separately to several different applications in the distributed computing environment. This seemingly trivial annoyance can quickly add up to many hours of unproductive time and can cost companies hundreds, or even thousands, of dollars per user per year. Many IT organizations have tried to address this problem with home-grown solutions (usually scripts of some type), but usually have less than satisfactory results.

There is a Unicenter TNG option called Single Sign-On that allows users to sign on just once and yet gain access to multiple networked applications, including UNIX-based, Windows-based, and mainframe-based services. This eliminates the need to maintain separate user registries, security environments, reports, or audit trails. From the user's perspective, it eliminates the need to remember different sign-on processes, user IDs, or passwords to do their job. When a user logs on to Single Sign-On (SSO), the Windows Program Manager group displays icons that represent the applications the user is authorized to access.

In addition to facilitating the logon process, SSO can make session usage available for reporting and chargeback. Data is maintained on each individual user, including log-on time to SSO and the connect time. SSO even allows the administrator to control and track user access to applications on client PCs.

Single Sign-On has three major components: Session Groups, Session Profiles, and Users. Session Groups and Session Profiles must be created; Users are then assigned to groups. Session Profiles defines the applications that are eligible for inclusion in a single sign-on process. Session Groups defines groupings of applications that can be accessed in a single logon. Finally, Session Groups are assigned to users, thereby giving them access to the required sessions with their one logon.

Creating a session profile begins with selecting Single Sign-On from the Unicenter TNG Main window. From there, select Session, Profiles; this causes the Session Profiles container to appear. In that container, select Session, New; the Session Profile - Detail window appears, as shown in Figure 8.9.

FIGURE 8.9
The SSO Session Profile - Detail window.

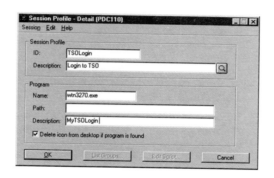

Enter the data requested. Key information on this window includes the following:

- Session Profile ID—This field identifies the name of the PC protected by this session profile.
- Session Profile Description—Description of the PC program (optional).
- Program Name—The name of the executable program to be protected.
- Program Path—The drive and directory where the executable program is located (optional).
- Program Description—The description of the program that appears on the client PC display.
- Delete Icon from Desktop if Program Is Found—If this option is checked, the icon for the Unicenter TNG–protected program is removed from the user's non-protected program group. If the icon is removed, users with access to the program will only see the icon in their Single Sign-On program group.

Save the profile and exit when the requested information has been entered.

The next step is to define the Session Groups. As noted above, Session Groups consists of collections of session profiles that may be accessed with a single sign on. Session Groups may contain any number of session profiles. To define a Session Group starting from the Single Sign-On window, select Session, Groups; this causes the Session Groups container to appear. From that container, select Session, Group, New, which displays the Session Group - Detail window (see Figure 8.10).

FIGURE 8.10

The Session Group - Detail window.

Enter the Session Group information, which identifies the unique name for this session group. Click OK to save the session group and exit.

In order for a user to have access to certain Session Profiles, the user must have a session group that contains the session profiles assigned. Single Sign-On assigns a default session group to each user. The default session group for a user can be changed in Unicenter TNG's Users component. The User Profiles container will appear when you click Users. From that container, select User Open, which causes the User Profile - Detail window (see Figure 8.11) to appear.

FIGURE 8.11

The User Profile - Detail window.

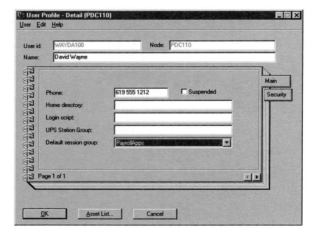

Enter the name of a Session Group definition in the Default Session Group field. Use the drop-down box to the right of the field to select a Session Group definition from the list. Click OK to save the profile and exit. The commit process must be run in order for this change to take effect.

This section was a brief description of what the Single Sign-On option can do, as well as basic information on setting it up. For more detailed information on installing and setting up the Single Sign-On option, refer to the *Single Sign-On Server Guide*, *Getting Started*, and the *Unicenter TNG Reference Guide*.

Testing A Security Policy

Unicenter TNG provides tools that allow the administrator to test a security policy before fully implementing it in a production environment. These tools are useful in determining whether the security policies that have been defined will result in the desired actions. There are several commands that assist the administrator to test the security policies. These commands should be entered on the command line. The commands that would be of use are as follows:

- CAUGUIEV   This starts the Security Rule Evaluator. After entering the asset type, the name of the asset, the node that the asset is on, the name of the user accessing the asset, and the asset mode, the program displays a window that indicates whether the policies in the database would permit or deny access. It does not test the enforcement decision, and the enforcement action is not executed.

- CAUSEC   This program provides a more complete means of testing security policy. It can test an attempt to log on to the system or access a resource against the current security policies, as well as test the enforcement actions.

- DSBULIST   Displays the list of users.

- ACBROWSE   Displays all of the access control rules in an exploded format.

Discussing each of these commands in detail is beyond the scope of this book. For more information on each of these commands, refer to the *Unicenter TNG Reference Guide*.

Virus Protection

Any enterprise that operates with external interfaces is in a position vulnerable to attack by a virus if it fails to take proper precautions. An external interface may be as obvious as an Internet connection not protected with a firewall. However, users can also introduce viruses from diskettes when loading software or data onto their machines. In addition, files downloaded by users from outside the company can be potential sources of infection.

The Unicenter TNG Framework includes a virus detection function. However, it is important to note that this feature is limited to just detecting a virus and reporting its detection. It cannot eradicate the virus.

The Unicenter TNG base product does not include any anti-virus functions. However, the more powerful anti-virus functions are provided by the Advanced AntiVirus Option (AAO). AAO features include the following:

- *Real-time components*. Protects all avenues of entry into the Windows NT enterprise. All files being loaded or exported from the server are scanned for viruses, including compressed files.

- *Virus wall*. Stops any infected file from being copied to a server and replacing an already existing clean version of the file.

- *Virus quarantine.* Gives the system administrator the option of automatically suspending any user who attempts to copy infected files to a server. This is intended to ensure that an infection is not spread beyond the user's system.

- *Floppy-drive protection.* InocuLAN scans a diskette's boot sector whenever a floppy disk is accessed to verify that a virus is not hidden there.

- *CD-ROM protection.* This media is also scanned to prevent this from becoming a source of viruses.

- *Network drive protection.* When files are copied from one mapped drive to another, InocuLAN scans all files moving between mapped drives.

- *Internet-enabled.* All file downloads from the Internet can be automatically scanned for viruses before they have the chance to infect the target machine. It will even scan compressed files.

- *GroupWare Messaging AntiVirus options.* InocuLAN protects Lotus Notes or Microsoft Exchange mail systems with its messaging options. Attached Zip files are also scanned.

- *Automatic software download, distribution, and update.* Automated downloading and distribution of the latest virus signature files and search engines using modem or FTP downloads.

- *Point-to-point management.* InocuLAN Servers can be managed by machine name.

- *Domain support.* Allows configuring servers into InocuLAN domains. Multiple servers can be configured simultaneously.

- *Scheduled scanning.* Administrators can scan networked servers at selected times.

- *Remote system event log support.* Uses Alert 4.0 to send alarm information to the remote server's system event logs.

Implementing InocuLAN

InocuLAN implementation is done with minimal effort. It consists of installing it and restarting the target system.

If Security Management will be used in a distributed environment, then Security Management's Domain Server component must be installed on the server machine that is acting as the Unicenter TNG domain controller. Keep these things in mind when Security Management is activated:

- It is important to activate Security Management on all server machines in the enterprise.

- Security Management's agent component must be installed on all machines in the Unicenter TNG domain, other than the domain controller.

- The Security Management logon agent should be installed on all the Windows NT workstation machines that can access the server machines in the Unicenter TNG domain.

- Set Define Security Policy to WARN mode. (This phase is described in more detail later.) When in WARN mode, any violations will be logged to the event console log and a warning message will be sent to the violating user, but users are still allowed access to the assets.

This allows the administrator to correct and fine-tune the security policy rules if they are in error, without stopping users from getting their jobs done. Once the policies are correct, re-execute the commit process. Security Management options should be run in FAIL mode for production operations after the policies have been tested and refined. This mode prevents users from accessing any assets they are unauthorized to use. Once this phase is completed, Security Management is operational. For more detailed information about this phase, refer to the *Unicenter TNG Administrator's Guide.*

■ When this security implementation occurs concurrently with production work on the same node, precautions must be taken to minimize any impact on the production work. Being able to set security policies and to see the resulting effects of those policies without adversely affecting productive work is critical to the eventual success of the Security Management solution. Therefore, it is recommended that Security Management be implemented in the following phased approach described in the next section.

Implementing Security Management

Set the Default Permission setting to DENY in order to deny an access attempt on any asset not referenced in a rule. This can lock everyone out, including the security administrators, if they are not careful.

We do two things to protect the organization from that eventuality:

1. Define a User for ourselves and another security manager (or two), and set the User Enforcement Mode to warn. Then even if an access control rule is mistakenly defined which denies the security administrators' access, it will not be enforced. Instead, a message will be logged, and we can investigate how our policy has gone awry.

2. Define a management user group including all the managers. (Note: There will most likely already be such a group imported from the Windows NT security database.) For this group we define a rule permitting access to the C:* in all access modes. This at least ensures that the default permission won't be applied to the system files.

Other settings we need to change are to set Implicit DENY Permission for Rules setting to YES, the System Violation Mode to QUIET, the User Default Violation Mode to SYSTEM, and the User Default Violation Action to CANUSER.

With these settings, we will explicitly permit specific groups access to files, and the users not in those groups will be denied access. We should plan to phase in the enforcement mode initially QUIET while we test the policy, WARN to try it out, and finally FAIL when we are ready to apply the policies.

Next define User Profiles for each user, and build User Groups for the various departments. We must also build asset groups for collections of files and directories that are used for various purposes. For example, we should build an asset group for the files shared by all the people in "accounting." Finally, we will write an access control rule permitting a user group to access the files used by that group. ●

Web Management

As the Internet marketplace approaches critical mass, the demand for Internet management infrastructure is about to explode exponentially. This is not only because Internet applications are more resource intensive (audio, video, chat, and VRML), but also because they will be increasingly linked to enterprise applications. Electronic commerce (e-commerce) will not happen in a vacuum; it will be linked to legacy databases and applications. As Internet applications become increasingly "mission critical," enterprise management solutions become crucially important in keeping them operational.

The imminent arrival of e-commerce implies that Web sites have already become companies' electronic front doors. Indeed, the World Wide Web has created an entirely new class of electronic services and information on a grand scale. Now users can conveniently span the globe in search of something. It may be information, or it may be an electronic commerce transaction.

Web surfing is as infamous as its predecessor, channel surfing. Web surfers are just as impatient as channel surfers, and yet response time is infinitely more variable. Surfers desire instant gratification, so delays mean moving on to the next site. Whether your site is dispensing information, goods, or services, attention span is a terrible thing to waste.

Being There

Most businesses create Web sites for marketing or sales purposes. Anyone visiting these sites is a potential customer. Every time a surfer gets impatient and leaves, it is a lost opportunity. Even more troubling is the distinct possibility that surfers will visit a competitor's site to find the same thing. Therefore, an effective Web presence requires professionally managed servers in terms of reliability, availability, and performance.

Professional management of Web sites has a number of implications. It means that servers should implement a "failover" capability, ensuring high availability (>99.96%). It means staffing by Internet specialists and 24×7 operations. It means eliminating single points of failure, whether they're network, system, database, or application dependencies. It means planning and distributing servers around Internet choke points to minimize traffic hops and application response time.

Hiring staff to manage mission-critical Internet sites will be challenging. Besides Internet backbone engineering specialists, management skills will be required for firewalls, encryption, digital signatures, IP multicasting, and "push" technologies, as well as intranet capacity planning and Internet performance analysis.

Security

Television, radio, and print advertising potentially reach wider audiences, but in terms of interactive media, the Internet is singularly accessible. It lets businesses conduct commerce with a more geographically distributed and diverse customer base than ever before. Furthermore, commerce on the Web can be quite efficient. As always, there are some tradeoffs to consider, because with accessibility comes exposure. Connecting to the Internet means taking the risk of being attacked. An attack can take the form of an Internet-borne virus, a break-in (to steal, snoop, or simply embarrass the organization), or the denial of network services. There are infinite permutations of these basic threats, so much so that a Web site exists for keeping track of hackers' latest Web site conquests!

Although general security was covered in Chapter 8, "Security," it is reviewed again here in a network context. Through the Internet, an organization can potentially provide computing services to remote employees, suppliers, commercial clients, and the general public. The open architecture exposes enterprises to security breaches ranging from simple mistakes to sabotage.

Ch
9

In order to protect valuable data and processes, an organization must set up a comprehensive security strategy to control access to the entire computing and communications infrastructure. This strategy begins with physical security for the resources (such as limiting access to the equipment and even to the buildings in which the equipment is located). It also includes access control implemented through the use of user IDs, passwords, and other user-authentication mechanisms. They also need to implement virus protection. If a company's network has even one point of connection to the Internet (as most do), it is necessary to set up firewalls to keep out unauthorized users while allowing authorized users open access to network resources. If dial-up access is permitted, this introduces further security requirements.

The Unicenter TNG Approach

Unicenter TNG can affect the management of an organization's Web site and services in a multitude of ways. Much of this has been discussed in prior chapters because a Web server is still, after all, a server. For example, Unicenter TNG Security Management provides a measure of protection for the files used by the Web server and for the application itself. The beauty of the system is that regardless of how someone enters the network, Unicenter TNG provides a filter to screen anyone accessing these resources. (For a refresher, revisit Chapter 8.)

A Web server needs to respond quickly and reliably to requests for information or attempts to process transactions. For a Web server to deliver HTML pages or transactions quickly, the underlying hardware and operating environment must contribute. Performance management for that machine is addressed in Chapter 4, "Server Management."

In addition to those functions discussed in other chapters, two components are particularly significant to Web management: the Network Security option and Web Management options. The Unicenter TNG Network Security option (NSO) provides a firewall and additional security layers over and above the system and application security provided by Unicenter TNG's Security Management component. NSO is designed to ensure that only authorized traffic moves between networks. It does this by examining packets crossing the boundary and preventing unauthorized packets from even entering the internal network. NSO can be set up to look at traffic between two internal networks, or with a supplier's network, or with the Internet.

An Internet connection requires more than additional security; it also requires the ability to manage the Web site itself. An organization may have thousands of Web pages spread across multiple servers, responding to the needs of diverse audiences. If such a Web site has not already done so, it will soon evolve into a mission-critical resource. In addition to access security, the site must be backed up, information must be verified for accuracy, and significant events must be logged.

Web Management options give the administrator an intuitive, easy way to monitor, maintain, troubleshoot, optimize, and repair Web sites. Through event and performance management, WMO ensures the reliability, efficiency, and security of Web sites accessed through intranets, extranets, and the Internet.

The remainder of this chapter is focused on the features and capabilities of the Java browser interface, NSO, and the Web Management options of Unicenter TNG and how these components facilitate Web site management.

Java Browser Interface

The Java browser interface allows you to manage a Web site with Unicenter TNG from virtually any Internet browser.

- It uses ordinary HTML to present (relatively) static information.
- It uses Java to build the more advanced user interfaces required to deal with all the complex information that Unicenter owns.
- It uses VRML—the Virtual Reality Modeling Language, the Internet standard for 3D information—to present the 3D views.

However, the Web browser does not connect directly to Unicenter TNG. There isn't anything to connect to. You need the Web browser plug to connect into a socket. A server provides the required socket.

Java Server

This server provides many valuable services. It presents the information that the browser needs: It formats reports and other information as HTML, it feeds the data to the Java interface, and it renders the network description from the repository into VRML files. It also acts as the initial launch point, delivering the Java applet down to the client.

To get its information, the server connects to all the services within the Unicenter architecture. Naturally, it gets the bulk of its information from the repository. Unicenter TNG does not send all *detail* information from the agents up to a centralized repository, however. Indeed, that much management traffic might well overload the network.

The agents and managers keep most detail information locally, sending only essential information, such as location, identification, object class, and status, up to the repository. The server needs to talk directly to managers spread across the network because Unicenter has a distributed architecture (see Figure 9.1). Still, for monitoring and managing a specific system, the browser can talk to an agent directly.

FIGURE 9.1
The Unicenter TNG
Architecture allows you
to manage from
anywhere.

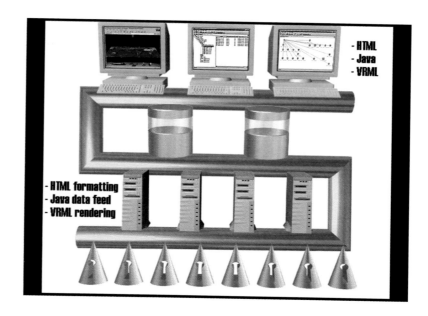

- HTML
- Java
- VRML

- HTML formatting
- Java data feed
- VRML rendering

Manage from Anywhere

This architecture allows you to manage your enterprise from anywhere.

The browser interface requires very little in the workstation. It needs connectivity to the network, a Web browser, a Java engine, and a VRML browser. These things are available everywhere these days:

Windows 95, including laptops

Microsoft Windows NT

UNIX systems like Solaris, HP-UX, AIX

Graphics workstations, like those from SGI

Macintosh systems

Network computers, like the JavaStation

Handheld computers

Soon even cellular telephones, wristwatches, and automobiles will support Java-enabled Web browsers.

Look and Feel

The look and feel of the browser interface is modeled on the standard Unicenter TNG interface. This user interface builds on the previous paradigm because it is well understood by thousands of users.

However, the structure of the interface has been consolidated to bring together GUI elements that better fit the browser metaphor. In particular, the system tries to present most information in a single window, which is the common approach in browsers.

Real World Interface

The browser interface included with the Real World Interface provides a 3D view of the world, the network, and the resources in it. The browser version of this 3D view is also quite similar to the "classical" version. In the browser interface, the Real World Interface is built using VRML, the Virtual Reality Modeling Language, which is an emerging standard for 3D content on the Web.

You can navigate through the world, either manually or in auto-pilot mode, by clicking on objects. The status of objects is displayed with the familiar red light. The 2D map navigation works identically, meaning that double-clicking on icons enters them and opens up details.

Unicenter Explorer

The tree browser lists the objects in the containment hierarchy, from countries, cities, and buildings, through networks and subnetworks, down to computers, disk drives, databases, and processes.

The right pane can take on various appearances, just like in the common Windows Explorer: detailed list, icon list, and small and large icons. In addition, the Unicenter Explorer—style interface provides the 2D map in the right pane as another arrangement of the contents of the tree. The Property notebook works in the Explorer-style browser as well; the detailed properties and status of any object in the tree are displayed in the right pane.

Infinite Drill Down

The tree browser, 2D map, 3D map, and notebooks represent information in the repository, which knows which objects exist and their main properties, including their status.

At times, you'll need to view detailed, real-time data. As mentioned before, this information is not resident in the central repository. The Explorer-style browser allows you to get at such data using the tree structure by drilling down into the system. By opening up the target computer's Unispace, the managers that are controlling the machine (or the agents that are monitoring it) become accessible. All the managed objects in the system—the file systems, memory, CPUs, and active processes—appear in the tree, seamlessly integrated with the larger objects such as computers, networks, and buildings.

Thus, the browser hides the data source distinction from the user: A network is simply viewed as a containment hierarchy, and the browser provides nearly infinite drill-down, regardless of the management component actually providing the data.

Real-Time Data

For second-by-second data on what is happening in the managed systems—how full the disk drive is, how busy the CPU is, and so on—the Explorer needs to talk to the agent that is actually monitoring the systems.

The browser offers an Agent View that displays dynamic metrics sent by the agent. The Agent View provides a number of pages, each with a number of controls. The actual configuration can be tailored depending on the situation: Each agent monitors different data and provides an appropriate representation updating its measurements. Agent View also allows management of the agent. For example, the user can alter alarm thresholds, the poll interval, and other agent policy specifications.

Performance Monitoring

The browser can also monitor performance data coming back from the Performance agent. For each object selected in the tree browser (or elsewhere), the performance monitor shows an appropriate metric. It also permits explicit selection of which metric to monitor. The performance scope shows the real-time metric, continually updated, compared with the historical data for the same parameter in the left pane of the chart.

Management and Administration

Inside Unispace, each system presents its management and administration functions: event management, storage management, workload management, software distribution, and so on. Most management disciplines display data in some form of familiar notebook. For example, under Event Management is Message Record, which displays a list of message records in the right pane of the Explorer. Opening a message record shows a notebook with the various categories of properties of that record.

Reporting and Documentation

The Report Browser shows the various categories of reports available. The report is displayed in the Web browser in the form of HTML text. The Web browser displays product help files and online documentation. The help system uses a similar split screen with a table of contents in the left pane, allowing you to select a chapter while presenting the detailed information in the frame on the bottom.

Unicenter TNG Network Security Option (NSO)

The Unicenter TNG Network Security Option (NSO) provides environmental protection against network security breaches. The basis of this protection is a firewall with additional security mechanisms that control the flow of network traffic to and from critical servers. NSO provides packet filtering, dynamic interface detection, anti-spoofing, and network address translation.

Beyond supplying a firewall, NSO acts as a user-aware IP network traffic security management tool. Additionally, firewall rules can be defined centrally and propagated to all firewalls on the network, regardless of manufacturer. Any subsequent security events can be routed back to the Unicenter TNG event console.

Administrators benefit from more granular control over who can access the company network (by individual server or the entire intranet), from where access is allowed, and when that access may occur. This grants the flexibility that administrators need to prevent users from accessing sensitive servers from unknown or untrusted entry points. The product does the following:

- Implements default security rules even before activation of the network connection, thus preventing breaches during initialization.
- Bases initial connection rules on user ID and IP address.
- Provides automatic spoofing protection by creating private routing tables within connection state tables, so that replaying captured session traffic will not fool the firewall.
- Creates state tables (tracking connections as well as packets) used for automatically shutting down traffic that violates policy, using as criteria which user sessions are allowed to access which addresses.

Another feature of NSO evaluates outbound network requests, prohibiting company employees from visiting unproductive or undesirable Web sites. Finally, NSO includes complete user auditing so that both permitted and denied network accesses are recorded for future reference.

NSO can also be fully integrated with the Unicenter TNG Single Sign-On option. Once installed, NSO is largely transparent to users (other than identification and authentication of users), and no applications need to be modified in order to implement and use NSO.

The NSO is designed to defeat a variety of network attacks. Following are some of the more common types of network attacks addressed by NSO and the defense techniques used to defeat them:

Attack   Spoofing—Impersonating an IP address different from the actual one (usually by replaying captured traffic from the impersonated site) in order to gain access.

Defense   Check against IP address, user authentication, and network interface. This prevents external users from claiming to be internal users because their packets are entering on the external network interface.

Attack   TCP sequence number prediction attacks—Establishing a session by predicting the TCP session sequence number and generating valid acknowledgments.

Defense   Require user authentication and continuously monitor active connections.

Attack IP options attacks—IP header options specifying explicit packet routing.

Defense Drop all packets with IP header options specified.

Attack RIP attacks—Requests to change routing information.

Defense An NSO policy can be defined to reject all RIP requests.

Attack ICMP attacks—Some ICMP messages can create network problems.

Defense An NSO policy can be defined to reject all ICMP messages.

Attack Data-driven attacks (SMTP and MIME)—Email messages with encoded and executable code.

Defense Filter based upon user ID and source/destination addresses and reject packets. A more complete solution would be to use bastion hosts for troublesome protocols, use address translation to hide the bastion host, and allow program execution only on the bastion host.

Attack DNS attacks—A DNS request could expose the internal structure of the network.

Defense Use a bastion host with an external DNS server and no information about internal structure.

Attack Fragment attacks—Packet fragments without a first fragment containing port numbers.

Defense Maintain information on connection states (pseudo-connections) and reject any packet fragments not associated with a first packet.

Attack Tiny fragment attacks—Overlaying packet headers with offset values in subsequent packets.

Defense Ensure header information is not changed when packet fragments are reassembled.

Attack Hijacking attacks—Taking over sessions from authenticated users. This requires hijacking software on the server.

Defense Standard NSO security prevents unauthorized root access to servers.

Attack Data integrity attacks—Interception and modification of packets.

Defense Verify header information, packet length, checksums, and other information.

Attack Encapsulated IP attacks—packets within packets.

Defense Extract embedded packets and subject them to the same packet-filtering rules.

The Unicenter TNG NSO provides firewall capabilities to protect a network from these and other types of unauthorized access.

NSO in Action

In this example, as the system administrator, you will work through steps necessary to control access to a confidential document server using NSO. The following table summarizes the steps in this scenario:

Step	Description
1	Define an NIC name in the `nso_svc_pol` file.
2	Define a Network Address Translation rule to hide the address of the confidential document server.
3	Define a Net Access rule using the new address.
4	Activate the new rules.
5	Define a new service policy.
6	Define a new rule based on the new service.

Defining a Network Interface Connection

Defining NIC names to represent actual network interface connections and then using the NIC names when writing Net Access rules makes it easier to adapt to changing requirements. This extra level of indirection, for example, prevents you from having to modify rules in the event of a network change.

Because writing and maintaining Net Access rules will be much easier if you start by defining NIC names, you will start by performing the following steps:

1. On the machine that functions as the confidential document server, determine which network interface connections exist. The response shows the following address and NIC name:

   ```
   hostname lan0
   ```

2. Edit the `nso_svc_pol` file, adding the following entry at the beginning, immediately after the `NSO_GREEN` statement:

   ```
   NIC hostname, external
   NIC_NAME lan0
   END_NIC
   ```

   In this entry, `hostname` is the name of the system where the NIC is installed and `external` is the name you will use to reference it.

3. Save the file and close it.

Defining a Network Address Translation Rule

The flexibility introduced through Network Address Translation comes in handy. It enables network setup to better reflect the organizational structure. When changing Internet service providers, Network Address Translation allows the organization to keep the same IP addresses internally, preventing lots of unproductive wheel-spinning. It can add an extra layer of security by obscuring the native address of network servers from hostile observation. This security dimension is what we will focus on next.

You want to make sure that the machine on the internal network where confidential document processing is maintained is not visible to the outside. You will write a Network Address Translation rule to automatically translate this node address into a different one. After finding an IP address on the same subnet that is not in use or planned for use, follow these steps:

1. Start Unicenter TNG Enterprise Management for the server.
2. After logging on to the server by way of the Logon icon, open the NetSecurity folder from the server's Enterprise Management window (see Figure 9.2).

Ch
9

FIGURE 9.2
Open the NetSecurity folder.

3. Open Address Translation from the NetSecurity folder window (see Figure 9.3).

FIGURE 9.3
Open the Address Translation container window.

The Net Address Translation Rules container window appears (see Figure 9.4).

FIGURE 9.4
The Net Address Translation Rules window.

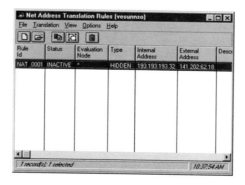

Because this is a new installation of Unicenter TNG/NSO, no existing Net Address Translation rules are displayed.

4. Next, choose New from the Translation menu.

The Net Address Translation - Detail window opens (see Figure 9.5).

FIGURE 9.5

The Net Address Translation - Detail window.

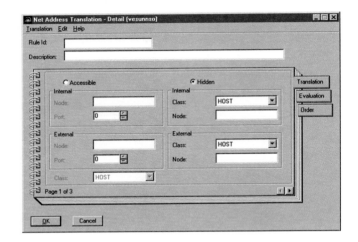

5. Enter the following data:

- For Rule Id, specify NAT_rule_1.
- For Description, enter test NAT rule 1.
- For Type, specify Hidden.
- For Internal Class, specify Network.
- For Internal Node, enter the subnet address for the confidential document processing systems.
- For External Class, specify Host.
- For External Node, enter the unused IP address on the subnet.

6. Click the Evaluation tab to bring up the Evaluation notebook page (see Figure 9.6).

7. You do not need to change the default values for Evaluation Class (Host) and Node (*).

Select the Active radio button to activate this rule and elect not to specify dates at this time.

8. Click on the Order tab to bring up the Order notebook page (see Figure 9.7).

Select First from the selections in the Order of Evaluation list.

9. Click OK to save the NAT rule definition and return to the Net Address Translation Rules container window.

10. Choose Folder Close to return to the NetSecurity folder window.

FIGURE 9.6

The Evaluation page of the Net Address Translation notebook.

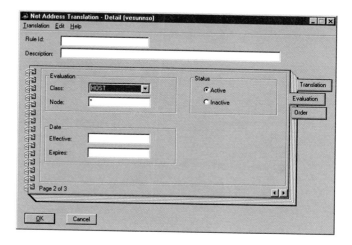

FIGURE 9.7

The Order page of the Net Address Translation notebook.

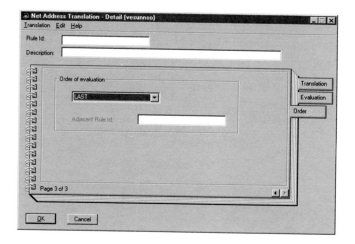

Defining a Net Access Rule

Net Access rules provide a bulk facility for administering, restraining, and confining server access. For example, if you defined network servers as stations belonging to station groups for workload scheduling (see Chapter 4), you could leverage those definitions. Net Access rules can be applied to those servers just as scheduling rules were applied to them.

For the time being, you want to make sure that users on the confidential document subnet can use only telnet to access the rest of our network. You will define a Net Access rule that restricts outgoing access to just telnet:

1. Open Net Access from the NetSecurity folder window.

    The Net Access Rules container window appears (see Figure 9.8).

FIGURE 9.8

The Net Access Rules container window.

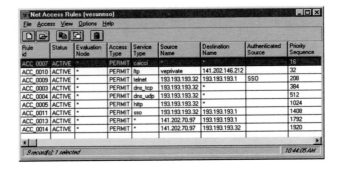

There are already a number of Net Access rules defined, so this container is populated with them. Now you're ready to bring in the confidential document subnet.

2. Choose New from the Access pull-down menu.

   The Net Access Rule - Detail window appears (see Figure 9.9).

FIGURE 9.9

The Net Access Rule - Detail window.

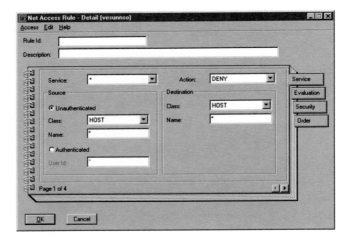

3. Enter the following data into the appropriate fields, using the Tab key or mouse pointer to move between fields:

   For Rule ID, enter `telnet_only`.

   For Description, enter `Limits access to telnet only`.

   For Service, specify Telnet.

   Click the Unauthenticated radio button to indicate that the rule is not being written for authenticated users.

   For Source Class, specify Host.

   For Source Name, enter the confidential document hidden external host address specified in the previous Net rule definition.

For Destination Class, specify NIC.

For Destination Name, specify external.

For Action, specify PERMIT.

4. Click the Evaluation tab to display the Evaluation notebook page (see Figure 9.10).

FIGURE 9.10

The Evaluation page of the Net Access Rule notebook.

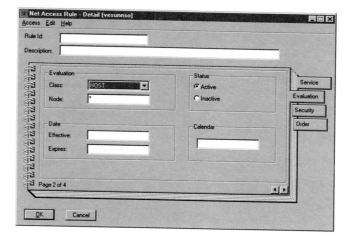

5. Enter the Evaluation node and Class information and choose Active for the Status.

6. Then click on the Security tab to bring up the Security notebook page (see Figure 9.11).

FIGURE 9.11

The Security page of the Net Access Rule notebook.

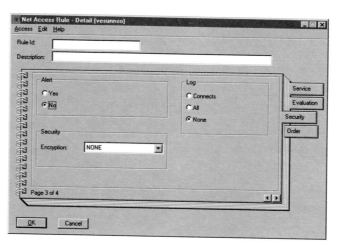

Specify values for Alert, Encryption, and Log.

7. Finally, click on the Order tab to bring up the Order notebook page (see Figure 9.12).

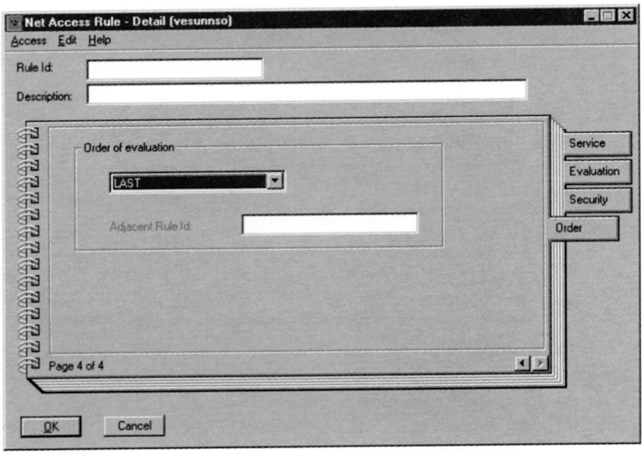

FIGURE 9.12

The Order page of the Net Access Rule notebook.

8. Specify FIRST for the Order of Evaluation for this rule. That means that all connection attempts from the specified source to the specified destination will be evaluated using this rule before any others.

   Click OK to save the test rule and return to the Net Access Rules container window. Although you could choose File, Commit to activate the new rule now, you'll perform this step later.

9. Close the window to return to the NSO folder window.

10. Close the window again to return to the server's Enterprise Management window.

Activating the New Rules

Another reason for Net Access rules is to handle idiosyncratic situations. If an organization uses some non-standard communication services, such as those embedded in legacy applications, it is convenient to add a service policy definition and then define Net Access rules for that service. After defining those rules, you need to activate them.

Exit the GUI and compile, load, and restart the new rules. Here is a sample:

```
nso_admin -compile
nso_admin -load
nso_admin_-start
```

See the *NSO Administrator's Guide* for complete syntax details. This makes the rules an active part of your NSO security configuration.

N O T E You should have access to the system console when restarting NSO, because it is theoretically possible to disable all network access to a system. ■

Defining a New Service Policy

Later, you may need to add a new service policy to the company's NSO security scheme. In this step, you define a policy for your own service, `my_svc_pol`, which is similar to telnet. First, you may want to make a backup copy of the `nso_svc_pol` file in the `$CAIGLBL0000\nso\config` directory:

1. Change to the subdirectory `$CAIGLBL0000\nso\config`:

   ```
   cd $CAIGLBL0000\nso\config
   ```

2. Edit the file `nso_svc_pol`. This file contains basic service policy definitions.

3. Define the new service policy as follows:

   ```
   SVC_POL, my_svc_pol,
      CHECK_TCP,
      CHECK_TO_PORT, 23,
      CHECK_FROM_PORT, PF_PORT_GE_1024,
      CHECK_FLAGS, CONNECT_FLAG,
      CREATE_CONNECTION, normal,
   END_SVC_POL
   ```

   Save the file and close.

4. Compile the rules, using the `nso_admin-compile` command, so that NSO can recognize the new policy.

Writing a Rule for the New Service Policy

Now you will see that if you open the Net Access Rules folder and choose Access, New to insert a new rule, the new service policy, `my_svc_pol`, will appear with the other services. This is the method you would use to define a rule for the new service.

You can define a rule for it, but since this is not a legitimate service and a real packet will never arrive, the rule evaluator will never select the rule. Nevertheless, you have carried out the steps required to define a service policy.

This brings up a novel way to discourage intruders. You can write network rules that *deny* access without sending any message to the sender. They have to wait until the attempt times out, which is annoying. However, specifying the more polite and timely DENY with ICMP for internal customers is a good idea.

Testing Security Rules

Testing out new rules before deploying them broadly is not only a good idea, it's absolutely necessary. While testing a new concept, it is possible to use temporary rules before instituting them as a set policy. For example, in protecting against shock-attacks, a rapid series of connections that can overwhelm your systems (also known as *denial of service*), you will want to install a filtering rule. This rule should block the source of the attack but not shut out the innocent, let alone everyone. You can use NSO to automatically protect your server by writing a temporary rule denying access to the intruder, refining it over time as necessary.

If you were actually carrying out the procedures described previously, you would now test whether NSO is working as anticipated. You would try to telnet to the confidential document server from outside the subnet. The attempt would time out. You would then attempt to make an FTP connection from one of the confidential systems to a node on the outside. This attempt would also time out. You would then attempt to connect to the same outside node using telnet instead of FTP. This time the attempt would be successful, verifying that NSO is operating as intended.

Unicenter TNG Web Management Options (WMO)

The Unicenter TNG Web Management Options enable comprehensive management of intranet, extranet, and Internet Web sites to make business processing reliable, efficient, and secure.

For example, agents provide true end-to-end management of the Web environment, timely notification of error conditions and performance degradation, and automated monitoring of all Web elements. Unicenter TNG/WMO makes it possible to manage Web site health and performance on an enterprisewide scale. It helps to control the total cost of ownership and improve the level of service by providing the following:

- A comprehensive model for integrated Web site management
- Site monitoring with (optional) automatic corrective actions
- Centralized event correlation and policy-based management
- Correlation of site health and performance from both end user and server perspectives
- Correlation of Web site performance with Web server OS and network response
- Reporting across multiple sites (real-time and historical)
- A Unicenter TNG Java-based Web interface for untethered management

Web Agents

Two key components of WMO are the Web Response Agent and Web Server Agent. The Web Response Agent provides automated, enterprisewide health and performance monitoring from the user (or Web browser) perspective. The Web Server Agents are intelligent, programmable agents that monitor the health and performance of a Web server/site. Events from the Web Response Agent can be correlated with information reported by the Web Server Agent. In addition, other Unicenter TNG agents, such as System Agent (which the Web server is running on), Network Response Option Agent, Database Agents, and Microsoft Transaction Server Agent, can be correlated to provide truly comprehensive end-to-end management.

Web Response Agents   Unicenter TNG/WMO includes a Web Response Agent that remotely monitors the accessibility of the Web server. This allows the site administrator to immediately detect and respond to server and network performance problems. The agent impersonates a Web browser by accessing the Web server from a remote Unicenter TNG server and periodically reports availability based on the response time of the server.

Web Response Agents can reside on one or more geographically distributed systems and can use standard Internet protocols to monitor the health and performance from the *user perspective*. The agent uses a combination of Ping, DNS protocol, FTP, HTTP, and HTTPS to determine the availability, round-trip response, and content of select URLs. The agent saves the route used to access the service as a string. The agent also automatically correlates the status of Ping, DNS, FTP, HTTP, and HTTPS for better problem resolution.

The features that apply to the overall operation of the Web Response Agent follow:

- **FTP**. The administrator can monitor URLs with an FTP scheme (such as `ftp://ftp.cai.com/readme.txt`). The agent will attempt to use FTP to copy the file and compute the delta time (from when the request was made) when the first byte was received and the last byte was received. The administrator can optionally specify a CRC to verify the content of the file.

- **HTTP**. The administrator can monitor URLs with an HTTP scheme (such as `http://www.cai.com/`). The agent will attempt to use HTTP to retrieve the URL and compute the delta time (from when the request was made) when the first byte was received and the last byte was received. The administrator can optionally specify a string or CRC to verify the contents of the URL. The agent can retrieve all of the components of the URL (page) or just the main body. Any components of the page that cannot be retrieved will result in an event report and content error status. The administrator can configure the number of concurrent threads to create when retrieving a single URL and the maximum number of URLs the agent will attempt to retrieve simultaneously. All caching is disabled, and the agent computes the total number of bytes received and the average throughput. CGI and ASP are handled just like HTML.

  The administrator can provide a script that permits posting input to the Web server. In the first release, the administrator can specify a "quoted string" or a file. If a file is specified, the agent encodes each line and sends an URL-encoded script.

- **Proxy**. The agent supports proxy configuration on a per-URL basis.

- **Diagnosis**. The agent issues a Ping and/or DNS test to diagnose service errors automatically. The administrator can control the operation for each status: normal, warning, and critical. For example:

  Normal—URL

  Warning—Ping, URL

  Critical—Ping, DNS, URL

  In the preceding example, the agent will normally access the URL. In critical status (a time out or unrecoverable error), the agent will issue a Ping test and a DNS test and will attempt to access the URL.

- **Correlation**. The agent automatically correlates Ping, DNS, FTP, and HTTP status. For each URL monitored, the Ping response, DNS response and accuracy, and FTP and HTTP response and accuracy are displayed.

- **Historical Reporting**. The default configuration for historical data collection is the URL name, the current and average time it takes to receive the first byte and last byte, and the total number of bytes transferred.

Web Server Agent   The Web Server Agent monitors the Web server for the Webmaster. The Webmaster can use the agent to monitor the same set of URLs as the Web Response Agent. Events from the Web Response Agent can be automatically correlated with information reported by the Web Server Agent. This also allows the Webmaster to engineer performance by correlating round-trip response time as perceived by the end user, with performance metrics generated by the Web servers. In addition, information from other Unicenter TNG agents, such as the System Agent (on which the Web server is running), NSO Agent, Response Manager Option Agent, and Database Agents can be correlated to provide end-to-end management.

The Web Server Agents are intelligent, programmable agents that can monitor the health and performance of a Web server/site. Web Server Agent will support the following platforms:

- Microsoft IIS
- Netscape Enterprise Server
- Netscape FastTrack Server
- Apache Web Server
- Sun Java Server
- Lotus Domino Web

The features that generally apply to the overall operation of the Web Server Agents follow. The Web Server Agents implement a consistent model for the monitoring and management of Web servers:

- **Status**. The agent maintains and reports three levels of status: normal, warning, and critical. Status (or state) is summarized at the component instance level and is propagated up to the component container and to the agent (top level). The administrator can easily determine the overall state of the agent by examining a single attribute. This propagation provides for progressive disclosure when drilling down to isolate the source of a problem. Summary status counts are maintained on a component basis, including the number of instances being monitored and the number that have warning and critical status.

- **Reset**. The administrator can reset the alert counts and statistics on demand. In addition, an automatic reset interval can be specified. The agent will reset the values to zero automatically at the specified interval. An interval of zero disables the automated reset.

- **Statistics and Availability**. The agent computes the current response time, high, low, rolling average, and standard deviation. In addition, the agent computes the availability of a service.

- **Thresholds/Actions**. The administrator can define warning and critical thresholds. A warning threshold must have a value that is less than or equal to the critical threshold. This is enforced by the agent. A warning or critical threshold can be enabled/disabled.

Corresponding to each threshold, a local action can be specified. A local action is simply a command line that is executed within the context of the system the agent is running on. An audit log is maintained by the agent, which includes the command line, a time stamp, and status. If the command line fails, an event is reported. Regardless of the status, an event is reported to indicate that the local action was taken, which provides a convenient audit on the manager.

- **Services**. The agent can automatically monitor and restart stopped services/daemons (such as HTTP, FTP, and so on) and can optionally reboot the Web server after n failed restart attempts.

- **Counters**. The agent can be customized to monitor a select set of counters, which indicate the performance of the Web server.

- **Disk Space**. The agent monitors workspace, log files, and Web content disks for available free disk space.

- **FTP**. The Webmaster can monitor select URLs with an FTP scheme (such as `ftp://ftp.cai.com/readme.txt`). The agent will keep real-time statistics and records the number of hits, invalid logins, IP disconnects, and response time, including the preceding statistics.

- **HTTP**. The Webmaster can monitor select URLs with an HTTP scheme (such as `http://www.cai.com/`). The agent will keep real-time statistics and records the number of hits, invalid logins, HTTP errors, IP disconnects, and response time, including the preceding statistics. The agent will record the peak number of simultaneous hits within a specified interval, such as 50 hits within 10 seconds. The agent can also be configured to reject a request if the number of simultaneous hits exceeds a threshold.

- **Web Crawler**. The agent uses a low-priority thread to crawl all of the links on the Web site, and reports any errors (bad links) into a "bad link" table. Real-time HTTP errors are reported in the table also.

- **Event Notification**. All errors and status changes result in an event report (SNMP Trap) to the DSM Manager, which in turn reports messages to the Event Manager component of Unicenter TNG. The DSM permits event correlation across objects and systems. Event Manager includes a number of methods for programmed event action.

- **Aggressive Retry**. When a warning or critical status is detected, the agent will automatically shorten the monitor interval, in effect performing an aggressive retry. The agent will automatically return to the regular schedule when status is normal. Put another way, three monitor intervals can be specified for each row in the table: normal, warning, and critical.

- **Correlation**. The Webmaster can define a cluster of Web servers, which makes up a Web site. DSM Policy will automatically correlate this information and create a Web site container. Each Web server is managed separately, but the status is propagated to the Web site.

Using the Web Management Option

To illustrate some of these features, this chapter uses a scenario to describe how to diagnose Web-related problems using the Unicenter TNG Web Management Option. Consider the following business process view.

In this business process view, the Web network is in Warning status, as indicated by the yellow Web Network icon. To determine the cause, double-click the Web Network icon (see Figure 9.13).

FIGURE 9.13
Select the Web Network icon.

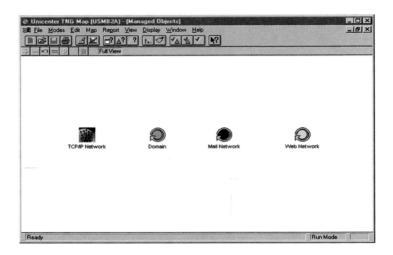

The map for the Web network appears, as shown in Figure 9.14.

FIGURE 9.14
The 2D map of the Web network.

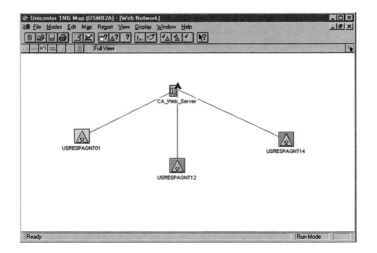

This window illustrates the Web environment with CA_Web_Server and three Response Agents. In this configuration there is a Web Server Agent on the Web server (CA_Web_Server) monitoring from the "inside." The three Web Response Agents are located throughout the network (USRESPAGNTxx) in different geographical locations, monitoring the Web server from the "outside" or the user's perspective.

Their status is shown by the coloring of the icon:

- The CA_Web_Server agent is in warning status.
- The Response Agent, USRESPAGNT01, is in warning status.
- The Response Agent, USRESPAGNT12, is in normal status.
- The Response Agent, USRESPAGNT14, is in normal status.

Because the state of a Response Agent propagates up to the Business Process View, the icon for the Web Network is warning. This reflects the most serious error condition of any of its components.

From this window, you can see the various components (both Server Agent and Response Agents) and their relationships, as well as their current states.

To determine the specific cause for the warning state, let's drill down into the components and look at more details through the user interfaces available in the Web Management Option.

Using the Web Response Agent

To open the Response Agent for USRESPAGNT01:

1. Click the right mouse button on the USRESPAGNT01 icon.
2. Select View Agent from the pop-up menu.

The Summary window appears (see Figure 9.15).

FIGURE 9.15
The Summary window.

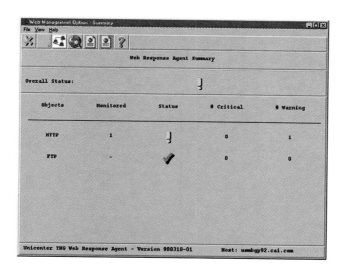

The Summary window for the Web Response Agent provides a view into how many URLs (either HTTP or FTP) are being monitored, the status of the URL(s), and the number of occurrences of each severity level.

From the Summary window, you can determine that an error was detected when polling an URL using HTTP and that the error is a warning-level error.

Examining HTTP Errors

To determine the precise error, drill down to examine the HTTP Errors window. To do this, click the HTTP Errors button on the toolbar. The HTTP Errors window appears (see Figure 9.16).

FIGURE 9.16
The HTTP Errors window.

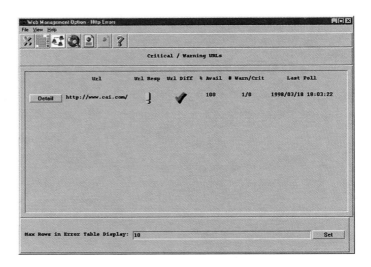

The HTTP Errors window lists all URLs being monitored by this agent that are currently in an error state. It displays the URL name and the source of the error (a response time error or a content difference error).

Additionally, the window displays the URL availability percentage for each URL (determined by the number of polls attempted and the number of timeouts that resulted). It also displays the number of warning and critical events since the last reset, and the date and time of the last poll.

From the HTTP Errors window, you can determine that the error condition exists because the expected response time for the URL being monitored, `http://www.cai.com`, was exceeded.

Viewing Detail Status

To get more information about the performance of the URL as a result of monitoring requests from this agent, drill down into the Detail Status window. To view the details, click the Detail button. The Detail Status window appears (see Figure 9.17).

FIGURE 9.17

The Detail Status window.

The Detail Status window shows the results of polling the specific URL using the different monitoring schemes available (URL, DNS, and Ping). This window displays a snapshot of URL, DNS, and Ping status, which provides an overall picture of the health of the URL from the client perspective.

In this example, the URL response time was greater than expected, but the URL content, DNS response and accuracy, and Ping response were within specified limits.

Viewing URL Details

To get more detailed information about the expected and actual response time for this URL error condition, click the URL button on the Detail Status window. The Detail window for the specific URL appears (see Figure 9.18).

FIGURE 9.18

The Detail window for the URL www.cai.com.

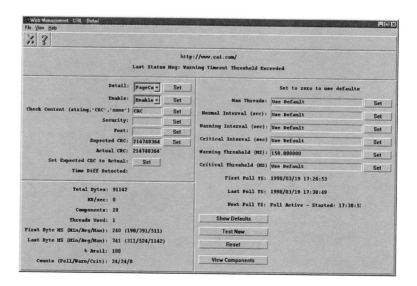

The following list describes the fields in the Detail window:

- **Title section**—Displays the name of the URL being retrieved and the status of the last poll.

- **Detail**—Selects which components are being requested from the URL. You can choose to retrieve the header, a component summary, or component details. If you choose component details, you can view statistics on each component in the URL.

- **Enable**—Turns on/off polling for this URL, based on the information in this window.

- **Check Content**—Describes how the information retrieved from the URL can be verified. You can choose a string (for dynamic content), a CRC (for static content), or none.

- **Security**—Sets security for user/password, SSL, or certificates.

- **Post**—Specifies the name of a file for input to the URL.

- **Expected CRC**—This is the CRC used to check the data received.

- **Actual CRC**—This is the CRC computed from the data received.

- **Set Expected CRC to Actual**—Loads the CRC used to check the data with the last computed CRC value.

- **Time Diff Detected**—Displays a timestamp of content check failure.

- **Total Bytes**—Displays the number of bytes of data received from the URL.

- **KB/sec**—Displays the calculated average transfer rate of the last poll.

- **Components**—Displays the number of URL components contained in the last poll.

- **Threads Used**—Displays the number of concurrent threads used during the last poll.

- **First Byte MS**—Displays the elapsed time, in milliseconds, from when the request was made to when the first byte of data was received.

- **Last Byte MS**—Displays the elapsed time, in milliseconds, from when the request was made to when the last byte of data was received.

- **(Min/Avg/Max)**—Displays the minimum, average, and maximum time, in milliseconds, since the last reset for First Byte and Last Byte.

- **% Avail**—Displays the number of polls divided by number of timed-out attempts (to determine the percentage that the URL was available).

- **Counts (Poll/Warn/Crit)**—Displays the number of polls, warnings (slow), and criticals (timeout) recorded since the last reset.

- **Max Threads**—Specifies the maximum number of threads to use to poll an URL.

- **Normal Interval**—Specifies the number of seconds between polls when status is not warning or critical.

- **Warning Interval**—Specifies the number of seconds between polls when status is warning.

- **Critical Interval**—Specifies the number of seconds between polls when status is critical.
- **Warning Threshold**—Specifies the number of milliseconds that, if exceeded by the measured response of the current value of Last Byte MS, set the status to warning.
- **Critical Threshold**—Specifies the number of milliseconds that, if exceeded by the measured response of the current value of Last Byte MS, sets the status to critical.
- **First Poll TS**—Displays the time and date of the first poll since the last reset.
- **Last Poll TS**—Displays the time and date of the last poll.
- **Show Defaults**—Displays the defaults for settable values.
- **Test Now**—Forces an immediate poll for the monitored URL.
- **Reset**—Resets the counters for the monitored URL.
- **Delete**—Deletes all the information in this window for the monitored URL.
- **View Components**—Displays a window of information on polled URL components.

From this window, you can see that for this URL, the Warning Threshold for response time was set at 150ms. During a poll of the URL, a response time of 741ms (for the Last Byte) was recorded. Therefore, because the Warning Threshold was exceeded, the status changed from normal to warning.

Other information of interest is contained in the First Byte and Last Byte (Min/Avg/Max) fields. These values show how the URL has performed (responsiveness) over time (since last reset) and how that performance has varied. This gives the Web administrator valuable information in analyzing the effects of server load and network latency on the server's performance, from the user's perspective. Additionally, the Counts (Poll/Warn/Crit) field tells the Web administrator the number of times the thresholds were exceeded for a given number of polls. In this example, the response to all polls since the last reset exceeded the Warning Threshold level.

Viewing URL Component Details

To look at the individual URL component response times, click the View Components button. The URL Components window appears (see Figure 9.19).

The URL Components window displays a list of the URL components, the status of the component download (OK indicates that the component was found and successfully downloaded), the CRC for the component, the size of the components, and the First Byte and Last Byte response times.

A Web administrator would look for any error status for a component and/or any significant gaps between First Byte and Last Byte, indicating a possible resource problem at the server.

From the information displayed in these last two windows, you can see that the data contained in the URL components was not delivered within the expected response time.

At this point, let's look at the Web Server Agent that is monitoring the server containing the URL to determine the cause of the unexpected slow response.

FIGURE 9.19
The URL Components
window.

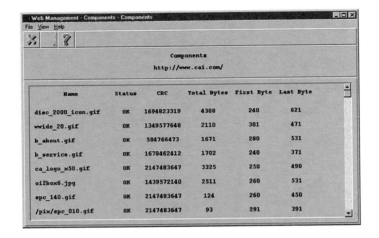

Using the Web Server Agent

To open the Server Agent from the Web Network window:

1. Click the right mouse button on the CA_Web_Server icon.

2. Select View Agent for the pop-up menu.

   The Summary window appears (see Figure 9.20).

FIGURE 9.20
The Summary window.

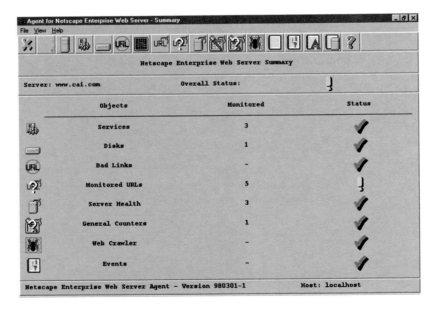

The Summary window for the Web Server Agent provides a view into the different objects of the server that are being monitored, how many instances of the object are being monitored, and the most severe state of any instance of the object being monitored.

The Web Server Agent can monitor and automatically restart Services (such as HTTP and FTP) and has the capability to reboot the Web server if necessary.

Disk space for workspace, log file, and Web content can be monitored, and warning and critical thresholds can be set.

Any requests that result in a Bad Link (not found) can be retained and listed.

URLs can be specified for a list of Monitored URLs, which can be monitored for disconnects, HTTP errors, hits, invalid logins, peak hits, and response time.

Server Health can monitor and display server CPU usage and number of processes, the number of requests per second, and the number of bytes transferred per second. Warning and critical thresholds can be set on these rates and CPU usage.

The Server Agent can monitor a set of General Counters, which track information like the number of requests (of various types such as HTTP, FTP, CGI, search, and post) in the form of rates and/or totals, the amount of data transferred as a result of requests, and server processes either idle or busy.

The Web Crawler traces paths through all of the links in the server and reports and retains all bad link information.

Events (which are specific to a vendor's Web server) can be selected for monitoring, and warning and critical thresholds can be assigned. Important events, along with context information, can be retained by the agent.

From this window, you can see that the Monitored URLs object is in a warning state. Drill down into these objects to see if there is a correlation between the Response Agent problem and the monitored condition of the server.

Viewing Details on Monitored URLs

Review the monitored URLs by clicking on the URL? button on the toolbar. The Monitored URLs window appears (see Figure 9.21).

The Monitored URLs window for the Web Server Agent provides a view into the specific URL and attribute being monitored. The status and attribute description is shown next to the URL, and the value the of the attribute is displayed along with the warning and critical threshold values.

In this example, you can see that the URL www.cai.com (shown in the upper part of the window as the Server: URL and represented by the / in the URL column) has exceeded its Peak Hits rate. Based on the information displayed, this URL received 15 hits in 10 seconds, which exceeded the warning level threshold of 14 hits in 10 seconds.

FIGURE 9.21
The Monitored URLs
window.

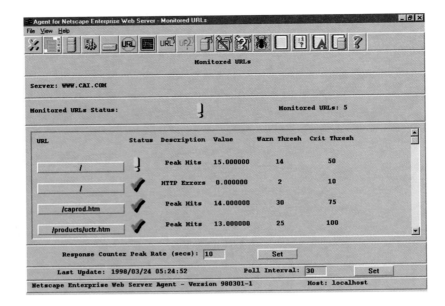

This condition shows that the load on the server exceeded the normal expectations and is likely to have caused the slow response time monitored by the Response Agent.

As a result of the Peak Hits and Response Time warnings that occurred at the Web Response Agent, the Web administrator decides to begin monitoring response time to requests. Now the agent will watch requests to the URL in question. This will give the administrator additional information in understanding the effect of load on server responsiveness.

By monitoring this URL (see Figure 9.22) from both the "inside" (Server Agent) and the "outside" (Response Agent), the administrator will be able to determine if actions such as increasing server capacity or limiting simultaneous connections are appropriate.

Additional Details and Functions of the Web Server Agent

In addition to the Summary and Monitored URLs windows, the Web administrator can select and view various counters for the server or an URL.

In the windows shown in Figure 9.23, the Web administrator can view the available general counters for the server and add a counter for monitoring.

Here the administrator has chosen to add a counter to monitor the number of GET requests received per second and has set warning and critical thresholds.

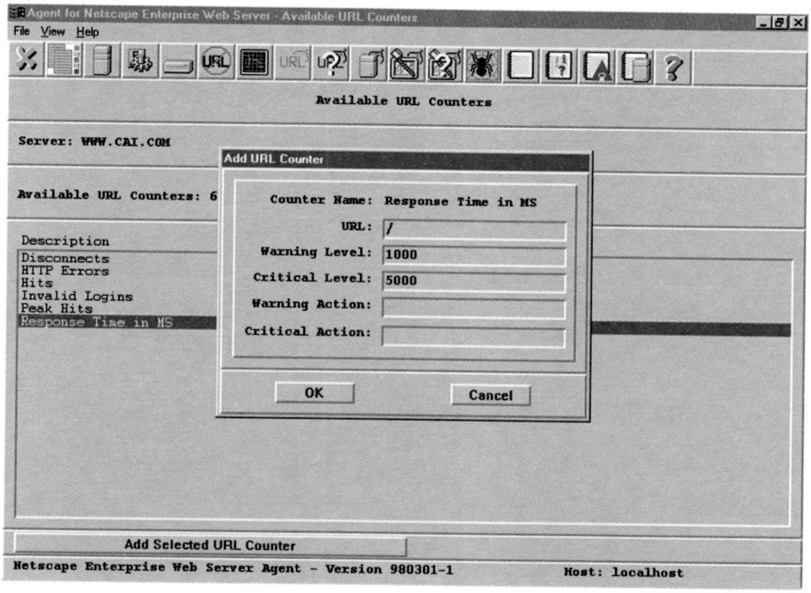

FIGURE 9.22
Monitoring the URL.

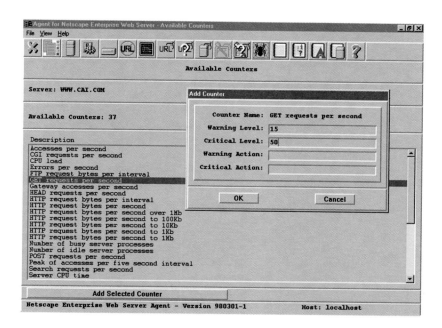

FIGURE 9.23
Viewing the available general counters for the server and adding a counter for monitoring.

Figure 9.24 is the view of the newly requested GET requests per second counter and its current status, value, and threshold information.

FIGURE 9.24
The Polled Counters
window.

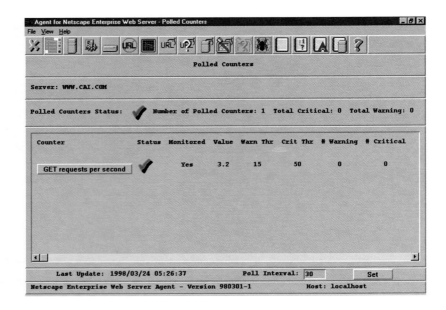

Application Management

Organizations live and die by information. More precisely, an organization's success depends upon how well it manages information. Applications and databases are the vehicles that organizations use for processing information in today's complex world. After all, if key business systems for communications, processing, order entry, customer service, and so on are down for any period of time, there is a substantial negative impact on the business. The key for enterprises today is to maximize the availability of mission-critical systems and make certain that all system components are effectively managed. Surprisingly however, applications are the least understood element of the management menagerie.

While the motive for managing applications is clear—more efficient and effective software implementation and maintenance—how best to accomplish it is being contested. Understanding obstacles to application management in general, and automated application management in particular, is essential for solving the problem. In short, application management is the next frontier to be explored and tamed in the information technology landscape.

New Applications

Enterprises are acquiring, developing, and integrating new breeds of distributed applications with components ranging from browsers to backend mainframes. An application can be software written 30 years ago in COBOL, yesterday in Java, or some combination of both. It can span the entire organization, such as an Enterprise Resource Planning (ERP) solution like SAP R/3, or consist of department data stored in Microsoft Access. Email (MS Exchange), groupware (Lotus Notes), and messaging (IBM MQSeries) are all *applications,* or components of applications, on which it is worth investing hardcore management assets. Obstacles to effective application management run the gamut, however. Architecture and implementation take on a new meaning with changes in technology, price, performance, networking environments, operating platforms, and database capabilities. It's hard to hit a moving target.

By nature, the IT environment is heterogeneous with multiple hardware platforms, operating systems, network protocols, and databases that—depending on their level of integration—all work together to deliver enterprise capabilities. Together they comprise the backbone of an application. This underlying structure determines the overall scalability, reliability, adaptability, and performance characteristics of the system. Seemingly unrelated decisions on development, deployment, access, and information affect the core capabilities of distributed applications.

Applications Never Meant for Management

For the vast majority of existing applications, no overt engineering was ever performed to make certain that an administrator (or console) could monitor the status of constituent software components as they executed. Monitoring program status and availability is only a basic starting point for application management but, even so, it is not simple. To make an application "manageable," the relationship of logical components (interface/desktop, application logic/server(s), and database/server(s) in a three-tier model) must be understood, and useful management metrics extracted from the components. As Internet and intranet applications are deployed with increasingly granular and interdependent components (the Java programming language is predicated upon this concept), the challenge of designing manageability into the software grows.

Market Evolution

Just a few years ago most organizations shopped for a management solution on a platform-by-platform, function-by-function basis. As the environment grew more complex, they began looking at common functions across multiple platforms. That is, if they needed scheduling, backup, network, performance, or event management, the tools provided needed to work on a variety of platforms. As distributed functions began to interrelate and multiple functions were required on a single platform, the focus on point platform solutions waned while enterprise management solutions waxed. Now organizations are no longer debating the need for enterprise management; they are pushing to acquire, deploy, and manage distributed applications and their associated management environment as quickly as possible.

Handling the New World

Enterprises need core infrastructure for successful deployment, development, and management of distributed applications. Distributed applications operate in a network environment, utilize client/server technology, and tend to operate on multiple platforms. It doesn't matter if you are dealing with thin or thick client, network, or traditional PCs, applications need to be designed to handle the new world.

The rise of the Internet, Java, network PCs, secure protocols, object databases, new operating systems, and platforms has provided a continuing set of challenges for application management. As new technologies appear, some or all existing code will eventually require interfacing or upgrading. The more scattered the development effort (different tools, architectures, and methodologies), the bigger the challenge of deployment, management, and maintenance.

Now that information is accessible via the Internet, extranets, and intranets, an important business metric will be time to market, whether delivering goods, services, or raw information. Constant changes in networking and applications will differentiate organizations that can harness these new technologies effectively.

There will be more focus on the deployment of new applications. Web technology, coupled with Java, provides a "build it once, run it anywhere" approach to application development. While solving some deployment problems, proper design, monitoring, and management remain IT challenges.

Instrumenting Applications for Management

At the minimum, applications could be said to be *instrumented* simply by virtue of the fact that they use system calls that, coincidentally, provide a clue as to their status. For example, programs frequently return integers to the operating system depending on the outcome of programming logic. As with nearly all aspects of computing, this was adequate for mainframe environments 20 years ago and, perhaps, standalone PCs now. Today, however, the complexity of networks and the complex network of dependencies fostered by distributed applications require far more sophisticated controls.

Currently, the three prominent ways to manage applications are

- Embedding application-monitoring APIs
- Inspecting network traffic for application transactions
- Monitoring all application-related components (out-of-band agents)

Embedding Application-Monitoring APIs   Often referred to as *instrumenting* an application, this technique involves the manual insertion of a set of monitoring (and potentially management) APIs directly into the application source code, similar to the way a program *fix* (or *patch*) is implemented in legacy environments. (It is interesting to note the more recent meaning of the term *instrumenting*, which refers to the use of agents to monitor and manage an application without altering the application.) Management tools call these APIs to establish an application's response time or provoke management actions, such as kicking off a backup operation.

The advantage of this approach is granularity and flexibility. Assuming a well-documented and understood list of application components, "roll your own" (RYO) applications can enjoy refined instrumentation. The associated drawback, however, is a lack of consistency (even a "standard" API may be inconsistently deployed within convoluted legacy applications) combined with intrusiveness. Many applications, especially older programs, are not well documented and understood, making instrumentation difficult, if not impossible. Moreover, the act of instrumenting applications is highly manpower intensive at a time when there is a shortfall of programming talent.

Ideally, instrumentation should be like security in that it needs to be designed in at the beginning. Unfortunately, there are too many applications running or being built without instrumentation that need management now. The large market of existing applications requires a low cost, low risk automated approach to application management.

Inspecting Network Traffic for Application Transactions   This method provides application-level monitoring by inspecting network traffic. As a tools-based approach, it is relatively "light- weight" in terms of deployment and monitoring overhead, but it does not provide active management functionality such as drilling down through the application dependency stack to reveal problems in the constituent components. The basic tradeoff for real-world applications employing this technique is giving up power for simplicity, such that advanced correlation or automated correction is not possible. Practically speaking, this approach, while convenient, is too little too late.

Monitoring All Application-Related Components (Out-of-Band Agents)   This methodology also involves instrumenting all application components, but in contrast to embedding APIs into the source code, the instrumentation is accomplished via external (often prepackaged) intelligent agent technology. Typically, the software monitoring agents report back to a consolidation point where the data is monitored for state changes and performance trends as well as translated into genuine management information.

An advantage of this approach is comprehensiveness, meaning that it is possible, with appropriate filtering and visualization techniques, to quickly grasp "the bigger picture." On the other hand, as more components experience deeper instrumentation, both complexity and the agent "footprint" increase. In addition, care must be taken in deploying the agents so the network is not burdened with unnecessary traffic.

Agents are useful to in-house and commercial application developers alike for creating and extending management-ready applications. A growing number of the most popular commercial applications—such as SAP R/3, Lotus Notes, and Microsoft Exchange—are made management-ready by application management agents. Overall, managing application-related components with out-of-band agents provides the most automated management capability, but is also the most resource intensive from a hardware perspective. It is worth noting, however, that this is an appropriate tradeoff, given the rate of development and economies of scale in the IT industry.

Exploring the Open Applications Management Initiative (OAMI)

The Open Applications Management Initiative (OAMI), an amalgam of the previously detailed application management approaches (with particular emphasis on agent technology), represents the pinnacle of CA's applications management strategy. OAMI offers two significant advances to help with the complicated task of application management:

- The facilities to unobtrusively instrument any application
- The facilities to completely automate application management

With OAMI, an administrator can manage anything from homegrown to shrink-wrapped applications across the enterprise in the context of a logical application topology. This topology depicts the environment where distributed application components exist and how they communicate with one another. This context helps administrators anticipate the impact of underlying system difficulties on an application. The end result is a more proactive IT staff and greater application availability.

Not only is application management considered from the perspective of a program in execution, it is also seen in the context of the life cycle of an application. For example, OAMI provides a full end-to-end process that covers change, configuration, distribution, security, backup, automation, and correlation of an application's impact on the environment. The full application coverage of OAMI provides users with the coverage they need to deploy distributed applications today. OAMI-managed applications and systems can derive benefits in all supported environments without changing the application.

The OAMI methodology and guidelines provide the first comprehensive approach to automated management of applications in a distributed world by offering a solution based on proactive, automated management of applications and databases. In managing applications across complex, heterogeneous environments, OAMI makes it possible to attain the fullest benefits by efficiently applying the services of the vital IT management disciplines, such as workload, security, storage, performance, problem, and output management.

The proactive application management offered by OAMI is made possible through a proven methodology of automatic and unobtrusive instrumentation, profiling, and monitoring of applications, combined with an integrated suite of management applications.

Application Management Demands

Application management is one of the most demanding disciplines in information technology. Creating an environment that provides for comprehensive application management, including optimal performance and high availability, must take into account many different factors.

The OAMI methodology organizes the bewildering array of factors that influence application management from a standard perspective. In other words, the first goal of OAMI is to transform the nearly insurmountable problem of application management—a conceptually and programmatically daunting task—into a methodology that makes it easier to comprehend and discuss both the challenge and its solution.

Fortunately, the problem of application management lends itself to decomposition, starting at the broadest and most abstract level, and then reduces into diverse sub-problems that eventually map to solutions. Just as fortunately, the constituent parts of the problem, once reconstituted, can then be recombined to produce a generic solution.

It is important to understand that even though there are many factors influencing application management, only a subset is *quantifiable*. For example, at the broadest and most abstract level, the *non-quantifiable* factors influencing applications concern

- The business using the application because businesses and their markets change.
- The problem the application is meant to solve because issues addressed a year ago may have substantially evolved.
- Information processing technology constantly progresses. This implies changes in price, performance, networking environments, operating platforms, and database capabilities.

Identifying and sorting out the non-quantifiable factors is an important step in focusing OAMI's implementation methodology. Having acknowledged this portion of the application management puzzle, the next step is to identify "quantifiable" factors and relate them to the wider picture of application management. The following are some factors:

- *The specific system upon which the application depends.* This includes hardware and software components, such as networks, servers, operating systems, and databases.
- *Application performance.* Determining why an application is "slow."
- *Application development stage.* Where is the application in its life cycle?
- *Discrete application processes.*

In order to provide practical application management, these factors must be considered holistically. OAMI explains how this is possible and presents a standardized approach required to make it work.

Discovering Application Common Denominators

While applications are different, they all have some common characteristics that will determine their success within the organization:

- Interfaces—User and data
- Environments—Development and runtime
- Trackability—Segmentation and specific interfaces
- Manageability

For each area in which multiple design choices exist for the architect, OAMI provides a strategy, technology, and open interface that make it easier to either build an application for management or proactively manage any present application without user changes. The capability to relate enterprise information and resources to specific applications, users, services, and functions without application changes is the heart of OAMI.

Mapping Distributed Applications

The common characteristics of today's distributed applications include the following:

- Multiplatform nature
- Network communications
- Internet capabilities
- Databases for information

In addition, distributed applications have special needs:

- To be distributed in the first place
- To be tuned
- To integrate with schedules on multiple platforms
- To integrate with configurations on multiple platforms
- To track changes
- For security
- For backup
- To be managed

Distributed applications impact any IT infrastructure, and the less tuned or conditioned the environment, the greater the impact.

The success of deploying and implementing any application including MS Exchange, Lotus Notes, or SAP R/3 is based on two things:

- Detailed understanding of the user environment
- Detailed understanding of the application's impact on the environment

Without the ability to fully understand both, users and the company will continue to suffer from

- Long implementation cycles
- Poor performance of deployed applications
- Difficult processes to change applications
- Unrecoverable failures

OAMI provides the core services, methodology, and capabilities to manage the applications that drive and impact business. After all, if the applications run reliably and are measured and managed efficiently, operations can accurately assess the impact of new applications and reserve resources to absorb change. The key guidelines for future success are to forecast and plan the impact based on architecture, number of users, existing environment, and planned usage changes.

Application management is a new concept for most organizations. Simply installing and using an application is (rightly) regarded as the achievement in itself. Managing a functioning application in order to derive the best possible return on the initial investment is often either an afterthought or completely ignored. Compounding this problem is the fact that the inherent complexity of distributed, heterogeneous environments makes application management impossible without sophisticated, automated solutions.

Every second of every day an application's performance and availability depend on

- The server or servers upon which it resides
- Numerous network hardware components
- The condition of underlying databases

In turn, these servers, network components, and databases—in order to remain operational and deliver optimal performance—depend on the availability and condition of other hardware and software.

OAMI in Action

The next section covers an actual implementation of OAMI to illustrate the impact of this initiative on specific applications. Lotus Notes was chosen because it is a widely deployed groupware, messaging, and electronic mail solution. A brief tour of the OAMI-compliant Unicenter TNG Lotus Notes/Domino Server agent is provided. While navigating through Agent View, it highlights some of the Notes agent components. This tour illustrates the out-of-the-box capabilities and benefits associated with instrumenting a third-party application in accordance with the OAMI initiative. Readers may profit by first reviewing Unicenter TNG's manager-agent architecture covered in Chapter 4, "Server Management," and Chapter 5, "Desktop Management."

The Lotus Notes/Domino Server Option

Enterprises rely on messaging systems like Lotus Notes as a principal mechanism for storing and distributing corporate documents and knowledge. Many organizations store gigabytes of electronic mail, documents, and information across a bevy of Notes servers. The need to effectively manage this environment has become more critical than ever to a business's success.

Mission critical business applications are often built around Lotus Notes. Downtime can mean loss of revenue, customers, and hard-won credibility in the market. Because of the growing role of Notes as an electronic repository for intellectual property and business applications, organizations now require robust management tools, such as event and storage management, to ensure system reliability, availability, and predictability.

Touring the Lotus Notes/Domino Server Option

Unicenter TNG WorldView provides the tools you need to assess the health of your Notes servers. From WorldView, you can view 2D and 3D maps and topological network structures and show the state of networks and nodes.

Notes servers appear in WorldView as managed objects and are automatically placed in a Mail Network Business Process View (BPV), which depicts the connection between servers (see Figure 10.1).

Ch

10

FIGURE 10.1
Unicenter TNG Map showing the icon for the Mail Network Business Process View.

Clicking the Mail Network icon drills down to the next level of detail that depicts the mail sites (see Figure 10.2).

Clicking the Mail Site icon drills down to the server level (see Figure 10.3).

Right-clicking the server brings up a pop-up menu from which you can access the MIB Browser, Agent View, or Node View (see Figure 10.4).

FIGURE 10.2

The enterprise from the point of view of the Mail Network Business Process View.

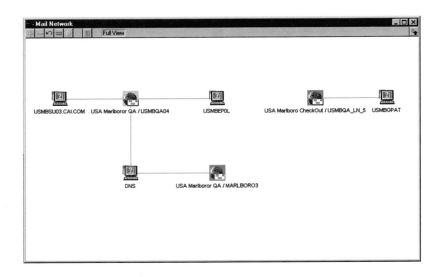

FIGURE 10.3

The map of the USA Marlboro Mail Network server.

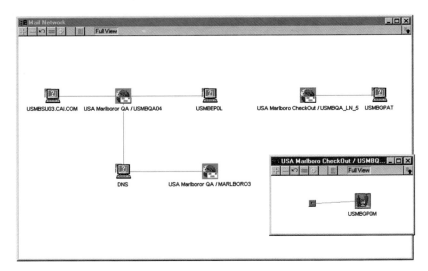

FIGURE 10.4

The pop-up menu.

Lotus Notes Agent Overview

The Notes agent periodically examines statistics about each Notes server and compares them against user-defined thresholds to determine the health of the server. If a threshold is exceeded, an SNMP trap is generated to inform Unicenter TNG about an exceptional condition. The trap will cause the server's status to be updated, which is represented by changing the color of the server icon represented in both WorldView and Node View. The status of an associated resource category (such as "Connectors," for example) is highlighted within Node View and Agent View. Working with the threshold values that triggered the trap is also possible through Agent View and the MIB Browser.

The Notes agent captures statistics for the following resource groups:

- Server
- Services
- Connectors
- MTA (Message Transfer Agents and Mail Router)
- Disks
- Databases
- Available Counters
- Polled Counters
- Monitored Events
- Event Log

Each metric within a category has associated warning and critical thresholds that determine the exception levels for a particular Notes server. By changing these thresholds, you can tailor the monitoring algorithm to match the processing profile of the system.

Let's start our tour with the Notes Agent Summary window (see Figure 10.5). This window automatically displays when you start up Agent View. It provides an at-a-glance status of all the mail server components monitored by the agent. Component status is propagated up to the Overall Status.

As indicated by the check marks (which display in green), the status of the MTA, Disks, Notes Databases, Counters, and Events groups are all normal. The status of the Services group is set to warning, as indicated by the yellow exclamation mark; the Connections group is critical, indicated by a red X. The Overall Status component is also designated critical because, by default, status propagates upstream according to the worst case.

Server

The Notes Server window enables you to reset historical counts and the server polling intervals, as well as providing a single control that can start and stop all Notes services. When you reset counts, the Notes Agent resets the historical number of warning and critical occurrences to zero in each window.

FIGURE 10.5

The Agent For Lotus Notes Summary window.

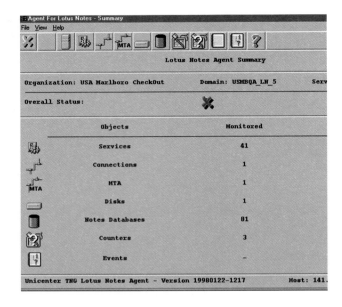

Look at the Server window in Figure 10.6 to see general information about the Notes server. To access this window, click the Server button on the toolbar.

FIGURE 10.6

The Agent For Lotus Notes Server window.

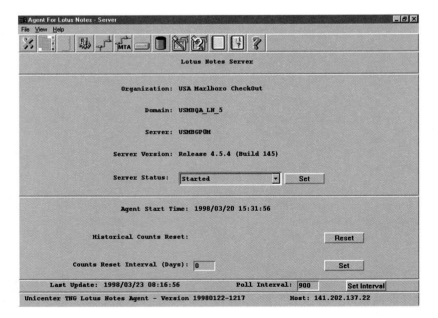

In the Server window, you can start and stop all Notes agent services with a single control. Additionally, you can manually reset the historical counts and set the time interval for automatic count reset.

Services

The Notes Services window displays the state and status of all Notes services or tasks monitored by the agent. You can manually start and stop services and set status from the Services window.

You can also specify whether you want automatic restarts and reboots and define a local action you want executed on the server whenever the specified number of reboot or restart attempts is exceeded.

Click the Services button to see which Notes agent services or tasks are started, stopped, or not installed.

In the Services window (see Figure 10.7), the traffic light identifies the service state of each installed component. Green indicates that a service is started; red indicates that a service is stopped; yellow indicates that a service is in the process of starting or stopping; and N/I indicates that a service is not installed. The status of each service component also displays. In this example, the services are in normal status, indicated by the green check mark.

FIGURE 10.7
The Agent For Lotus Notes Services window.

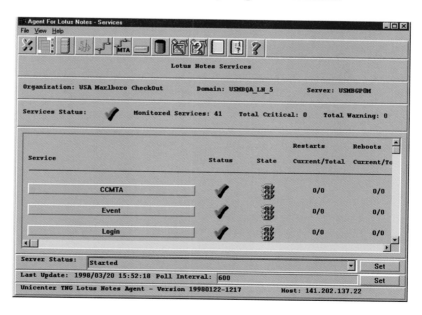

By clicking the Service box for any of the monitored services (for example, Event), you access the View/Modify Service dialog box (see Figure 10.8) where you can change the service state (turn the service on or off) and define thresholds for automatic restarts and reboots. You can also define a local action to take on the server. A local action can be an executable file, a command interpreter action (`cmd/C copy file1 file2`), or a Notes console command (`$console load addin`).

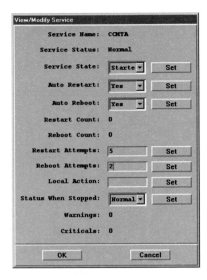

FIGURE 10.8
The View/Modify Service dialog box.

The Event service is automatically restarted and rebooted. If the Event service stops, the agent will attempt to restart it five times. If that doesn't work, the agent will attempt to reboot five times. If the reboot attempts fail, the agent executes the local action (`NOTIFY.EXE`) on the server that pages an administrator. When the service stops running, its status (in this case, warning) will be automatically propagated upwards.

Connectors

The Connections window displays the service status and heartbeats missed for each server connection. This window is used to verify that connectors are functioning properly and allowing mail to be sent between servers.

Connectors are defined by the Notes administrator to connect servers in different Notes sites or to connect to SMTP Internet servers. They are monitored using heartbeat messages sent between servers where agents are running. The Notes administrator can specify the send and receive interval and the number of consecutive failed-to-receive messages for warning and critical status.

Click the Connectors button to display the Connections window. The Connections window lets you monitor the service status and heartbeats missed for each server connection (Notes "connection document").

In this case, `USMBGPAN.CAI.COM`, a local connector, is started and in normal status (see Figure 10.9).

FIGURE 10.9
The Agent For Lotus Notes Connections window.

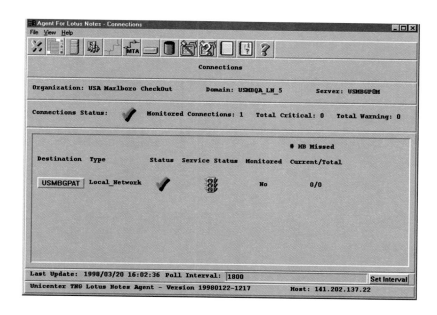

By clicking the Destination button, you can change various properties of the connector (see Figure 10.10).

FIGURE 10.10
The View/Modify Connector dialog box.

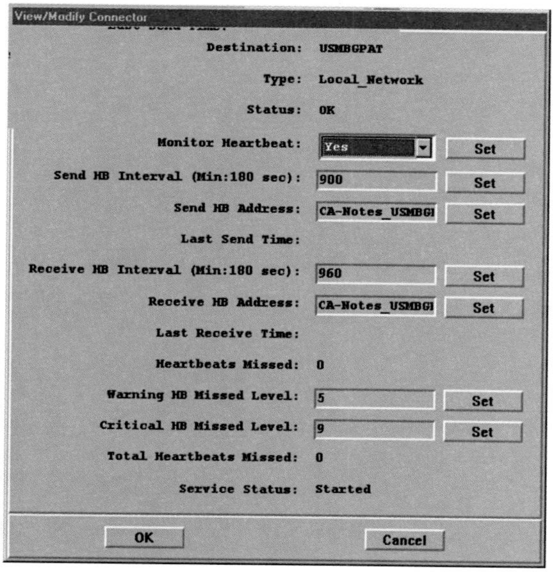

Ch
10

In Figure 10.10, heartbeats are monitored for the connector. When a single heartbeat is missed, the connector status changes to warning; when three consecutive heartbeats are missed, the connector status changes to critical. No heartbeats have been missed since the last heartbeat was received.

Each Notes/Domino agent expects an agent on the destination server named `CA-Notes_(machine name)`. Agents that send heartbeat messages to and receive heartbeat messages from the agent use this destination user's Notes mail address. If the agent is installed on Notes server `US01` in the `CAI_DOM1 Notes/Domino` domain, other Notes/Domino agents would use the address `CA-Notes_US01@ CAI_DOM1`.

The following example shows a CA Notes/Domino agent exchanging heartbeat messages with another CA Notes/Domino agent.

```
Notes/Domino agent on US01
Send address:     CA-Notes_US02@ CAI_DOM1
Receive address:  CA-Notes_US02@ CAI_DOM1
Notes/Domino agent on US02
Send address:     CA-Notes_US01@ CAI_DOM1
Receive address:  CA-Notes_US01@ CAI_DOM1
```

The following example shows a Notes/Domino agent exchanging heartbeat messages with a Unicenter TNG SMTP (UNIX mail service) agent. Both servers are in the `cai.com` Internet domain. SMTP agents all use the same mailbox name.

```
Notes/Domino agent on US01
Send address:    CA-SMTP Agent@unix01.cai.com
Receive address: CA-SMTP Agent@unix01.cai.com
SMTP agent on UNIX01
Send address:    CA-Notes_US01@us01.cai.com
Receive address: CA-Notes_US01@us01.cai.com
```

Mail Transfer Agent (MTA)

The MTA window displays information about traffic on the mail network. By using this window, the Notes administrator can set limits to monitor the amount of traffic and to determine whether queue sizes are getting too large, perhaps indicating a problem with delivery. The Notes agent maintains a rolling average and high and low values. It also tracks the number of warning and critical status changes.

Click the MTA button to check mail traffic on the Notes server (see Figure 10.11).

To change the threshold values for the MTA or Router queue, click the Queue button to display the MTA Queue Detail dialog box (see Figure 10.12). By using this dialog box, you can also set what local actions to take when the warning and critical thresholds are achieved.

The MTA Queue for Lotus Notes Mail has a warning threshold of 50 messages and a critical threshold of 75 messages. When the warning threshold is achieved, the local action, `NOTIFY.EXE`, is taken. When critical threshold is achieved, `ALARM.EXE` is executed.

FIGURE 10.11
The Agent For Lotus
Notes MTA window.

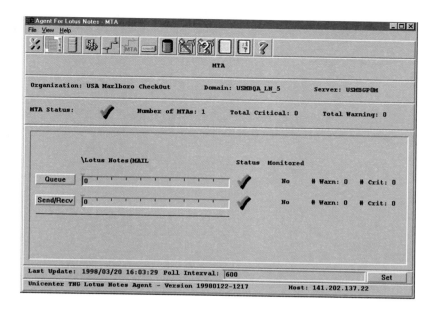

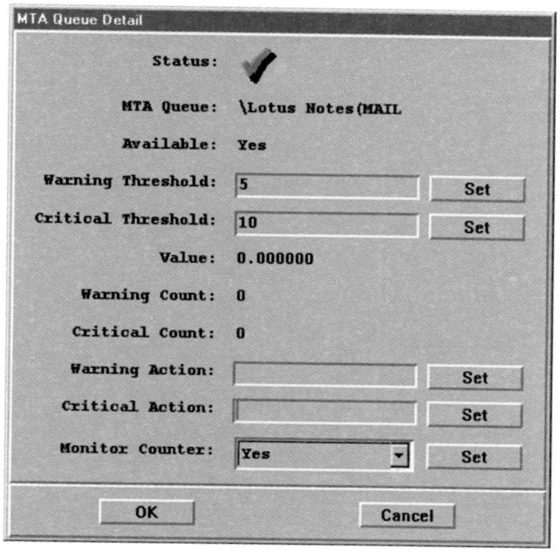

FIGURE 10.12
The MTA Queue Detail
dialog box.

Disks

The Disks Used by Notes window displays disk utilization. The Notes agent calculates the percentage of total disk space currently in use. If the percentage exceeds the warning or critical threshold, the disk status is changed accordingly.

To check your disk utilization, click the Disks button to display the Agent For Lotus Notes Disks window (see Figure 10.13).

FIGURE 10.13.

The Agent For Lotus Notes Disks window.

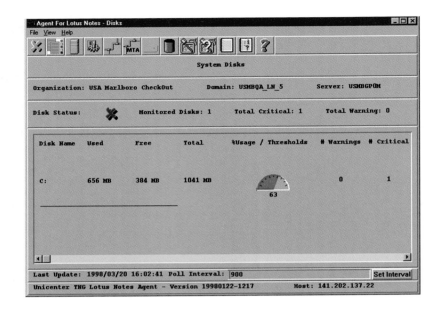

The disks are in normal status, indicated by the green color of the usage gauges. To change the critical and warning thresholds for the C: disk, click the gauge to display the Disk Space dialog box (see Figure 10.14).

FIGURE 10.14

The Disk Space dialog box.

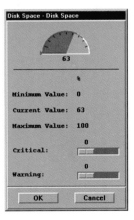

You can easily adjust the thresholds by moving the sliders along the strip charts.

Databases

The Database window (see Figure 10.15) provides information about server databases, including their size, file name, status, percentage used, quotas, and the number of times that a warning or critical status was reached. If the database size exceeds the warning or critical threshold, the database status is changed accordingly.

FIGURE 10.15

The Agent For Lotus Notes Database window.

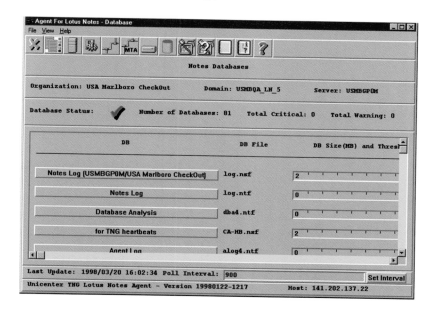

Click the Databases button to view the size of the databases used by the Notes agent.

The tick mark on the strip chart shows the threshold value. In this case, the warning and critical thresholds have the same value, so only a single tick mark appears on each chart. To reset the warning and critical thresholds for the Notes Log database, click the DB button to access the Modify Thresholds dialog box (see Figure 10.16).

FIGURE 10.16

The Modify Thresholds dialog box.

Available Counters

The Available Counters window displays a list of counters, enabling you to select which parameters to monitor. The list includes all Lotus Notes–specific NT system counters. The Notes administrator can pick and choose which ones to monitor from this list.

Click the Counters button to access the Agent For Lotus Notes Available Counters window (see Figure 10.17). From here, you can select counters to be monitored and set warning and critical thresholds.

FIGURE 10.17

The Agent For Lotus Notes Available Counters window.

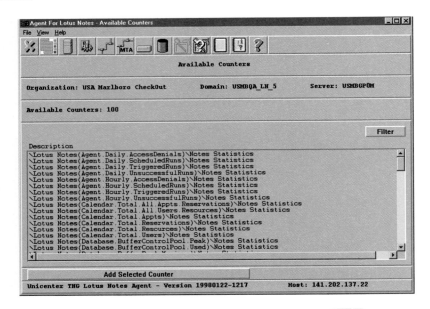

To select a counter to add to Polled Counters, highlight the counter to add and then click the Add Selected Counter button to display the Add Counter dialog box (see Figure 10.18). Here, you define the warning and critical thresholds and the local action to take on the server when these levels are achieved.

FIGURE 10.18

The Add Counter dialog box.

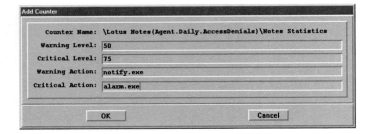

Polled Counters

Once a counter is selected, it is monitored in the next window, Polled Counters.

The Agent For Lotus Notes Polled Counters window (see Figure 10.19) displays a list of all the counters monitored by the agent.

FIGURE 10.19

The Agent For Lotus Notes Polled Counters window.

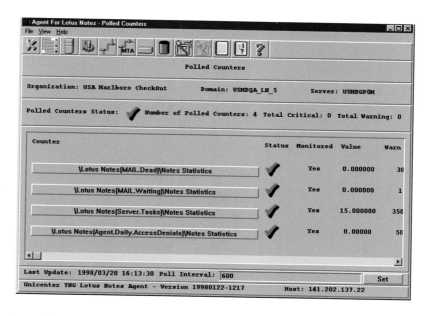

To define warning and critical thresholds, click the Counter button to access the View/Modify Counter dialog box (see Figure 10.20).

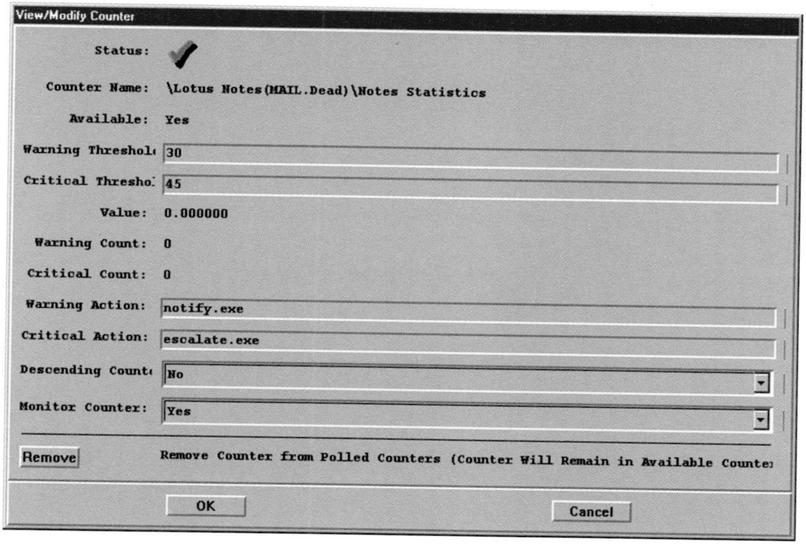

FIGURE 10.20

The View/Modify Counter dialog box.

For this counter, the lower the value, the more critical the need for attention. By setting the Descending Count value to Yes, you can define a critical threshold that is lower than the warning threshold.

Monitored Events

The Agent For Lotus Notes Monitored Events window displays a list of events that have been selected for monitoring. You can associate a severity level (warning or critical) with each event.

Click the Events button to display the Agent For Lotus Notes Monitored Events window (see Figure 10.21). In Windows NT, the monitored event ID is the event ID used in the NT Event Viewer.

FIGURE 10.21

The Agent For Lotus Notes Monitored Events window.

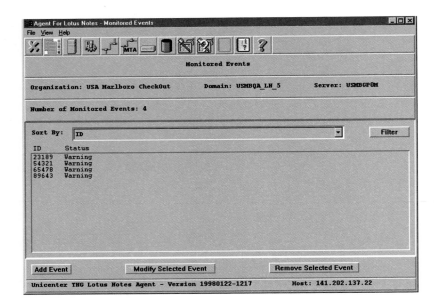

To change the severity status propagated when the event occurs, highlight the event and click Modify Selected Event to display the Modify Event Status window (see Figure 10.22).

FIGURE 10.22

The Modify Event Status dialog box.

Event Log

The Event Log window displays a list of events that have occurred with event IDs matching those in the Agent For Lotus Notes Monitored Events window. From here the Notes administrator can manually reset the overall status to normal.

Display the Agent For Lotus Notes Event Log window (see Figure 10.23) by clicking the Event Log button on the toolbar.

FIGURE 10.23
The Agent For Lotus Notes Event Log window.

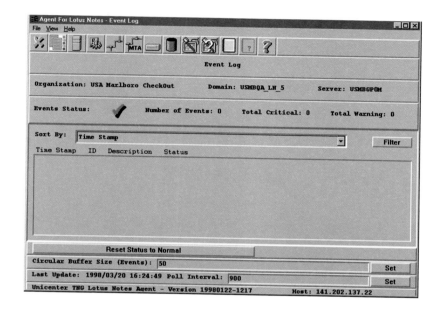

In this example, you are displaying Event Log information in time stamp sequence. You can change the display sequence by choosing a different value in the Sort By list box. Event ID 1 propagates up a warning status that displays as a yellow exclamation mark.

OAMI Summary

The Open Application Management Initiative (OAMI) is a strategic initiative from Computer Associates that provides definition, strategy, and guidelines for the design, deployment, and end-to-end management of applications. For these purposes, application management is defined as the science of transferring vital management data concerning business applications and middleware to an operations department or enterprise management infrastructure.

Full coverage of applications is provided by OAMI, which includes, among other elements, an object model, the means to reduce application complexity, APIs, and methodology. OAMI was developed to apply to all applications within the enterprise, including legacy applications, whether developed internally or purchased from a third party. You can find additional information on OAMI programming specifications and APIs by requesting technical white papers from Computer Associates. ●

Ch
10

Unicenter TNG Options

In this appendix

This book discusses several Unicenter TNG options. However, there are many more options available. These options enable users to tailor the management functionality of Unicenter TNG to their specific management requirements. For example, if an organization has implemented a specific database such as Ingres II or an application such as SAP R/3, Unicenter TNG provides the optional components to manage these particular IT assets. This appendix provides an overview of each of the Unicenter TNG options. Many of the options take advantage of Unicenter TNG by integrating with enterprisewide functions such as Event Management, Agent Technology, Security, and so on.

Security Options

The Unicenter TNG security options provide organizations with complementary functionality needed to secure today's distributed environments. Security, already a primary concern for organizations, has become even more critical with the growth of heterogeneous IT infrastructures and the rise of the Internet. To meet these challenges, Unicenter TNG comes complete with a series of security options that meet the broad spectrum of challenges facing today's security-conscious organizations.

Unicenter TNG Advanced AntiVirus Option

The Unicenter TNG Advanced AntiVirus option is an integrated anti-virus solution for complex enterprise environments. This option provides the following:

- Real-time virus scanning and cure
- A central console for anti-virus administration
- Hands-free monthly virus signature updates and software downloads, testing, and deployment
- Protection of Internet/intranet servers, workstations, and messaging systems
- A central virus activity log
- Advanced AntiVirus option agents for Lotus Notes and Microsoft Exchange Server

With its Java-based interface, this option enables platform-independent management, including universal access and centralized anti-virus management across the Internet or corporate intranets. The Unicenter TNG Advanced AntiVirus option is certified by the National Computer Security Association to detect 100% of the viruses that have been identified.

The supported environments are as follows:

- Messaging systems—Lotus Notes and Microsoft Exchange Server
- Client platforms—Windows, DOS, Macintosh, and OS/2
- Network platforms—Windows NT and Novell NetWare

Unicenter TNG Network Security Option

The Unicenter TNG Network Security option is a network security product that combines the high-level security of a proxy solution with the performance characteristics of a packet filter. This option works at the packet level by examining the packets' content, not just the header information. Because of this capability, it can maintain session state information even for *connectionless* protocols, such as UDP.

NSO's main functions are as follows:

- Controls, audits, and restricts access to all systems on intranet/Internet networks
- Maintains connection state information in tables
- Anti-spoofing detection via private routing tables
- Dynamic interface detection
- Enables network security policies and rules to be defined centrally and enforced across the entire enterprise
- Controls access based on user ID and password authentication for accountability
- Default rule load before NIC is activated to prevent breach during initialization
- Need for Web or FTP proxy server eliminated
- Can exploit Unicenter TNG calendars

Unicenter TNG Encryption Option

Unicenter TNG uses a proprietary encryption algorithm for its communication. Protection for client applications can be realized through the use of optional encryption products available from CA. These products perform encryption at the endpoints of a network without requiring changes to existing applications; they also secure all data transmissions whether they are on the same LAN, across a WAN, or even across the Internet. Additionally, they perform encryption/decryption on a connection basis via policies and support three modes of encryption: LOC, DES, and DES3.

Unicenter TNG RACF Option

The Unicenter TNG RACF option is a solution for security monitoring and control of RACF-based systems. Together with Unicenter TNG, it provides enterprisewide security policy management and reporting. Password violations, file access violation, incorrect user ID, and all CICS violations are monitored. These events are passed on to the Unicenter TNG Event Manager, where they are correlated. Unicenter TNG then either automates a response or alerts a security administrator of the violation.

This enables centralized management and control of systems running IBM RACF for MVS, a component of the OS/390 Security Server, through integration with Unicenter TNG.

Software	Requirements
Server or Workstation	MS Windows NT Server or Workstation, TCP/IP
MVS Software	CA 90s services 1.0 9611 or later
TCP/IP	IBM RACF for MVS Release 1.8 or later

Unicenter TNG Single Sign-On Option

The Unicenter TNG Single Sign-On option provides Windows-based users with the ability to log on to multiple applications with a single, secure sign-on process. This option eliminates the need to remember different user IDs and passwords for each system. The enhanced security and usability features benefit every level of the organization with decreased user errors, heightened productivity, fewer Help Desk calls, and more manageable and secure systems.

The supported environments are various UNIX platforms, Windows NT Server, and Microsoft Windows for client machines.

Network Options

The Unicenter TNG Network options provide organizations with the particular functionality needed for their individual networked environments by enabling organizations to tailor their Unicenter TNG management resources to meet their specific management needs.

Unicenter TNG DECnet Manager Option

The Unicenter TNG DECnet Manager option manages DECnet networks, which includes network discovery, status monitoring, and other management capabilities. This option enables organizations to gain control over their DECnet network by showing, at a glance, what devices are on the network and whether they are available. Additionally, it centralizes and integrates DECnet management with the rest of the network and enterprise management.

Integration with the Unicenter TNG Real World Interface map provides intuitive representations of the network topology, the status, and the impact on business applications with the aid of Business Process Views.

The Unicenter TNG DECnet Manager option offers the capability to successfully manage your entire digital networking environment, including support for DECnet Phase IV and Phase V (OSI) end nodes, digital bridges, routers, terminal servers, and SNMP-compliant devices.

Microsoft Windows is the supported environment.

Unicenter TNG Response Manager Option

The Unicenter TNG Response Manager option provides end-to-end response times from the end-user perspective and discovers network resources and users. This option is a proactive management application, collecting networkwide performance metrics for TCP/IP, NetBIOS, IPX/SPX, and SNA networks (through integration with the Unicenter TNG SNA Manager option) with the Response Manager agent.

The Response Manager option analyzes end-to-end response times and provides automated recommendations to optimize service levels for client/server applications in a multi-vendor environment. It monitors intranets as well as Internet performance. It shows exactly which users are accessing what servers and applications, as well as what kind of response times they are experiencing. Response Manager identifies, isolates, and helps resolve response-time problems on LANs, remote links, and servers.

The supported environments are as follows:

- Server—Windows NT
- Networks—TCP/IP, IPX/SPX, and SNA (requires the Unicenter TNG SNA Manager option)

Unicenter TNG SNA Manager Option

The Unicenter TNG SNA Manager option provides a graphical interface for viewing enterprisewide information pertaining to SNA network subsystems. This option is a client/server application that integrates CA-Netspy on the MVS platform, with SNA Real World Interface and SNA Manager Problem Analysis components on Windows NT workstations. It also enables CA-Netspy to feed performance and alert data to Unicenter TNG.

The SNA Manager discovers all SNA nodes and presents the information in easy-to-read network topology maps.

MVS is the supported environment.

Options for Operational Efficiency

Unicenter TNG is replete with operational management functionality. However, Unicenter TNG also provides additional operational management functions that allow organizations to adapt Unicenter TNG to their particular management requirements. As with all Unicenter TNG options, they leverage the Unicenter TNG framework and integrate with other management applications offered in the Unicenter TNG management suite.

Unicenter TNG Automation Point Option

The Unicenter TNG Automation Point option provides extensive event automation, problem notification, and escalation capabilities for IBM and non-IBM legacy environments. It consolidates events from multiple platforms for correlation and cross-platform management and automatically corrects system problems within the data center infrastructure. These capabilities also extend to non-IT devices, such as environmental equipment.

Automation Point automates tasks such as responding to messages, invoking time-based procedures, communicating with host-based products, sounding alarms when critical messages appear, activating a beeper, and executing REXX procedures. When running on Windows NT, the Automation Point option emulates various IBM terminals.

The supported environments are as follows:

Console types supported:

MVS

JES3

VM

VSE

CA-Remote Console sessions

Asynchronous terminal emulation:

Telnet

DEC VT52

DEC VT100

DEC VT320

Tandem 6530 (conversion or block mode)

It also provides access to MCS consoles and multiple mainframe sessions, including TSO, IMS, and OMEGAMON.

Unicenter TNG Advanced DocServer Option

The Unicenter TNG Advanced DocServer option provides quick and easy access to all documents regardless of their origin in the enterprise. It offers a single repository for managing documents produced in the mainframe, LAN, or UNIX environment. This tool facilitates document management through centralized administration, enabling collection and classification of documents for printing, viewing, and archiving. Combined with CA-DocView, it provides a single point of view and a single point of control for distributed environments.

CA-Unicenter/Advanced DocServer gathers documents from any system supporting the NJE application protocol-mainframe, UNIX, and LAN environments, while preserving source file identification.

The supported environments are as follows:

Server

Windows NT Server

Clients (with CA-DocView)

Windows

Windows NT Workstation

Networks

TCP/IP

SNA LU6.2 (for mainframe communication)

Unicenter TNG MVS Event Manager Option

The Unicenter TNG MVS Event Manager option is an extension to CA-OPS/MVS II to provide graphical, real-time monitoring of MVS resource status. As an integrated part of Unicenter TNG, this option consolidates MVS events with enterprisewide events managed by Unicenter TNG. This provides a consolidated view of the enterprise as objects on the map or Real World Interface.

The Unicenter TNG MVS Event Manager option also provides consolidation of MVS resource status information, with the resource status monitored and managed by all of the Unicenter TNG enterprisewide management disciplines.

MVS and Windows NT are the supported environments.

Unicenter TNG Data Transport Option

The Unicenter TNG Data Transport option provides data transport technology designed to optimize network traffic, leverage the Internet and intranets, and support the widest range of platforms and protocols for today's business. The new capabilities include support for broadcast and multicast technology to speed delivery and reduce overall network traffic. In addition, the new route optimization technology automatically determines the optimal route and methods to deliver all information fast, efficiently, and with full management. All data transport nodes are automatically discovered by the Data Transport service.

Unicenter TNG MLINK Option

The Unicenter TNG MLINK option is designed to provide Data Transport option capabilities to CA-MLINK users. In addition, this option enables integration of Data Transport and Unicenter TNG for increased management and control of MLINK operations.

Unicenter TNG XCOM Option

The Unicenter TNG XCOM option incorporates the new Data Transport option capabilities for CA-XCOM users. In addition, this option provides life cycle management integration, including integration with CA-Endevor and Unicenter TNG Software Delivery.

Desktop and Server Management Options

The desktop and server management options extend Unicenter TNG's management capabilities for virtually any type of desktop or server. These options provide additional controls and automation of functions, which reduces the total cost of ownership of IT resources.

Unicenter TNG Directory Management Option

The Unicenter TNG Directory Management option provides central administration of directory objects such as user accounts across a network of multiple directory types and environments.

This option's administration policies facilitate the consistent administration of a large number of objects. These policies define defaults and rules for groups of objects, eliminating the need to specify details for individual objects.

With this option, groups of objects can be defined according to business function, allowing administration to be organized along business lines. The Unicenter TNG Directory Management option also enables administrators to audit and make directory changes offline without affecting performance during working hours.

The supported environments are as follows:

Directories

Microsoft Windows NT SAM

Microsoft Exchange Server

Lotus Notes

Novell NDS

UNIX NIS, NIS+

Databases

OpenIngres

Microsoft SQL Server

Oracle

Sybase

Informix

Unicenter TNG Asset Management Option

The Unicenter TNG Asset Management Option provides a set of hardware and software inventory functions, configuration control functions, and software metering functions. Built-in hardware-detection using DMI and proprietary inventory capabilities automatically discovers and records all appropriate devices. In addition, the software inventory scanner can detect over 3,000 brand name applications. Administrators can also secure desktop configuration files and prevent a user from making unauthorized changes.

Any application can be metered and audited regardless of whether the software is located on the desktop or the server. Asset management can control and deny the use of unauthorized software, which ensures that no user can access or install applications not approved by the IT department.

The capability to centrally administer system configuration files, meter or audit software usage, and define systemwide policies for the PC and server environment are among its features. The Unicenter TNG Asset Management option has heterogeneous support for all networking environments and all major databases.

Supported environments for Unicenter TNG Asset Management clients include the following:

DOS

Windows

OS/2

Macintosh

UNIX

VMS

NetWare

Banyan VINES

Unicenter TNG Software Delivery Option

The Unicenter TNG Software Delivery option is a tool for installing, configuring, distributing, activating, verifying, updating, and uninstalling software from a central point. Administrators can configure software and data into packages for delivery to one or more users or groups. By defining groups of target computers according to business function, administration can be organized along business lines. Groups can also be defined using hardware or software inventory information to deliver software according to target configuration.

Software Delivery supports both pushes (server-initiated) and pulls (target-initiated) deliveries. This option provides both local and enterprise control with the scalability to support tens of thousands of nodes. Enterprise managers can administer the complete environments, while local administrators can manage individual domains. The Unicenter TNG Software Delivery option supports the wide range of diverse platforms and protocols found in today's heterogeneous environments.

Unicenter TNG Remote Control Option

The Unicenter TNG Remote Control option provides control over the remote PC. This option enables remote control functionality, enabling system administrators, Help Desk staff, trainers, and telecommuters to assume control over one or more desktops and servers from any remote location. For example, administrators can restart Windows or log on to an NT server, simultaneously view several PCs, or have several end users simultaneously view one PC. The Remote Control option supports multiplatform, multiprotocol remote capabilities and includes advanced remote access features for dial-in, printing, file transfer, and session recording.

Groupware Options

The Groupware options enable users of groupware and groupware-applications to manage them under the Unicenter TNG umbrella as they would any other IT resource. All key groupware components such as Microsoft's Transaction Server, Microsoft Exchange, Lotus Notes, and UNIX/SMTP are manageable through Unicenter TNG with these components.

Unicenter TNG Microsoft Transaction Server Option

The Unicenter TNG Microsoft Transaction Server option provides intelligent agents to simplify management of Microsoft Transaction Server 1.0 in large enterprise environments. It enables organizations to secure, manage, and maintain their MTS applications with business-based policies, while ensuring the availability of internal and external business communications.

This option's policy-based agents provide real-time monitoring of Microsoft Transaction Server processes in order to detect their operational status and resource utilization, real-time monitoring of transactions, response times, allocation of threads, and real-time alarm generation.

Unicenter TNG Microsoft Exchange Option

The Unicenter TNG Microsoft Exchange option ensures the reliability and availability of Microsoft Exchange environments by monitoring and automating the functions required to keep Exchange servers up and running. This option extends Unicenter TNG's capability to manage Exchange servers, their associated databases, and connected UNIX Internet mail servers running the UNIX SMTP option. This option provides agents for monitoring the Exchange server for disk utilization, number of mail messages, mail queue length, the availability of other Exchange servers, and much more. The agents automatically populate a Business Process View of the mail network.

Microsoft Exchange and Microsoft Windows NT are the supported environments.

Unicenter TNG Lotus Notes/Domino Option

The Unicenter TNG Lotus Notes/Domino option provides automated, enterprisewide health and performance monitoring for Lotus Notes and Domino servers and inter-connected UNIX Internet mail servers running the UNIX SMTP option. This option extends Unicenter TNG's capability to manage Lotus Notes and its associated databases and provides various agents to monitor the Lotus Notes server for database whitespace, database replication accuracy, mail queue length, the availability of other Notes/Domino servers, and so on. The agent automatically populates a Business Process View of the mail network.

Lotus Notes/Domino Server is the supported environment.

Unicenter TNG UNIX SMTP Option

The Unicenter TNG UNIX SMTP option provides automated, enterprisewide health and performance monitoring for UNIX SMTP Sendmail servers. It monitors the Sendmail server operation including services (SMTPD), counters for MTA message queues, mail traffic, mail store (database) size, and available disk space; it also sends MTA (Message Transport Agent) heartbeat messages to verify end-to-end operation among heterogeneous mail systems and the availability of other mail servers. This option provides an automatically populated Mail Network Business Process View (BPV), depicting the mail network topology.

Sendmail for various UNIX platforms is the supported environment.

Application Options

The ability to manage the development, deployment, and ongoing functions of business-critical applications is essential to the success of any organization. If applications are not available for use, then business ceases. These Unicenter TNG options enable users to manage the critical applications that are essential to their success.

Unicenter TNG Change and Configuration Management Option

The Unicenter TNG Change and Configuration Management option (CMO) is a software configuration system developed specifically for Unicenter TNG clients. This option supports managers and developers by visually tracking, managing, and automating the workflow of small to very large software development projects. CMO tracks and manages change control, version management, parallel development facilities, release management, and configuration management. This allows developers to continue using their existing equipment, tools, and data while the system tracks and stores the changes made throughout the development life cycle.

Various UNIX platforms are supported.

Unicenter TNG SAP R/3 Option

The Unicenter TNG SAP R/3 option is an integrated solution for managing complex SAP R/3 systems. It extends the SAP Computing Center Management System (CCMS) through Unicenter TNG's management functions, enabling cross-platform, multisystem management and control. This option provides central administration of multiple SAP R/3 instances from one console, online (hot) backup capabilities, automatic error detection and correction, and more.

SAP R/3 3.0C or later as well as Windows NT and various UNIX platforms are supported.

Help Desk Options

The Unicenter TNG product suite contains highly functional help desk capabilities. To provide even more functionality, Unicenter TNG offers the Advanced Help Desk Management option for complete Service Desk capabilities. This option is utilized as an essential component of an organization's integrated service management infrastructure.

Unicenter TNG Advanced Help Desk Option

The Unicenter TNG Advanced Help Desk is a high-end help desk management Unicenter TNG extension that provides automated Call and Problem Management. Automatic logging creates a detailed record that allows the analyst to rapidly gather information with a minimum of keystrokes. Service desk calls are logged and tracked through automated Call and Problem Management.

A built-in self-learning knowledge tool enables end users to see how a particular problem was resolved in the past. This option also features automatic problem capture, incident generation, notification, call escalation, auditing, security, and the capability to integrate seamlessly with other applications.

Advanced Help Desk keeps track of all internal and external support agreements. It also has the capability to trap events from any source in the distributed environment and to automatically generate incident reports. The filtration facility extracts irrelevant information.

Unicenter TNG Advanced Help Desk is an integrated solution that supports and enhances the following Unicenter environments:

- Unicenter TNG Advanced Help Desk server
- Unicenter release 1.1 or later running on HP-UX, Sun Solaris, IBM AIX, and Silicon Graphics IRIX
- Unicenter TNG Advanced Help Desk client
- HP-UX, Sun Solaris, IBM AIX, and Silicon Graphics IRIX
- Microsoft Windows and Windows NT

Internet Options

With the advent of the Internet, there has been a full-scale charge by organizations to move their marketing and distribution channels to the World Wide Web. Web servers, in addition to requiring the same care as any other server, have some special requirements. The Web Management component of Unicenter TNG addresses these issues to ensure that electronic business initiatives are reliable, serviceable, and manageable.

Unicenter TNG Web Management Option

The Unicenter TNG Web Management option secures and manages Microsoft IIS and Netscape Web servers. It automatically archives infrequently used Web pages for efficient storage utilization. Web Management performs real-time analysis to isolate a problem, report the event, and either fix the problem automatically or send a message to the Unicenter TNG Event Manager. Web server performance is monitored.

This option extends Unicenter's management functionality to ensure reliable and secure electronic commerce on both the Internet and within corporate intranets. Unicenter TNG functions such as storage, security, event, performance, and problem management guarantee control, audit, and restricted access to all systems and traffic on a corporate network.

The supported environments are as follows:

Microsoft IIS Web servers
Windows NT
Netscape Web servers

Netscape Commerce server

Netscape Communications server

Various UNIX platforms

Storage Options

The Unicenter TNG storage options provide organizations with additional capabilities for protecting and managing their mission-critical information—whether that data is stored in a centralized or distributed fashion. These options extend the robust storage capabilities that are inherent to Unicenter TNG.

Unicenter TNG Advanced Storage Option

The Unicenter TNG Advanced Storage option is a complete storage management solution for the enterprise's data backup, restoration, and disaster recovery needs. It offers advanced capabilities such as centralized administration and intelligent alert notification; it is designed to perform high-speed backup and restore across single or multisite enterprises via RAID tape support, hot backups of databases and messaging scripts, and much more.

Unicenter TNG DASD Manager Option

The Unicenter TNG DASD Manager option enables viewing of enterprisewide information pertaining to storage, cache, and DASD performance via an easy-to-use graphical interface. It combines CA-ASTEX on the MVS platform with the Unicenter TNG DASD Manager option Agent and the Unicenter TNG DASD Manager option Problem Analysis component on Windows NT workstations. The DASD Agent maintains real-time performance status of network and storage resources on the Unicenter TNG map. The DASD Manager Problem Analysis component enables viewing of active and historical alerts. It can also display or print historical performance reports for each mapped resource monitored by the Unicenter TNG DASD Manager option.

The supported environments are as follows:

MVS

Windows NT

CA-ASTEX 2.5

Unicenter TNG DFSMShsm Option

The Unicenter TNG DFSMShsm option allows the administration, management, and control of MVS disk resources in a DFSMShsm-managed environment from a Windows NT workstation. This option provides an extensive set of disk management functions including file and disk-volume maintenance services, displays of the MVS catalog structure, the current DFSMS configuration, and more. DFSMShsm is invoked for all archive, backup, and recall services, as well as to list the available backups and archives. The DFSMShsm option brings the MVS storage objects managed by DFSMShsm into the Unicenter TNG environment. Information is presented using the Microsoft Explorer paradigm.

Reference to Unicenter TNG's Agents

In the context of Unicenter TNG, agents are small, specialized programs that work in coordination with the Distributed State Machine to monitor and control managed objects. A managed object may be a database server, a workstation, a device, or a network that will be managed by Unicenter TNG. The Distributed State Machine is the manager component that communicates with and controls the managed object through agents.

Communications between the Distributed State Machine (DSM) and the agents use four common Unicenter TNG services:

- Distributed Services Bus
- Object Store
- SNMP Gateway
- SNMP Administrator

The agent generally monitors the object's essential resources. The types of resources that it may monitor are those that affect the object's performance, availability, and reliability. The Unicenter TNG intelligent agents also monitor the resources for adherence to predefined policy. Critical thresholds may be set; the agent will send a notification that the threshold has been exceeded and the status of the object is set to "critical" when the thresholds are exceeded. Depending upon how it is set up, the Unicenter TNG Event Manager can automatically initiate a predefined action in response to the event.

Computer Associates and a number of third parties have written several generalized and specialized agents. Some agents are provided with the Unicenter TNG installation software and some can be ordered separately from Computer Associates, while others can be obtained from the appropriate manufacturer. The CA agents that integrate with Unicenter TNG are listed in this appendix in alphabetical order, with a brief description of their capabilities.

Unicenter TNG CA-Datacom Agent

The Unicenter TNG CA-Datacom Agent integrates performance monitoring of multiple CA-Datacom databases on the mainframe with Unicenter TNG's enterprise management capabilities. The CA-Datacom Agent monitors important areas of database and application performance, notifying the Unicenter TNG console when thresholds are reached or exceeded. Unicenter TNG will then automatically correct the problem, open a problem ticket, or notify the system administrator. This agent can also enforce complex policies that monitor and correlate multiple events. The Unicenter TNG CA-Datacom Agent enables integrated management of OS/390 and key subsystems like MQSeries, MVS, IDMS, DB2, and CICS, with all of the distributed computing resources in the enterprise.

The supported environments include OS/390 and CA-Datacom/DB Release 9.0 with SQL option.

Unicenter TNG CA-IDMS Agent

The Unicenter TNG CA-IDMS Agent enables administration of CA-IDMS central versions from the Unicenter TNG platform. This option provides an MIB to identify CA-IDMS resources to be monitored and managed by the agent. The performance areas monitored include CPU, I/O, buffer pool, log and journal, lock, workload, memory, DC resource and network. Monitoring of each of these MIB performance groups can be turned on or off to meet specific requirements. The Unicenter TNG CA-IDMS Agent enables integrated management of OS/390 and key subsystems like MQSeries, MVS, DB2, Datacom, and CICS, with all of the distributed computing resources in the enterprise.

OS/390 Release 2.0, CA-IDMS/DB 12.0 or later, and IBM TCP/IP 3.2 or later are the supported environments.

Unicenter TNG CICS Agent

The Unicenter TNG CICS Agent provides continuous monitoring of important event, status, and configuration information. The agent monitors essential resources and emits alerts when user-defined thresholds are exceeded. System resources, DSA utilization, memory utilization, and CICS transactions are among the monitored performance areas. The Unicenter TNG CICS Agent enables integrated management of OS/390 and key subsystems like MQSeries, MVS, IDMS, Datacom, and DB2, with all of the distributed computing resources in the enterprise.

Unicenter TNG DB2 Agent

The Unicenter TNG DB2 Agent integrates the performance management of DB2 databases with the distributed enterprise. The Unicenter TNG DB2 Agent performs continuous monitoring of essential event, status, and configuration information. The agent monitors important resources and emits alerts when user-defined thresholds are exceeded. DB2 address space CPU and I/O utilization, logging status, locking status, workload utilization, database/pageset status, EDM pool status, applications status, and more are among the monitored performance areas. The Unicenter TNG DB2 Agent enables integrated management of OS/390 and key subsystems like MQSeries, MVS, IDMS, Datacom, and CICS with all of the distributed computing resources in the enterprise.

OS/390, DB2 for MVS or OS/390, and IBM TCP/IP are the supported environments.

Unicenter TNG DCE Agent

The Unicenter TNG DCE Agent monitors the Distributed Computing Environment (DCE) and performs proactive maintenance and failure recovery. In doing so, this option has the potential to detect pending failures before they become service outages. The Unicenter TNG DCE Agent checks for problems such as data inconsistency, data corruption, and software malfunctions that can be caused by incorrect software behavior, operator error, or hardware problems.

In addition, the Unicenter TNG DCE Agent monitors the activity within the DCE cell. It can provide reports on server activity and can send alerts to the Unicenter TNG map when designated thresholds are exceeded or errors are detected.

Unicenter TNG Informix Agent

The Unicenter TNG Informix Agent automatically monitors important RDBMS resources for adherence to user-defined thresholds. This option provides RDBMS monitoring of such parameters as tablespace utilization and sequence number rollover. The agent alerts Unicenter TNG when warning or critical thresholds are approached. This option also provides configuration management and status management for Informix databases.

Unicenter TNG MQSeries Agent

The Unicenter TNG MQSeries Agent provides status, event, and configuration information about the MQSeries server. The MQSeries Agent monitors the performance of essential MQSeries resources and emits alerts when user-defined thresholds are exceeded. This agent monitors Queue Manager, Queues, Channels, Dead Letter Queue, paging data sets, application errors, threads, processes, and channel initiators. With this agent, management for OS/390 and key subsystems like MVS, CICS, IDMS, Datacom, and DB2 can be integrated, along with all of the distributed computing resources in a comprehensive enterprise management environment.

Unicenter TNG MVS Agent

The Unicenter TNG MVS Agent ensures the reliability and availability of mission-critical MVS subsystems through continuous monitoring of important status and configuration information. With the Unicenter TNG MVS Agent, management for OS/390 and key subsystems like MQSeries, CICS, IDMS, Datacom, and DB2 can be integrated, along with all other distributed computing resources in a comprehensive enterprise management environment, for the first time.

Unicenter TNG NetWare Agent

The Unicenter TNG NetWare Agent ensures network resource availability and performance by providing event and performance management. The NetWare agent monitors status, event, and configuration information for critical operating system parameters. It also monitors selected Desktop and server operating system resources for adherence to user-defined thresholds and policy. The NetWare Agent detects deviations from profiles and, if necessary, escalates events to Unicenter TNG for appropriate action.

Unicenter TNG OpenEdition Agent

The Unicenter TNG OpenEdition Agent provides a complete UNIX environment within MVS (OS/390), enabling most UNIX applications to run on the mainframe. The OpenEdition Agent monitors the status of key OpenEdition resources, detecting deviations from user-defined policy and escalating events to Unicenter TNG for action when appropriate. The resources monitored are similar to those available on typical UNIX systems: use of kernel services, processes and threads, file systems, and memory usage within the kernel and user address spaces. These unique OpenEdition metrics are fully integrated with more traditional MVS statistics, such as paging, CPU, and memory usage. The result is complete, end-to-end monitoring and control of the OpenEdition environment.

Unicenter TNG OpenIngres Agent

The Unicenter TNG OpenIngres Agent complements this powerful relational database management system by automatically monitoring and managing its databases and applications, as well as other IT resources. Its intelligent agent monitors the performance of key OpenIngres resources, including status, event, table and log space, performance, and configuration information. An alert is sent to the Unicenter TNG Event Manager when user-defined thresholds are exceeded. Unicenter TNG correlates these events with system, network, and application events to determine the cause of a problem, and then either corrects the problem or notifies the database administrator. The capability to anticipate problems before they impact production ensures the reliability and availability of mission-critical OpenIngres applications.

The supported environments include various UNIX platforms and Windows NT.

Unicenter TNG OpenVMS Agent

The Unicenter TNG OpenVMS Agent monitors status, event, and configuration information for critical OpenVMS parameters. The agent monitors key operating system resources for adherence to user-defined policy. It detects deviations from profiles and, if necessary, escalates events to Unicenter TNG for appropriate action.

Unicenter TNG Oracle Agent

The Unicenter TNG Oracle Agent simplifies administration and enhances the manageability of multiple Oracle databases. It continually monitors critical RDBMS parameters, including status, event, tablespace fragmentation, I/O workloads, and table and log space. This agent can anticipate problems before service is interrupted and can take automated corrective action when events occur. Database administrators can set thresholds for important performance indicators, lessening the chance that performance will be impacted by increasing workloads.

The supported environments include various UNIX platforms and Windows NT.

Unicenter TNG OS/2 Agent

The Unicenter TNG OS/2 Agent ensures network resource availability and performance by providing event and performance management. The OS/2 agent monitors status, event, and configuration information for critical operating system parameters. It also monitors important Desktop and server operating system resources for adherence to user-defined thresholds and policy. The OS/2 Agent detects deviations from profiles and, if necessary, escalates events to Unicenter TNG for appropriate action.

Unicenter TNG SQL Server Agent

The Unicenter TNG SQL Server Agent continually monitors critical RDBMS parameters, including file storage space, system resource utilization, configuration, locking system, and server processes. This agent anticipates problems before service is interrupted; it can take automated, corrective action when events occur.

Unicenter TNG Sybase Agent

The Unicenter TNG Sybase Agent monitors critical RDBMS parameters, including file storage space, system resource utilization, configuration, locking system, and server processes. This agent anticipates problems before service is interrupted; it can take automated corrective action when events occur, or notify the database administrator.

Windows NT and various UNIX platforms are the supported environments.

Unicenter TNG Tandem NSK Agent

The Unicenter TNG Tandem NSK Agent monitors status, event, and configuration information for critical tandem NSK parameters. The agent monitors important operating system resources for adherence to user-defined policy. It detects profile deviations and, if necessary, escalates events to Unicenter TNG for appropriate action. It also monitors files, processes, and other system resources.

Unicenter TNG UNIX Agent

The Unicenter TNG UNIX Agent monitors status, event, and configuration information for critical operating system parameters such as CPU utilization, disk space availability, swap file activity, and memory usage. It also monitors important desktop and server operating system resources for adherence to user-defined policy. This agent detects profile deviations and, if necessary, escalates events to Unicenter TNG for appropriate action.

Unicenter TNG Windows 3.1 Agent

The Unicenter TNG Windows 3.1 Agent enables system administrators to control this environment by monitoring status, event, and configuration information for critical operating system parameters, as well as key desktop and server operating system resources for adherence to user-defined policy. The Windows 3.1 Agent detects deviations from profiles and, if necessary, escalates events to Unicenter TNG for appropriate action.

Unicenter TNG Windows 95 Agent

The Unicenter TNG Windows 95 Agent facilitates control of the Windows 95 environment by monitoring status, event, and configuration information for critical operating system parameters. This system agent also monitors essential desktop and server operating system resources for adherence to user-defined policy. It detects deviations from profiles and, if necessary, escalates events to Unicenter TNG for appropriate action.

Unicenter TNG Windows NT Agent

The Unicenter TNG Windows NT Agent monitors status, event, and configuration information for critical operating system parameters. It also monitors essential desktop and server operating system resources for adherence to user-defined policy. The agent detects deviations from profiles and, if necessary, escalates events to Unicenter TNG for appropriate action. The agent monitors and reports on such user-defined resources as file system space, file accesses, processes, services, printers, memory, CPUs, registries, and event logs.

Index

C

W-Z